Praise for **Boom or Bust!**

"I applaud **Boom or Bust!'s** practical career planning guidelines for the mature worker. For nearly a decade, Spherion has been providing thought leadership on the evolving U.S. workforce. Findings from the Spherion® Emerging Workforce® Study show that attracting the right mix of workers will be the defining factor in the future success of U.S. companies. As predicted labor shortages loom, understanding the Baby Boomers' transition to flexible work schedules and alternate careers will become an important factor in the coming war for talent. **Boom or Bust!** illuminates ways that both Boomers and employers can benefit from the coming workforce changes."

> **Roy Krause**
> *President and CEO, Spherion Corporation*

"Forget the Golden rule. From now on it is the *Boomers* rule! And it is all about taking charge of your next career(s). Read **Boom or Bust!** This fabulous guide will help you re-think, re-design and re-vamp how you look at work and play during your golden years."

> **Gerry Crispin**
> *Chief Navigator & Author, CareerXroads*

"**Boom or Bust!** guides the reader to create, plan and manage the next phase of their career. Mature work life is a fact. With over 40% of the adult American population now over 50, you can bet that the Baby Boomers will put their stamp on mature work life just as they have on so many other important social issues in our history. This is the book to help them do just that. As a work lifestyle expert, author and life coach, I value the message that **Boom or Bust!** is sending. Mid-course is the perfect time to plan if you wish to enjoy a longer, more meaningful work life. This is the book to help you develop that plan."

> **Kimberly Fulcher**
> *President and CEO, Compass Life and Business Designs*
> *Author, Remodel Your Reality; Seven Steps to Rebalance Your Life and Reclaim Your Passion*

"While good books frequently appear about what is happening in a maturing America, **Boom or Bust!** is the only one that describes "How to Navigate your Career" if you are a Baby Boomer or older in this new American workplace. This is the book for each and every person who seeks to continue to work, in some capacity, in their maturity."

> **Richard Katz**
> *Founder & CEO, SeasonedPro.com*

BOOM OR BUST!

New Career Strategies In a New America

CAREER MANAGEMENT GUIDE FOR BABY BOOMERS AND BEYOND

Carleen MacKay and Brad Taft

Cambridge Media, LLC
Scottsdale, Arizona

© 2006 by Carleen MacKay and Brad Taft

Printed in the United States of America. All rights reserved. No part of this publication may be reproduced, distributed, or transmitted in any form or by any means, electronic or mechanical, including photocopying, recording or by an information storage and retrieval system- except by a reviewer who may quote brief passages in a review to be printed in a periodical or on the Web – without permission in writing from the publisher. For information, contact Cambridge Media, LLC, 6520 E. Cholla St., Scottsdale, AZ 85254. Tel: 480-315-0372 Fax: 480-315-0373

ISBN 0-9773408-0-5
LCCN 2005934482

Although the authors and publisher have made every effort to ensure the accuracy and completeness of information contained in this book, we assume no responsibility for errors, inaccuracies, omissions, or any inconsistency herein.

A number of words, including brand names and product names, used in this book are trademarks, trade names or service marks of their respective holders. The inclusion, exclusion, or definition of a word or term is not intended to affect, or to express any judgment on the validity or legal status of any proprietary right which may be claimed in that word or term.

CORPORATIONS, UNIVERSITIES, COLLEGES AND PROFESSIONAL ORGANIZATIONS:
Quantity discounts are available on bulk purchases of this book for training, educational and gift purposes. Special books or book excerpts can also be created to fit specific needs.
For information, contact:

Cambridge Media, LLC
6520 E. Cholla St. , Scottsdale, AZ 85254
Tel. 480-315-0372; Fax 480-315-0373

Designed by Steven John Koeppe, Dada Advanced Design Associates

To my children, Chuck and Lorraine, Steven, Heather and Steve, and their children, Charlie, Sam, Carleen and Vivian who are everything I ever hoped for in terms of who they are and who they are becoming.

— Carleen MacKay

To my father Jack, who through his hard work and dedication to family, organizations and community, has lead by example and continues to make contributions during his active 3rd Act.

— Brad Taft

Table of Contents

PREFACE XI

ACKNOWLEDGEMENTS XIII

ABOUT THE AUTHORS XIV

Intro **WHAT WORKPLACE CHANGE MEANS FOR YOU** 1
THE PLANNING PROCESS ENCAPSULATED – 8 EASY STEPS

Step 1 **LETTING GO OF THE PAST** 13
End of your 2nd act. Intermission is over. Let the 3rd act begin…

Step 2 **INTERNAL ANALYSIS** 17
How do you view your future today?
What are the principles you live and work by?
What talent do you offer?
What skills do you offer?
What is your preferred work environment?
What is your unique style?
What motivates you?
Come down from the clouds – Pull together Steps 1 & 2 of your plan

Step 3 **MARKETPLACE TRENDS** 33
Test your knowledge of changing demographics – a quiz
History's lessons learned – A retrospective journey of work in the USA
What's next according to the youth of America?
What's next according to the mature population of America?
What's next according to the Scientists, Futurists and Economists?
Sound bites from the trend watchers
Additional resources
Carleen MacKay's top picks for what's next
Who is most likely to work in any meaningful way?
Come down from the clouds – Discover your marketplace opportunities
Reflect

Step 4 **WHAT CAREERS ARE HOT? 49**
What are the realities of change and their influence on work in America?
What's "hot" according to the Department of Labor?
What's "hot" in your opinion?

Step 5 **YOUR CAREER OPTIONS 63**
But, first, a few words about research
And, just a few more thoughts on new strategies for maturity

Angel Investors **66**
Boards of Directors **68**
Coaches **73**
Consultants **79**
Entrepreneurs **85**
Fancy-Free Workers **93**
Franchisees **97**
Government Workers **102**
Home-Based Business Owners **107**
Independent Professionals **112**
Learners **120**
Mentors **126**
Non-Profit, Foundation and Philanthropic Contributors **131**
Phasers **139**
Pieceworkers **143**
Portfolio Career Jugglers **148**
Revolutionary Reinventors **157**
Small Business Owners **160**
Stipend Workers **163**
Stress-Free, Easy Does It Workers **167**
Teachers **171**
Teaming...The Ensemble Players **175**
Temping **178**
Traditionalists (Traditional re-employment with a twist) **181**
Venture Capitalists **189**
Volunteers **191**
Web Merchants **194**

Step 6   GAP ANALYSIS - CHALLENGES AND BARRIERS   197
Time out
Challenges
    Yesterday's workplace vs. the new workplace
    Meeting the challenges of change:
        Your shifting workplace
        Facts work
        Humor works
        Planning works
        A good jolt works
        Read, reflect and respond
            Financial implications
            Spiritual implications
            Physical implications
            Intellectual implications
        Final thoughts about the fear of risk and the risk of fear
Barriers
    Overcoming barriers:
        Skills or educational gaps.
        Networking
        Interviewing
        Negotiating
        Selling

Step 7   GOALS, OBJECTIVES, BRAND & YOUR WRITTEN PLAN   231
Goals – Guiding beacon
Objectives – What you need to do to get where you are going
Written plan – Pulls together your actions

Step 8   **YOUR MARKETING TOOL KIT**   **241**
    A writer's checklist
    Biographies
    Branding statement (one more time)
    Brochures
    Business cards
    Business plans for small business
    Contracts and agreements for independent agents and executives
    Proposal development
        Sales proposals
        Grant writing
        Responding to Requests for Information (RFI's)
        Responding to Requests for Proposal (RFP's)
    Resumes
    websites

Next Steps...

    WHERE IN THE WORLD DO WE GO FROM HERE?   **272**

    Ah...fellow traveler...but that's the fun of it.

General Index   **273**

Name Index   **275**

x

Preface

You recall from your history books when the original 49ers struck out for California to find gold. Burdened with picks, shovels and pans, they were fueled by large doses of hope, strong backs and wishful thinking. Some hit pay dirt – that is, they lined their pockets with gold. Most failed and lost their shirts. A smart few began businesses to supply the lusting, gold seeking 49ers. A smart few others had the foresight to buy land.

The Boomers were the "few" who saw other ways to benefit from all that gold in the hills of California. This book's title, "**Boom or Bust!**," came to mind because of the original 49ers - that "smart" generation in 1849 who used the magical discovery of gold to their advantage by exploring alternative paths and more creative ways of finding "gold" than by simply wielding picks and shovels.

Today's Boomers, you and your colleagues born between 1946 and 1964, as well as some of us who were born before the official start of the boom, are faced with a new challenge. If you wish to thrive, you will be forced by circumstance to figure out how to work in a largely "de-regular, full-time jobbed" economy – one that has radically redefined the nature of work and for which your experience has not prepared you.

Boom or Bust! will help you to find your own best alternative path and to develop the skills to succeed. It is today's smart answer to the challenges we are facing. To use a metaphor, it will help you to find gold in the new and unexplored hills of the 21st century.

If you are reading this book...

...You are one of today's smart "49ers" – the new Boomers, if you will. Whether you are 40, 50, 60, 70 or beyond, this book is for you!

...You are one of an increasing number of people who, like you, have noticed the extraordinary changes in both the private and public working sectors.

...You know, even if you are still working in a regular, full-time job, that just by virtue of growing older, you are increasingly at risk for layoff or "organization-sponsored early retirement."

...You recognize that you are likely to live a longer, healthier life than most people of your parents' generation. This knowledge will influence your decisions as to when, and at what age, you should completely retire from work.

...You are, like the savvy earlier 49er's, willing to open your eyes to imagine, to see and to plan new ways to thrive in a future that looks different than the past.

...You worry about your need to meet your financial commitments and to sustain your established life style.

...You need doses of inspiration as well as a practical guide to get you started on your future.

Who will benefit the most from reading this book?

You will if you plan to continue to work in America throughout your maturity. Or, to quote President John F. Kennedy – you will if you understand that: "The time to put on a new roof is when the sun is still shining."

Lest we limit your dreams of the future at an arbitrary chronological time, we believe you will benefit from reading the book at any age that is old enough to understand that good work matters.

Later in the book, you will read a few short stories by people who are well into their maturity and who are, today, contributing in new, different and better ways than in their youth or middle years.

Why is this book vitally important to you?

It is precisely because of your longer life expectancy that you are likely to outlive your savings and investments. You may find that you need some form of gainful work to see you through this longer lifetime.

Since you have so much of a lifetime ahead of you, you may feel that one of the most important of life's secrets is finding something meaningful to do. We are here to show you that "creating" something meaningful to do is within your grasp.

In fact, we believe that it is only through a lifetime well lived and well spent that any of us can, for certain, measure the value of our existence at all.

And, you will find the book important if you agree with the growing body of evidence that suggests that working longer will be a positive influence in ensuring a longer and more vital lifetime.

This book will guide you to understand the changes in the workplace and to succeed in a new world of work; a world you did not choose, do not always understand, and where your expectations may have been dashed by the lightening-fast, changing realities of our economy.

If you are confused as to how to start to create a meaningful and joyful mature career, this book will offer you food for thought, strategies, tactics and themes to help you identify and achieve your goals.

How is the book "laid out?"

This book is laid out in eight steps filled with substantive, easy to read and useful information that will show you how to get started, where to go for help or inspiration, and what to do when you are stalled. It is both an informational resource and practical guide to taking the first steps in your creative career planning and life changing process.

The book initially focuses on helping you to find the motivation to get moving with your own mature career plans. It offers reasons for you to pay close attention to the changes that affect you. By understanding the fundamental changes in the U.S. world of work, it is our expectation that the facts and figures, as well as some assumptions, will speak volumes by themselves.

The book then presents "working" sections that include a body of information that will help you to learn more about the need for planning, managing, and making dramatic adjustments or small changes to your thoughts and goals for your own future. Exercises will help you to integrate each topic's key lessons with your thought processes, unique points-of-view and strategic goals. You will identify your strengths and determine your readiness for meeting the challenges of a changed world. You will be given the opportunity to develop a working plan to systematically achieve your goals. It includes information on today's hot career paths and businesses, new opportunities that are in the pipeline as well as information as to how to get to where you are going. Real life stories from people who have met the challenge of making significant changes to their own lives and careers will inspire you to move forward with your own plan and to stay the course until you reach your goal.

Acknowledgments

We would like to thank family, friends, colleagues and clients who provided inspiration, motivation and specific contributions to this endeavor.

Our spouses, Hector (a member of the Silent Generation) and Pam (Boomer); Carleen's children, Chuck and Lorraine, Heather and Steve, and Steven (the Sandwich Generation & Generation X); Brad's daughter, Taylor (Gen Z); and Carleen's grandchildren, Charlie, Sam, Carleen and Vivian (Gen Y {We like "WHY"} & Gen Z) provided the support necessary to get through the trying times and helped us celebrate the many small successes along the way.

Colleagues, friends and contributors to the book – The Baby Boomer and the "Not so Silent" Generation themselves whose names and contributions appear throughout its pages, provided valuable ideas and experiences. Colleagues like Anette Asher, John Arslain, Jim Dodgen, Mike Freccero, Noha Garas, Pam Grosicki, Kirk O'Hara, Carolyn Parrott, Manville Smith and Pete Tzavalas believed in the course of change and fought for the future during a time of (almost) insurmountable challenge. Steven Koeppe at DADA Advanced Design Associates provided his creative brain power in the design and put up with our many changes in the development of the book.

The many clients we've been honored to assist over the years who have shared their challenges and successes as they navigated the turbulent waters of career transition.

Thanks also to the endorsers of the book – we still cannot believe our good fortune in attracting such well-known authors and experts to endorse this first book in a trilogy on the subject of working older in America.

About the Authors

Carleen MacKay is the subject-matter expert on all aspects of the maturing workforce for Spherion, a leading staffing, recruiting and workforce solutions provider in North America. As Spherion's expert on 3rd careers, Carleen leads the development and delivery of a comprehensive suite of career transition and career management services for mature professionals. As a nationally recognized expert on developing the mature career, she is often quoted in the media and is always provocative in her responses to the press. Her purposeful lifework is based on the premise that experienced workers both need and want to continue working long beyond the traditional retirement age. Her roles as co-author of Boom or Bust!, writer/editor and producer of 3rd Careers - HOT TOPICS, a weekly newsletter for individuals seeking additional knowledge about this stage of their work lives, and an active career consultant fill Carleen's days with a sustainable state of fun that some people call "work."

Brad Taft is the founder and president of Taft Resource Group, a career management and outplacement consulting firm. He has over 25 years experience in the employment and career consulting fields where he has developed, delivered and marketed executive search, career transition and organizational development services. His early career was in executive recruiting with firms including Korn/Ferry International. Brad then moved to the outplacement industry, where in addition to founding two of his own companies he held senior level consulting, management and marketing positions with three national firms. He received a B.A. in communications and a M.B.A. from the University of Southern California. An accomplished public speaker and writer on career and organizational issues, he has written numerous articles and has been quoted in various publications including the Wall Street Journal, Money, Los Angeles Times and the Employment Law Letter.

Introduction

What Workplace Change Means for You

Employability of the maturing workforce in America – Now at "Red Alert."

A spine-tingling problem confronts the U.S. In the last decade of the last century, the majority of the U.S. workforce labored in reasonably stable jobs and lived in relative isolation from the rest of the world. As a result, many of us missed noticing the first large waves of workplace change - the growing tsunami of corporate mergers and acquisitions. Some of us were intently focused on the dot.com revolution, a mere blip in time that created new organizations into which we quite literally poured our hearts and emptied out pocketbooks. Others, especially those of us who lived and worked in the American heartland, labored on as in the past. A few of us felt the first tingles of concern.

Fast forward to today. This is the time and place where many of us find ourselves trapped in the torrential current of a different economy, paddling furiously in the waves of technological change and drowning in the whirlpool of remarkably increased global competition.

As the waves of change rock the U.S., private organizations try to squeeze every penny they can out of their thinning pocketbooks in the hope they will weather the storm of change and maintain enough profitability to last until the next wave of innovation.

Still, many of us hoped for the return of a mythological kingdom where all would be as it had once been.

> *"Things will soon be as they were"* some dreamers still say.

"Things will never be as they were" a growing number of realists are saying today.

The facts are that employers will continue to 'do whatever it takes' to effectively cut costs, and they will not return to the past, nor will we. Employers will accelerate their efforts to control their variable costs. "People" are the variable costs over which employers have the most control.

Even now, the public sector is being rocked by many of the challenges the private sector experienced a few short years ago. The truth is that our world – public and private – is forever changed and we should have seen it coming.

Workforce reductions and organizational restructurings will continue. This workforce fall-out has completely unraveled the regular, full-time employer/employee relationship.

This is what the change means to you.

Boomers, many of whose work lives were spent in a so-called merit (longevity) based economy, are the most costly to employ and, as a result, are the most likely to be affected by this unraveling. The same employers who have long used age and "early-retirement" as reasons for reducing headcount through massive lay-offs, are now doing so at an *accelerated* pace.

Cost cutting measures include the transition from employing long-term, full-time employees to a new kind of workforce model — one composed of flexible, part-time or just-in-time staff and outsourced, insourced or shared sourced solutions.

What is to be made of this spine-tingling problem?

Is all the news as gloomy as a recent joint study conducted by AARP and the Society for Human Resource Management (SHRM) suggests? In their study, they found that the majority of employers—65%—do not actively recruit older workers in any capacity!

Or, does the fact that the Bureau of Labor Statistics estimates that by 2006, 40% of the adult U.S. population will be over 50 concern you? How about the fact that one American is turning 50 every 7 seconds? Finally, if Boomers are laid off at 4 or 5 times the rate of other employees, yet we are almost 50% of the population, what is to become of this segment of the workforce?

These facts should, at the very least:

- *Raise the hairs on the back of your head*
- *Cause your spine to tingle*
- *Give you bad dreams*
- *Instill fears for your future, and that of your children to new heights*

Concern is too soft a word to apply to the situation. Scared to death may be a more realistic response – especially, if you have no clue as to how to navigate your future. But, then again, why should you know how to do this? This is a NEW day in America.

Of course, this book wouldn't mean much to any reader if it focused on the gloom and doom of change or failed to suggest new ways to cope and to thrive in a new economy.

There are answers to working successfully in a new era – they are not difficult – but they are very different than our experience suggests.

The blueprint and process for effecting your own change is in the book. How you manage the personal impact of change is your challenge.

You will "Boom or Bust" depending upon the choices you make.

Here is the good news.

There is a pot of gold at the end of this particular rainbow!

But, like the savvy 49ers of yore, you will have to look in a *different* and new direction to find it!

My story by Carleen MacKay...

In 1989, I happened to be switching planes on a long ride between eastern cities. As was, and is, my habit, I bought a plane-reading book that turned out to be pivotal to the new dawn of my thinking about a very different future than my experience suggested.

The book was *The Age of Unreason* by Charles Handy, a self-described philosopher and widely acknowledged writer, broadcaster, oil executive, economist, professor, lecturer and consultant. In his book, Mr. Handy suggested that the developed countries' world of work was forever changed and that the changing nature of organizational life was already underway and we had but to see it to catch up! Remember that this was written in the 80's.

Encapsulated, Mr. Handy gave strong voice to other's softly whispered suggestions that the industrial age was over for the developed countries, including the U.S. The lifetime job, he wrote, was gone...or, at least, dying. He suggested that there were new meanings to explore and new ways to work and that we had better be listening to the challenges and the opportunities if we were to thrive.

Fascinating reading — but, what was most important to me about the book only occurred to me a few years later when I read the book again, woke up with a start and realized that virtually everything he described regarding the developed countries' world of work and their organizational structures had happened – or was happening.

One of the themes I came to understand from his book was his attention to the meaning surrounding the word "worklife." Mr. Handy described our work lives as a shamrock, the three-leafed symbol of the Christian Trinity, as three or four leaves representing a work portfolio, one where we would be balancing several tasks, some of them simultaneously, over a working lifetime.

I believed him.

At the same time, and with respect to Mr. Handy, I rephrased his new concept of worklife to the term "lifework" – a much more rewarding and seductive term to my ears than the term worklife. It was the concept of lifework in a changed economy that helped me to create new themes and patterns in my own life and in my own "work." When I think of lifework, it attaches a meaning – a passion, if you will, to the idea of work.

I continued to read and to learn and, ultimately, I came up with three key truths about myself as the result of reflecting upon Mr. Handy's words and the rising chorus of voices of other authors, poets, economists and futurists. The following is what was true for me then and is still true for me now.

#1

I believed that my mental and physical health would benefit from staying actively engaged in some form of work throughout most of my lifetime.

I now know this belief does not apply to me alone. Growing evidence, by various U.S. and worldwide centers for study on topics associated with aging populations, routinely reports connections between longer work lives and longer life spans.

Much of the research has been focused on genes, advances in medical science and lifestyle - yet, the links to psychological factors such as a positive self-image and the sense that there is still more meaningful work to do may be equally important to extending life.

I wondered what the outcome for me would be if all of that was taken away at some arbitrary age labeled "retirement." It felt ominous. Think about the stories we all have heard about people dying shortly after retirement. Why wouldn't they? Bored and depressed, perhaps? Undervalued and lonely?

What is the secret of attaining great age? Is it, in part, work? Is it here that our positive self-perception is often well nurtured? And, when we lose not just our jobs but also our work lives, do we not feel the blow to our self-worth?

*It became clear to me that
we are meant to be productive, well connected
and valued for our contributions throughout our lives.*

The Institute for the Study of Aging and the International Longevity Center (ILC-USA) studies cognitive loss due to aging. It has found that *lifelong learning* allows for intellectual stimulation and *leads to brain growth*. If you are interested in reading what ILC-USA has to say about various topics related to the aging brain, go to www.ilcusa.org.

*I asked myself where does learning happen best for me?
It is in the workplace that I find myself mentally challenged – not in the schoolroom.*

What influence does the type of work we do have on increasing our lifespan? Is it through the right choice of work that we can find the meaning of life? Is good work, in part, what adds to our relevancy to society, to our community and to our families?

*I needed to find out what type of work meant the most to me.
I knew that it was my learning mind, not an aging back,
that would see me through to longer productive years.*

#2

I knew that I both wanted and needed a continued income if I hoped to remain independent and enjoy a longer, reasonably comfortable life.

I wondered about what I might do to ensure a continued income stream for my family. I knew that early retirement and its increased benefits might relieve employers of guilt, but I also knew the thinly disguised perquisites of early retirement would not provide for inflation, nor would they overcome boredom, nor, as it turned out later, would they bridge the gaps lost by strangled pensions and sickly 401k's.

As time went by, I thought about what the impact of a strong blip in the economy might have on accelerating my own unplanned early retirement. I was right to wonder because, as it turned out, stock market "adjustments" significantly reduced, or literally wiped out, retirement portfolios for those of us who sought support for our savings in the stock market. Jobs were eliminated – careers came to an abrupt end.

I thought about other savings. How much would I need to live a longer life in relative comfort?

Research quickly demonstrated that roughly half of us have failed to save much toward retirement. Well, I was saving, but was it going to be enough? What was enough?

I studied organizations with defined pension plans and saw the quiet erosion that was taking place. Today we know that some pensions from previous generations have even been eliminated in the private sector. And, we now know that the public sector is suffering from the early stages of pension reform as whole cities face deficits in pension plan fundings.

I gave some thought to Social Security benefits and took the time to check what my benefits might provide. The Social Security Act of 1935 was created at a point-in-time when only one in four workers even lived to collect their benefits at age 65. It dawned on me that social security was never linked to longevity – not only this, but I ultimately realized that social security's effectiveness was reliant upon a scheme in which current social security recipients were sponsored by current workers. Population rises and drops and, most importantly, medical technology and our ever-increasing life spans were not taken into account when the system was set up.

There will soon be 77-78 million people over 50. By 2006, 40% of all American adults will be 50 or older. It seems obvious that the next (and much smaller) generation cannot feasibly sustain us.

Alone, financially dependent, uninspired by each waking morning...
Not the picture I want to paint for my future!

According to an AARP study in 2002, over 80% of the maturing population would like to continue to work in some capacity, but most baby boomers have been caught in a dilemma of how to change and accommodate to new ways to work gainfully in the largely de-jobbed world of the mature worker. Other emerging workforce statistics reinforce this point-of-view: For example, according to AARP, only 33% of today's workers expect to retire between the ages of 55 to 64. 40% of workers expect to retire between the ages of 64 to 69. The rest of us would like to plan to work past the age of 70. Furthermore, mature workers (baby boomers and WWII generation adults) make up 70% of employees who say they are most likely to want to stay with their current employer for the next five years. This worker data is almost in direct contrast with employers' actions.

With the average lifespan in the United States approaching 82.5 years (depending on which statistical table you source), it is no wonder people want and need to work longer. Even if you can stay healthy, there seems to me to be simply too many of us to slide gracefully into too long a downhill ride into retirement. There are certainly too many of us to spend 1/3 of our remaining lives bored, depressed, ill and – dare I say it – poor?

Continuing to work is not only essential to keeping mature workers mentally engaged, but also considering the ever-rising life expectancy, fallout of retirement portfolios and unreliability of social security, it is vital for our very survival!

#3

I knew intuitively that work had to transcend mere drudgery in the last third of what I hoped was my own long life.

The words of George Elliott began to play over and over in my thoughts. "It is never too late to be what you might have been."

I wanted something more from work than simply work itself.

I thought about what I loved, what my passions were and what I could make money doing. For me, the answer as to what I loved was reading and researching – then the obvious connection surfaced. I was not only interested in reading and researching but I was compelled to study about work, workplace trends and shifts. And, since I was maturing in a society that has not particularly valued older workers (or older people for that matter), I was interested in learning how to thrive as an older working person in an aging population. The trip to the future began almost (but not quite) that easily.

Three unyielding truths – and a belief in the changes in the world of work that Charles Handy wrote about; could this be the beginning for me? Did I need a plan?

Next, I developed a mission statement based on the 3 truths.

"I will find my lifework's passion and get paid for doing it. I will stay true to my commitment to doing only that work which matters to me and, at the same time, meets an emerging marketplace need. And, I will – for the rest of my life — pay close attention to trends and changes that affect my choices."

I posted the mission on my refrigerator.

From that day to this, I have never changed the statement – awkward phrasing and all.

I identified a personal interest.

Although I was far from certain that career management was my life passion, it seemed like a good starting point since I really needed to manage my own career anyway.

I began to simplify my life by working my way out of debt.

Ultimately, (today) I am unencumbered.

I studied the stories of others who had made their own "lifework" journeys.

Their stories are shared with you in a later chapter of the book. They inspired me because many of these friends started relatively late to actually plan their mature lifework. They paid the price to get what they wanted. I trust you will find the inspiration you need from these hearty pioneers.

I discovered the value of self-assessment and journaling.

Easy exercises in self-assessment and journaling suggestions are shared with you in this book.

The work I did to complete these short tasks confirmed what I already knew. The exercises gave me descriptive language to use with others and provided much needed reinforcement for my own thoughts and dreams.

I decided to use a simple business-planning model as my blueprint.

It was the model with which I was familiar. A scaled down model is in the book and it will guide you step-by-step, set your timelines and help you through the process of self-discovery and into a world of work of your own creation.

Our story...the story of a working generation is captured throughout this book in Step 5, the section entitled "Your Career Options." It will help you to see how others, who have made a transitional career journey, accomplished their objectives.

Adapt or fail, dear reader.

We are moving from a perceived 'safer time' to today — where firms are attempting to stay as small as possible and layoffs occur at any time or place for any reason. With this, the maturing workforce is faced with a choice...adapt or fail.

But could this forced adaptation be opportunity knocking?

Is it possible that as the old door closes, new windows of opportunity are being flung open?

Can it be that the early adapters of our species are finding new challenges, more fun and highly profitable endeavors in this changed world of work?

The answer is...yes...opportunity is knocking in many ways.

There are alternative ways to contribute other than time and place oriented, regular, full-time, same career jobs.

*Consider the following options, which represent **some** of the alternative work choices you will explore in the second section of the book:*

1. Part-Time, casual or scheduled work
2. Long-term temporary assignments, contracts and "gigs"
3. Interim, independent professional, free agent roles
4. Coaching, consulting and mentoring
5. Starting a small business or a home-based business
6. Buying a franchise
7. Selling products on the Internet
8. Phasing into retirement
9. Re-positioning your career by pursuing new educational opportunities
10. Sage work, i.e., specializing, such as in startups and turnarounds
11. Volunteering
12. Non-profits
13. Government opportunities
14. Stress free jobs
15. Fanciful work and fun options

This list hints at some of the choices we have presented for you to explore. It is not complete. For a complete list, you will have to read Step 5.

Your story.

If statistics hold true, it may turn out that my journey to discovery may be, in some part, your story. If so, the challenge the book proposes to you is to learn how to continue to work and how to find y*our life's purpose* and *meaning* in the world of the mature worker.

It is possible that you know why you want or need to continue to work. Your reasons may be monetary, or you may be bored by the work you are doing today. You may be tired of a demanding job and need a change to a slower pace. You may have given up an important dream that you would like to pursue. You may be at a point in time that you realize the work you are doing now will not be available in the future because of workplace change. You may simply want to pursue a new adventure – one that might take you into the world of Internet sales or starting a home-based business. Whatever your reason or reasons, this is a good place to capture your own journal of truth or truths.

_____

_____

_____

_____

NOTES

Whether you are working today in any capacity or, if you are retired, laid-off or between "gigs," the work we will do together will take you to a destination of your own choosing.

The 8 Steps of this workbook will help you to:

Reflect on your values, principles, motivations and who you are today.

Learn the latest information about how work has changed and is changing.

Explore new opportunities that are "hot" today.

Integrate marketplace information with your future work choices.

Overcome perceived challenges and real barriers.

Apply what you have learned.

Receive practical, step-by-step techniques and tools to help reach your goal.

For the proverbial picture "worth a thousand words" consider the growth in the U.S. workforce, by age, for the calendar years 2002-2012 according to The U.S. Department of Labor's Bureau of Labor Statistics.

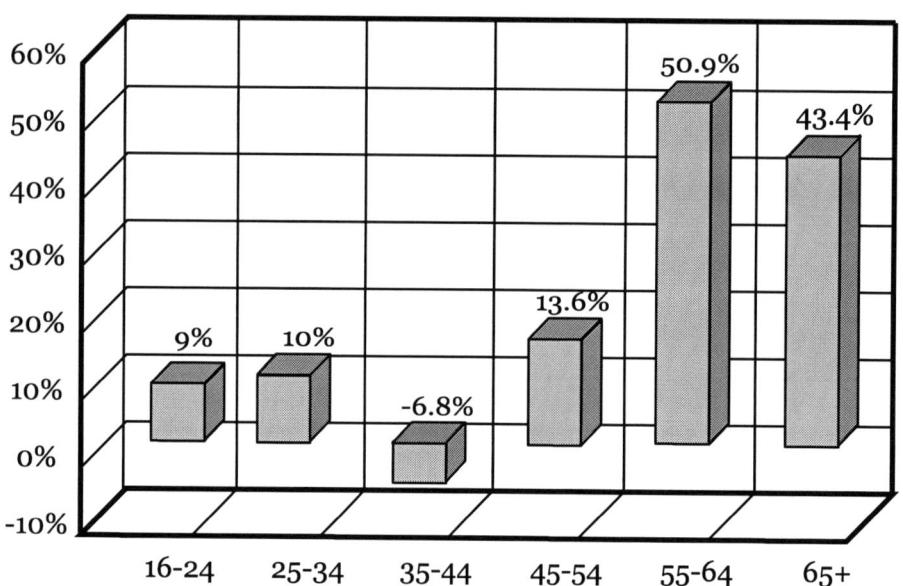

We recommend that you view this process of experiential learning as a journey and that you take the time to complete each step in the order it is presented. Should you encounter an obstacle or run head on into a real barrier, seek additional help from a qualified Career Coach who will add value to those difficult side paths you may encounter from time-to-time in your journey.

BOOM OR BUST! *New Career Strategies In A New America* 11

If you would not start a business without a plan why would you run your career without one?

Year in and year out that is exactly what most people do! They let chance — not choice — drive their work and, consequently, their lives.

The planning process is anchored by a series of 8 easy to follow steps. Reading from the bottom of the page to the top, the steps look like this:

"A GOAL
WITHOUT A PLAN
IS SIMPLY A WISH UPON A STAR"

Step 8 Marketing Tool Kit — Beyond resumes

Step 7 Your Plan — Organizing my campaign

Step 6 Challenges Barriers — What is in my way?

Step 5 Your Career Options — What works for me today? Which options should I pursue?

Step 4 Today's Hot Opportunities — Which careers are hot and what are my alternatives?

Step 3 Marketplace Trends — What has changed, or is changing, in the world of work? Do I need to change priorities or perspective?

Step 2 Internal Analysis — What are my competencies, skills, values and interests? Where is my best fit?

Step 1 Letting Go — What do I want to stop doing? What is no longer important to me?

NOTES

Letting Go of the Past

> *Our clients said...*
>
> "When I joined the workforce, I thought - there was a there - and now, I realize that not only was there not there, the thought that there was something there at all was a myth and I had lost myself somewhere along the way."
>
> *If you can figure this out...you've worked in corporate America.*
>
> "I am through working for insecure people who use their management roles merely as narcissistic tools to make themselves feel important at the expense of others."
>
> *A common sentiment regardless of your experience in either private or public organizations.*
>
> "I worked hard to take care of my family in a job that, while it was somewhat interesting, didn't really fulfill me. I don't know where I am going next, but I am going to take the time to find out what matters to me."
>
> *Hearing this is a source of great sorrow, as well as great hope, to career coaches everywhere.*
>
> "Maybe I just need to find some way to continue to do what I have always done in order to maintain a reasonable income to support me in my old age. Then again, if I could learn something new, maybe I can overcome my fears and have some fun. I am willing to try."
>
> *Good news....This person was ready to learn.*

Someone else once said...
"It's never too late unless you think it is."
We agree with that statement.

And, we add:

If you can let go of the past,
you will find that you can move ahead
no matter what your chronological age is today.

Since you will be bringing your "self" into your future, it is important to take a hard look at the opportunities and challenges the future portends for you, for your family and for your unrequited dreams.

When you were young and new to the adult world of work, you were like the puppy, the youngster for whom every experience was novel. You learned by trial and error. You were adventuresome and foolish. You were independent and optimistic. When you did not like doing something, you stopped doing it, changed jobs — or changed companies — and went on. Change was more about getting rid of what you did not like rather than taking the time to discover what you wanted! You made mistakes but corrected course readily. You were not stopped by fear and uncertainty and had little to lose as everything lay ahead of you and there seemed to be plenty of time to change or adjust. Think of this time of your life as time spent in your first career or, metaphorically, as your 1st Act in a 3 Act play!

When you were in your early mid-life, you were apt to take a more cautious approach to work than during your youth. Perhaps you were caught up in consumer games of acquisition and one-upping the neighbors. You might have been raising children. This was also a time when the boomer generation was more likely to be changing spouses than jobs. During this mid-time of life you may have settled for "good enough" in your work life, confusing your security needs with the perceived risks that stood in your way of achieving a richly rewarding future. If you were part of a lucky few, you achieved what you went after and it was good. Yet, lucky or unlucky, wise or hard working, there are aspects to the work you once did that no longer matter. Think of this time of your life as time spent in your second career or, metaphorically, as your 2nd Act in a 3 Act play!

Now that you are in your mature working years, jobs you didn't like, work whose meaning has long since faded from your list of important memories, things you did for gain but that were not fun or worthwhile, the youthful ambitions that, once achieved, rang hollow - all of these may be unpacked from your "baggage" of long ago and left behind in the past where they belong.

If you are alive, everything still lies ahead. There is still time to be the best of who you might have been. There is still time to do good work.

Following a short intermission,
while you let go of the past and strategically plan your third career,
you will come to see that your 3rd Act is your opportunity
to pull your life play together for a grand finale.

You are, at long last,
both the author and the central character
of your 3rd Act.

End of your 2nd act. Intermission is over. Let the 3rd act begin...

The 3rd act signals the moment in time when you are given the opportunity to align yourself with good work that you define based on this moment in your lifetime.

Your first exercise is to let go of what you no longer want in your work portfolio. The following exercise, in letting go of past experiences that no longer serve you well, will help you to get started.

Note what others have said they no longer want from their past work experience. Reflect on their thoughts. Is there a grain of truth in others' words that rings true for you?

"Don't like 80% of what I used to do and here's the laundry list of those things..."
"Tired of travel and don't want work that involves commuting long distances"
"The sun has set on bad management – I won't tolerate jerks again"
"Get me out of the corporate political environment"
"Want to give up the long hours"

Take a metaphorical "time-out." Reflect on work you don't want to do again or what doesn't work for you any longer. Capture your thoughts in the space provided.

1

2

3

For more information on "letting go" of the past, read *Repacking Your Bags* by Richard Leider. His story will help you to unpack those items from your backpack (i.e., your working past) that no longer matter to you. Richard Leider has a more recent offering entitled *The Power of Purpose: Creating Meaning in Your Life and Work* that may inspire you. Tom Peters' recent book, *Re-imagine*, is also a provocative reading experience and a guide to both letting go and imagining your future.

Get ready for Step 2! Step 2 will propel you into a future of your own choosing.

Be prepared to be deliberate and bold.

The work ahead will help you to abandon senseless fears.

NOTES

Step 2

Internal Analysis

How do you view your future today?
What are the principles you live and work by?
What talent and skills do you offer?
What is your preferred work environment?
What is your unique style?
What motivates you?

Come on down from the clouds of retrospection.
Get a toehold on today's reality.
Welcome to Step 2 of your plan.

How do you view your future today?

How do you feel about your future at this moment in time?

> Are you eager, optimistic, or self-confident?

>> Are you cautious, curious or uncertain?

>>> Are you discouraged, anxious, or struggling?

Can you think of one word — just one word that accurately describes how you feel about your future at this particular moment? Write it down.

Your One Word: _____

It is *always* useful to know what you are feeling because your feelings often govern how you will act. Many times, it is *only* our feelings that set our limitations or, conversely, allow us to achieve new heights – even beyond our wildest wish list.

Regardless of where you are today, your confidence and optimism will grow as you put together your plan for your future.

Recall the words of Henry David Thoreau when he wrote: *"I went to the woods because I wished to live deliberately, and not, when I came to die, discover that I had not lived."*

Copy and Clip

> *A note for your refrigerator.*
>
> *Living and working well are deliberate choices, they are not random happenings.*
>
> *It takes skills and self-confidence to do both and you only get what you want if you are willing to do the work.*

What are the principles you live and work by?

Principles are not the words you say.

They are the actions you demonstrate each and every day.

Think for a few minutes about other people you have known and whose "principles" you have observed throughout the years.

For example, do you know someone whose integrity is beyond question? Is there a person whom you would describe as the salt of the earth and another who is devoted to a cause?

Principles, as they relate to work, may be thought of as describing the best of who you have become and it is likely that you have already earned a reputation for your principled actions.

Here is a simple way to help identify your most important principles. If others had to describe you, what would they say or, what would you hope they would say?

Your response: _____

_____

_____

_____

_____

_____

_____

_____

_____

_____

_____

_____

Next, read the following list, select and **check ( ) 2 or 3 phrases** that are most like you at your principled working "best." If you don't find your best view of yourself from our list, add your own definition.

Be certain to include your response from the previous page.

You are best known and respected for your:

1. _____ Unswerving action
2. _____ Widely acknowledged business ethics
3. _____ Absolute integrity in everything you do or say
4. _____ Truthful, straight-forward ("tell it like it is") communications
5. _____ Extraordinary persistence
6. _____ Commitment to a cause
7. _____ Courage "under fire"
8. _____ Ability to face risks
9. _____ Strength of character
10. _____ Calm, well-balanced approach to solving problems
11. _____ Decisive, fast response to tough challenges
12. _____ Disciplined work style
13. _____ People-centered concern
14. _____ Persuasive, influential presence
15. _____ Flexibility and accommodation to frequent change
16. _____ Extraordinary responsiveness
17. _____ Always doing the job right the first time
18. _____
19. _____
20. _____

What talent do you offer?

At last, you have lived long enough to know what you are really good at, what you have learned and what you have done consistently best over the years.

In Part 1 of the following exercise, please identify the special, inherent talent that you have contributed to others throughout your career.

For example, a particularly creative person would want to communicate this talent to any prospective organization before making a commitment to a new job or role.

By using language that accurately describes your talent (not to be confused with your skills or competencies), you have a better chance of making a good career choice and shining as a star in your next "gig" wherever it might be!

On the next page is a list of choices.

From the following list, please **check ( ) 2 or 3 words** that most accurately describe your natural born talent. Add your own adjectives if our choices do not accurately capture what you want to communicate.

1. _____ Conceptual
2. _____ Empathetic
3. _____ Friendly
4. _____ Steadfast
5. _____ Adaptable
6. _____ Creative
7. _____ Organized
8. _____ Systematic
9. _____ Trendsetter
10. _____ Flexible
11. _____ Visionary
12. _____ Persistent
13. _____ Collaborative
14. _____ Innovative
15. _____ Original thinker
16. _____ Compassionate
17. _____ Structured
18. _____ Accommodating
19. _____ Spontaneous
20. _____ Precise
21. _____ Interactive
22. _____ Reflective
23. _____ Analytical
24. _____ Logical
25. _____ Practical
26. _____ Pragmatic
27. _____ Independent
28. _____ Intuitive
29. _____
30. _____

Next, from your "top 2 or 3" descriptors, please provide one past career accomplishment that accurately describes each talent you have identified. If you wish you may use more than one descriptor in each accomplishment statement.

> For example, a *creative* friend might write something like this: "I am particularly proud that I was able to **conceptualize** and write a comprehensive and **unique** book on behalf of every "boomer" working in America just at that precise moment in time when the marketplace need was highest. While the book was based on my personal and professional experience, it was the **novel** approach I took in **designing** its content that resulted in the book's reaching the top of the business book bestseller list in the first month it was published."

> The writer used descriptors of inherent conceptual and creative talent to detail an accomplishment and quantify a result.

> For example, a highly *structured, analytic* individual might write about the same accomplishment in the following way: "I **systematically studied** the changes in the U.S. workforce and with great care and **attention to the facts** presented by **quantifiable data**, wrote the **definitive** book on planning and managing your career in a vastly different world of work than experienced by most of us in the recent past. It was as a result of this careful **research** and **analysis** that the book reached the top of the business book bestseller list in the first week of the first month it was published."

The same scenario but different descriptors, message and inherent talent.

The point is that language matters. The language you choose sends specific messages about who you are as well as what you have accomplished.

Now it is your turn to capture your top 2 or 3 identified inherent talents in statements that support your career accomplishments to date. Please do not offer personal accomplishments, stay true to your accomplishments in the work setting.

Accomplishment #1 _____ (talent you choose to illustrate)

I am particularly proud of the time when:

_____
_____
_____
_____
_____

Quantify the result:

_____
_____
_____
_____
_____

Accomplishment #2 _____ (talent you choose to illustrate)

I am particularly proud of the time when:

_____
_____
_____
_____
_____

Quantify the result:

_____
_____
_____
_____
_____

Accomplishment #3_____(talent you choose to illustrate)

I am particularly proud of the time when:

_____
_____
_____
_____
_____

Quantify the result:

_____
_____
_____
_____
_____

What skills do you offer?

Not to be confused with inherent talent, skills are what you have learned to do through experience and practice.

List your skills. For example, you may be able to type very fast. You may be a whiz at Word, PowerPoint, Excel or other aspects of the computer-user's skills. You may know certain programming languages. You may have worked in a call-center using sophisticated telephone equipment. You may be highly skilled in retail sales.

Select 2 or 3 skills from the list that describe your most significant skills and add a description in the space provided.

If you wish to self-identify a skill that is not on our list, please add your own at the end of the exercise.

Computer Skills:

_____
_____
_____
_____

Selling Skills:
_____
_____
_____
_____

Negotiating Skills:
_____
_____
_____
_____

Networking Skills:
_____
_____
_____
_____

Public Speaking Skills:
_____
_____
_____
_____

Business Writing Skills:
_____
_____
_____
_____

Interpersonal Skills:
_____
_____
_____
_____

Language Skills:

Cross-Cultural Skills:

Artistic Skills:

Technical Skills:

Mathematical Skills:

Scientific Skills:

Research Skills:

Other Skills:

What top 2 or 3 skills do you consider to reflect you at your very best?

What is your preferred work environment?

Check ( ) the top 2 or 3 statements, or add your own statements, that most accurately reflect the work environment you prefer.

I would ideally like to work in an environment that provides me with the opportunity to:

1. _____ Research and analyze ideas and concepts
2. _____ Work alone
3. _____ Interact frequently with a collegial team, customers or clients
4. _____ Experience frequent change
5. _____ Invent or create something new
6. _____ Travel extensively
7. _____ Help someone in need
8. _____ Implement structure and processes
9. _____ Influence others
10. _____ Freely offer ideas and suggestions to improve products or services
11. _____ Receive public recognition for good work
12. _____ Be open and direct with people of like persuasion
13. _____ Work from home, at least some of the time
14. _____ Clearly understand the expectations of the day-to-day work itself
15. _____ Enjoy a very, very fast pace
16. _____ Keep up a moderate, steady pace
17. _____ Enjoy the utmost flexibility in my daily schedule
18. _____ Improve the community (or world) in which I live
19. _____ Continue to learn and develop
20. _____
21. _____

What is your unique style?

Check ( ) 2 or 3 words/phrases (or add your own) that accurately describe your work style:

1. _____ Direct
2. _____ Authoritative
3. _____ Collegial
4. _____ Tactful
5. _____ Patient
6. _____ Impatient
7. _____ Driven
8. _____ Collaborative
9. _____ Hierarchical
10. _____ Entrepreneurial
11. _____ Non-hierarchical
12. _____ Wild and impetuous
13. _____ Empathetic
14. _____ Solicitous
15. _____ Mentoring
16. _____ Structured
17. _____ Fun-loving
18. _____ Accommodating
19. _____ Flexible
20. _____
21. _____

What motivates you?

Another way to look at your future from the inside out is to reflect on words and language that come closest to describing your motivations.

Your words are that lifeline of language that gives structure to what motivates you. Carefully chosen words help you to communicate these motivations to others.

By acknowledging your authentic feelings at this moment of your time out, you will gain insight into your high needs, opportunities and, possibly, your barriers to reaching new goals.

The exercise on the following pages is designed to help you express your current motivations about work.

Remember:

There are no right or wrong answers because the feelings you express are simply your facts!

Or, put another way; reflect for a moment, on the words of Frank Zappa who said:

> "Fact of the matter is, there is no hip world, there is no straight world. There's a world, you see, which has people in it who believe in a variety of different things. Everybody believes in something and everybody, by virtue of the fact that they believe in something, uses that something to support their own existence."

Place a **check mark ( )** **by the top 3 statements** that best support what motivates you at this stage of your career.

I would like to:

1. _____ Find something secure that will last long enough to meet my financial needs
2. _____ Explore government jobs in order to ease into a later retirement
3. _____ Find a solid, part-time job, one that does not add to life's stresses
4. _____ Slow down in my present field within my current organization
5. _____ Have someone else, preferably a recruiter, find a job for me, even if it pays less
6. _____ Have one more chance to do something "big" within the scope of my experience
7. _____ Use my experience and further develop my competencies as a "specialist"
8. _____ Work in my previous career field, but as an independent contributor
9. _____ Work in a consulting capacity for an established consulting firm
10. _____ Use my targeted experience to start a small business
11. _____ Do something wildly different that I have yet to identify
12. _____ Return to school and learn something new
13. _____ Re-investigate a dream, something I have always harbored a secret "yen" to do
14. _____ See the world and be paid to do it
15. _____ Change direction by buying a franchise or launching a business
16. _____ Create a legacy, such as found through writing a book or joining the lecture tour
17. _____ Volunteer to help the less fortunate or to improve my community
18. _____ Mentor others, to bring the benefits of my experience to the younger generation
19. _____ Work for pay in a not-for-profit corporation where doing good matters
20. _____ Create a Foundation or Philanthropy
21. _____ Embark upon an area of study that has long interested me
22. _____ Upgrade my skills before I go charging into the future
23. _____ Go back to school and get a degree
24. _____ Teach full-time
25. _____ Get out of the house

List your top 3 responses in descending order of preference:

1. _____

2. _____

3. _____

Review your top 3 responses.

If at least 2 of your top 3 responses are found in the statements #1 through #5, your feelings and thoughts appear to reflect your security needs.

While you may be ready for, or forced into, some changes in your work life, it is likely that you will be very conservative in your approach to dealing with what feels like radical new ideas about work. You will be offered the opportunity to see new ways to help you take small, but powerful, steps into the next stage of your career. *Think of your driving motivation as* **security!**

If at least 2 of your top 3 responses are found in the statements #6 through #10, your feelings and thoughts appear to reflect your interest in maintaining your investment in the past. While you may be ready to explore unfamiliar options, it is likely that you will be most comfortable with using fairly traditional approaches to the job market. Once you understand the benefits, you appear to be ready to learn some new "tricks" to position yourself in any one of several alternative approaches to a largely familiar job market. *Think of your driving motivation as* **experience!**

If at least 2 of your top 3 responses are found in the statements #11 through #15, your feelings and thoughts appear to reflect your curiosity about a future that looks, feels and, in fact, is very different than your past. Since you are an explorer in a new world and ready to look at the many options available, we suggest that you investigate all of the ideas around new ways to work before settling on one. *Think of your driving motivation as* **change!**

If at least 2 of your top 3 responses are in statements #16 through #20, your feelings and thoughts suggest that you are ready to bring the wonderful gift that is you to the world. Many people find that their search for life's meaning is in the helping professions. What better time to explore the satisfaction that service to one's neighbors and local or global communities can provide? That time is now if this is your driving force. *Think of your driving motivation as creating a legacy through* **service!**

If at least 2 of your top 3 responses are in statements #21 through #24, your feelings and thoughts suggest that you are ready to learn something new or to upgrade your skills in order to compete in a new world. What better time is there to learn when learning has been made so easy for you? *Think of your driving motivation as* **learning!**

If your top 3 responses are all over the board, you are ready for a broad-brush approach to learning more about the future as it unfolds. You are the one who is likely to look at the future first and then back at yourself to determine where you fit. *Think of your driving motivation as that of being a* **pioneer!**

Did you check the 25th item — "Get out of the house?"

Did you think we had forgotten to include a definition for this choice?

The reason we included this choice is because this response applies to most of us in less than 90 days of so-called, full-out retirement.

You are ready to pull the pieces of the puzzle together and to think about the themes and patterns you have self-described.

Copy and Clip

> *A refrigerator note for security seekers...Consider the following:*
>
> *You want security but you may be looking in the wrong place.*
> *It does not exist "out there."*
> *No organization will give this to you.*
>
> *Shhhhh....Security lies within you.*

Come down from the clouds – Pull together Steps 1 & 2 of your plan.

Use your words or phrases from the work you have done so far and insert below. Then, try to create a simple paragraph about you by pulling your thoughts together.... Don't worry if the phrasing is awkward. This is an exercise to help you remember what you have said about yourself.

How do I view my future today? (one word)

What motivates me?

What competencies, talents and skills do I offer?

What is my preferred work environment?

What is my unique style?

Pull it together in a short paragraph about you!

Step 3

Marketplace Trends

> *For the first time ever we must learn to learn from the future that is upon us, not just from the lessons of the past.*
>
> *In fact, it has been said by some that we must even unlearn our lessons from the past.*
>
> Let's take a short journey through the trends that shaped today and then, together, explore the future in keeping with our philosophy that we must align our work with the marketplace as it is and as it is becoming.

Test your knowledge of changing demographics – a quiz.

Take our true or false quiz to determine what you know about the changes in the U.S. that affect you.

_____By 2006, 40% of adult Americans will be over 50.

_____By 2015, workers over 50 are projected to comprise 20% of the workforce.

_____By 2008, the median age of the U.S. worker will be 40.

_____The total U.S. population tripled from 1900 to 2000.

_____People in the 45 to 64 year old range outnumber the population under 15.

_____Life expectancy at the turn of this century approached 80, regardless of gender.

_____Married couple households are now at an all time low.

_____Research has found no significant relationship between age and job performance.

_____Population over 65 has increased 10 fold in the past 100 years.

_____People 55 and older take fewer sick days than their younger counterparts.

_____At the beginning of the last century, life expectancy was 47 years.

_____When Social Security eligibility for full benefits was set at age 65, life expectancy was 62.

_____Today, 3.8 out of every 4 workers are expected to live until age 65.

_____By 2012, more people are projected to be leaving, rather than joining, the regular workforce.

_____The fastest growing users of the Internet are people over 50.

_____Social Security benefits are the primary source of income to over 50% of people over 65.

_____By 2020, there will be double the number of people over 85 than there were in 1990.

Total your True _____and False_____ responses and turn the page for the answers.

> ## ALL THE ANSWERS ARE TRUE
> *And many of these truths affect you or your loved ones.*
> *From a political, societal and economic perspective, the implications are huge.*
> *Read on to learn more about the marketplace trends that affect you and yours.*
>
> (All statistics are courtesy of the Department of Labor and the Bureau of Census)

History's lessons learned-
-A retrospective journey of work in the United States of America.

Were you born in the '30's? There were 48 states and life expectancy was close to age 60. Secretary Frances Perkins helped Franklin Roosevelt to make wages a campaign issue and, during the first year of the Fair Labor Standards Act, covered workers were provided with a minimum wage of 25 cents per hour based on a 44-hour workweek. This baseline was raised to 40 cents per hour in the second year of the program. The Social Security Act of 1935 created the unemployment compensation program and provided maximum benefits at age 65 to covered workers. Of course, since life expectancy was around age 60, few people lived to "enjoy" Social Security benefits. The average annual salary was around $1,500 and unemployment stood at around 25% in much of the nation. Men worked in blue-collar jobs and women stayed at home. Labor Unions were strong. You might describe the typical American family as survivalists, not consumers, in the 30's. We were perfectly suited to factory work; and workers, such as those in the canning industry, often worked 10 hours a day for $4.50 per week. The "lucky" men worked in the automobile industry, railroads, steel companies and mines. The rest worked hand-to-mouth at whatever they could find.

Were you born in the 40's? Men went to war and women went to work. The bombing of Pearl Harbor created the American Nursing Association and over 179,000 women enrolled in the U.S. Cadet Nurse Corps. Other women labored in woolen mills to make blankets for our soldiers and in factories to produce munitions and tanks. 1946 marked the official start of the baby boomer generation as men returned home from war and we produced the largest boom in birthrates in the history of the U.S. Because of the G.I. bill, an emphasis was focused on higher education, at least for the men. The Industrial Age was in full swing and the first signs of the emerging, educated White Collar workforce were seen and felt. The minimum wage was raised to 43 cents per hour and new industries, such as the plumbing industry took off as 55% of American homes had indoor plumbing by the '40's. The 1940's saw the beginning of "Right to Work Laws" – simply stated – American workers did not have to join unions in order to work in unionized factories. Today, 22 states offer Right to Work Laws. We welcomed the behemoth...IBM to the world of work and Americans took their first, unknowing and hesitant steps away from the industrialized age into the age of knowledge workers.

For a sweet story about a woman who epitomized the lifestyles of women during the war years, go to http://www.stg.brown.edu/projects/WWII_Women/Grandma.html. Kathy O'Grady interviewed her grandmother Katherine O'Grady for a real life description of what it was like to live and work during the 2nd World War.

Were you born in the 50's? For the first time, the middle-class dominated the economy and male college graduates were told that by "keeping their noses to the grindstone," they would soon forge their way as leaders of manufacturing firms in our lightening-fast, industrial-based economy. The post-war baby boom continued in full swing. Women were entering college to become teachers or health-care professionals or, simply, to snag better educated husbands than they might otherwise find. The first universal credit card was issued by Diner's Club in 1950 and, thus, began a full-out swing to consumerism as American debt began to rise at an unprecedented rate. The average salary in the 1950's was $2,992/year – a number that allowed William Levitt (founder of Levittown in Long Island) to build affordable houses in the suburbs for the new middle-class. Congress created the Small Business Administration. The number of workers providing services began to catch up with the number of workers producing products.

The '60's – the years the last of the baby boomers were born. "We stand today on the verge of a new frontier" said President John F. Kennedy as he took office following a narrow defeat of Richard M. Nixon due, in large part, to his success on the first televised political debates in which he clearly outsmarted and outclassed RMN. TV changed the way we saw the world and it fueled consumer buying to a feverish new pitch. The minimum wage was raised to $1.00 per hour in the '60's and the average American salary was $4,730/year. It was in 1964 that the Civil Rights Act was enacted, paving a way for certain changes on behalf of the previously disenfranchised minority groups in America. More and more women entered the workforce; divorce rates zoomed and married couple households declined. Youth migrated West and the older generation migrated South. We noticed the older generation for the first time as advances in medicine ("better living through chemistry") began to dramatically increase life expectancy to 65 years. Birth rates began a steady decline. This reduction was the start of a decline that continues today.

Percentage-wise, our share of the world's population shrunk as our consumption of the world's resources grew. A few people noticed and the first baby steps of the infant environmental movement were taken. Great changes occurred in the '60's. Federal spending increased dramatically with the launch of Medicare, food stamps and educational initiatives. Military spending increased. Labor contracts began including cost-of-living clauses. We ended the '60's with uncomfortably high unemployment rates. As for you, if you were born in 1946, the official start of the baby boomer generation, you turned 18 in 1964, the official end of the birth dates for members of this generation.

If you were growing up in the 70's, you were here when Apple Computer and Microsoft were founded. You were here when 18 year-olds were given the right to vote. You were here when computer games flooded the youth market and the microprocessor was developed. Deregulation occurred in the airlines and other industries. As David Frum stated in his wonderful book, "The '70's – How We Got Here" – this was the decade that brought us modern life "for better or worse." Take the time to read this book because this is the definitive work that changed what and who we are today.

To glide over the '70's in your journey through the world of work is to miss the obvious. For example, did you miss that fact that it was in the '70's when imported manufactured goods began to overtake American made products? It was in the '70's that the computer began to change everything, even where workers would sit as they performed work for multi-national companies. Did you miss the changes in world demographics – the time when third world countries outgrew their ability to care for their own populations and what this meant to American labor? Did you miss the fact that our younger population was diminishing even as China, Bangladesh, India and other countries' populations were exploding? Are you concerned that these countries were, and are, focused on educating their best and brightest while we have been focused on providing a one-size-fits-all education for everyone?

By the end of the 1970's average salaries soared to $7,564 and our national debt rose to $382 billion. Disillusionment began to set in and we lost faith in many of our leaders.

If you were maturing in the 80's, you were here when IBM introduced its PC model, the MTV generation gradually took over much of TV, layoffs in the manufacturing sector gained national attention as cost-conscious executives quietly outsourced lower-level tech jobs abroad to take advantage of lower wages. The rich grew richer, the poor received more entitlements and the middle-class was squeezed. The nation was in recession for the first two years of the '80's and Savings and Loans faltered. Corporate restructurings, fueled by mergers and acquisitions, began in earnest. You were here when Microsoft launched Windows, which, as it later turned out, was another world-changing event in our history of work. You were here when we went on a binge-buying spree and the "status seeker" generation was in full swing. Bigger houses, larger mortgages, more credit buying, and average wages of $15,757 were the norm.

Welcome to the 90's. Fondly thought of by many as the "electronics age," the Internet moved front and center into our daily lives. From 3 million users in 1994 to over 100 million users by 1998, the Internet now commands and controls much of our lives. The minimum wage was increased to $5.15/hour in 1997 and several states became "majority-minority" states. The labor force was revolutionized. The Dow jumped thousands of points as the so-called dot.com revolution swept our major cities, such as Silicon Valley (not a city, but a Northern California state-of-mind) and Boston. Familiar goods disappeared soon to be replaced by more gadgets than most folks would ever need. World markets were linked in ways never anticipated even a few years earlier. Higher-level technology jobs accelerated their march overseas.

Small businesses produced 75% of America's new jobs between 1990 and 1995. The number of women-owned businesses climbed into the lower stratosphere between the beginning and end of the '90's. Small firms began to hire older workers, many of whom preferred part-time work. The 1990's brought new waves of mergers, acquisitions and hostile takeovers changing the landscape – forever, as it turned out, from one of lifetime employment to one of shorter tenure in our larger corporations. Restructuring resulted in significant employment reductions in manufacturing, banking and finance. The term "rightsizing" became commonplace in our business language. A vast variety of stocks boomed. Americans bought many things on margin, including stock.

Here we are in the early 2000's. Investments turned bitterly sour by the early 2000's. Corporate volatility became the name of the business game. Business leaders demonstrated a preference for early retirement programs in favor of younger, cheaper workers. The only workers who grew older in their jobs were the "C" level officers at the very corporations that were laying-off older workers. Annual bonuses for many of these "C" level officers jumped into the higher stratosphere. Information technologies allowed ever-faster delivery times, medical diagnostics became more accurate, and a new range of technologies appeared. We bought more prescription drugs. Our houses grew larger and our bodies grew fatter. All these facts altered the way we do business, work and live today.

Look back over the past 50 years and you will see that we have changed more in every social, economic and cultural sense than we could have imagined. We have lost much of our trust and faith in each other and in the leaders of our organizations. We have discovered or committed ugly new white-collar crimes. In short, we've endured more events than in the entire history of our world before that precious moment you first appeared on the scene.

All so-called Boomers (those born between 1946 and 1964) were here when:

- Manufacturing declined and the service sector grew.
- More workers were in gold-collar jobs than in white or blue-collar jobs.
- The gold-collar (highly skilled) worker adapted daily to more changes.
- The marketplace demanded, and got, previously unimagined customizations of products.
- Unions, except government unions, were increasingly viewed as compressing ever smaller organizational profitability.
- Bonds between employers and employees grew weaker.
- Many employers stopped offering defined benefits that guaranteed payments to retirees.
- The end of the age of paternalism was conceded by employers/employees alike.
- Employers began managing increasingly diverse, including global, work forces.
- The issues of equal pay for equal work continued to be felt by women and by minorities.
- Joining the workforce became a fact of life for over 60% of married women.
- The shift continued from product to service industry employment.
- Technological innovations profoundly impacted how we work today and how we will work tomorrow.
- Biological sciences exploded on the scene increasing life spans and quality of life.
- Substantial numbers of Americans lacked health insurance.
- The aging population began to tax our health and pension systems.
- Stocks soared to new heights, slipped back to pre-boom times and began to seesaw back and forth.
- We became an economy of full-fledged, avaricious, consumer-driven, market gluttons.
- We began to wonder if we could (or should) keep up our spending habits.
- We watched the beginning of the end of corporate and government bamboozling 24/7.

What's next according to the youth of America?

According to a recent Gallup Poll, virtually all teenagers use a computer and most use the Internet for research rather than reading books and magazines.

66% consider that space explorations, new advances in computers and advances in the medical field are the most important subjects for them to pursue. 60% would prefer to live in a "smart" house and over 50% report that they (or their siblings) program all electronic equipment in their households.

According to the same Gallup Poll, 80% believe that we will vote for President on the Internet and almost as many believe that cancer will be cured in their lifetimes. 60% believe AIDS will be cured and 45% believe that space travel will be common for ordinary Americans. Half believe that longevity will exceed 100 years and almost half think human cloning will be common. 40% believe that advances in technology will be developed to prevent wars.

Of course, there are robots; e-toys and creative future think items that rightfully belong in this section.

Is the day coming where the robots will take over the low level jobs the undereducated youth need? Or, have you noticed that many fast-food restaurants are now employing older workers who, although marginally slower, more than make up for this by being more reliable than youth and....we can make change. Watch out! The low-tech members of the youthful generation are beginning to lag behind, working increasingly in low-level jobs for low-level pay.

Since this book is about you and our generation, suffice it to say that youth will change the world of the distant future and we are here to change our world today as well as the world of the near future.

But, the seeds for that distant horizon are being sown now and it is useful to remember that time is moving faster than it used to in that once-upon-a-time fairytale memory of your youth.

You can be part of the start of what's next.

What's next, according to the mature population of America?

Remember: According to the U.S. Census Bureau in May 2003, the number of Americans 45 to 64 increased sharply in the 1990's. The population of those 65 and older either working or looking for a job has grown by 50% since 1980.

Check it out:

- Loneliness alone will prompt more of us to work for free or to work for fees.
- There is growing evidence that the image of American workers retiring completely is unlikely today. For example, a Fall 2003 survey by AARP claims that 7 in 10 Americans expect to work past the once typical retirement age of 65 and nearly half expect to work well into their 70's. Interviews of people between 50 and 70 showed that the main reason for continuing to work past so-called normal retirement is most often the result of financial need.
- By several estimates, at least 1 in 10 people over 65 lives in poverty and this number is steadily growing. Many of these people will have to find whatever they can in order to escape the dreariness of the single room in a down-and-out section of town.

- More and more middle-aged adults are now taking care of their aging parents. Their pocketbooks will be stretched further than ever as they raise children, born later in life, and care for parents who will live longer than anticipated.

- Trends suggest that most seniors will continue to be forced to take low-level administrative or service jobs because of widespread myths and prejudice about their ability to contribute. In part, this book is about reversing that trend, at least, for you.

- Focused, deep expertise will be saleable at high cost by seniors. Subject matter experts will be in demand at any age; in fact, age will be an advantage for those who understand that this type of work is the venue of the sage.

- People 50 and older are the fastest growing users of technology and this trend suggests that many mature adults will enter the field of Internet sales and re-tool into emerging fields, such as nanotechnology and Wi-Fi.

- It is anticipated that those of us who understand that continued learning is key to our future will flood universities and other institutions of higher learning. One expectation is that online accredited universities will be the domains of the mature adult.

- The trend to work for another decade or more after the traditional retirement age of 65 is a relatively new phenomenon. While the economic implication is a large part of the story, it is also true that we are more energetic and going to be living longer – anticipating an old age without something meaningful to do, either full-time or part-time, is not exactly a desired outcome for many.

- In the near future, companies will not want to offer desirable health insurance to retirees and, in the short term, retirees will use this fact to their advantage to return to work while saving firms the considerable cost of these benefits.

- There will be lowered costs of prescription drugs for chronic illnesses associated with maturity and, in the short term, additional prescription drug coverage through Medicare.

- On the horizon are breathtakingly rapid advances in the treatment of adult onset diabetes and hypertension.

- Physical fitness salons and trainers will be specifically suited to the older adult.

- Older, well educated people will be teaching our youth and participating in the home schooling movement.

- Expect to see a strong focus on wellness and prevention, instead of repair of used body parts.

- The explosion in the workforce will be in the area of Just-in-Time (JIT) employment opportunities for some of us who will be used to fill in, or bring much needed experience to the workplace, on demand.

- An abundance of franchises and small businesses will compete globally and locally. They will be owned and, in many cases, operated by Baby Boomers.

> *Opportunity knocks on many doors.*
>
> *Which one of these opportunities is knocking at your door?*

What's next according to the Scientists, Futurists and Economists?

Jane Lubechenco, writing on behalf of the National Science Foundation, stated:

"We are modifying physical, chemical, and biological systems in new ways, at faster rates, and over larger spatial scales than ever recorded on Earth. The world is changing in myriad other important ways as well. Inequity within and among all nations has increased; new infectious diseases have emerged; there is dramatically more technology, communication, and information systems have undergone revolutionary changes; markets have become global; the biotic and cultural worlds have been homogenized; the rate of transport of people, goods, drugs, and organisms has increased around the globe; multinational corporations have emerged; and nongovernmental organizations have increased. Most of these changes have profound implications for our future. Integration of the human dimensions of these global changes with the physical-chemical-biological dimensions is clearly needed. The challenges for society are formidable. **Business as usual will not suffice.**"

This is the moment when crisis and opportunity are converging. For better and for worse, the U.S. economy is hard-wired to the future.

Indeed, the trends are clear - the choices we make now will affect our children and our children's children. Is your work to be found in fighting for a cause? Well, here you go — *cause choices* — right in front of you!

For example, there is a revolution coming in the environmental area – Older people will have a great deal to do with changing attitudes. To paraphrase Rabbi Zalman Schachter-Shalomi, as we age we will question our relationship with the planet and we will come to know that the quality of living is not material. We will consume less of the Earth's resources, reducing further damage to the planet.

If you wish to reflect on the suggested trends and other perspectives regarding the meaning of lives well spent into very old age, read both *The Longevity Revolution* by Theodore Roszak and *From Age-ing to Sage-ing* by Rabbi Schachter-Shalomi.

This is what Watts Wacker, the founder of FirstMatter, LLC and the futurist at SRI International, one of the nation's foremost think tanks, Jim Taylor, the Executive Vice President of Iomega Corporation, and Howard Means, Senior Editor of the Washingtonian, had to say about work in their 1997 book, *The 500 Year Delta*.

> "Shed the notion that any loyalty is to be given or received in a business relationship, realize that you are a freelancer moving from deal to deal even when you are in someone else's employ, and understand that there is only one person you are working for: yourself. You're the boss. You're the only person in charge of the only career you can control: your own. This may be scary. If you have been taught to be primarily defensive, it may even be debilitating. **But, this isn't servitude, this is freedom.**"

This is what Peter Peterson, chairman of The Blackstone Group, a leading investment bank, former secretary of commerce and chair of the Federal Reserve Bank of New York posed as a central question in *Gray Dawn*, a book whose message you cannot afford to ignore.

> "Can even the wealthiest of nations afford to pay for such a vast number of senior citizens living a third or more of their adult lives in what are now commonly thought of as retirement years?"

He added:

> "The United States has two major disadvantages. The first is its very low national savings rate, which will severely restrict the ability of future Congresses to deficit-finance any sizable portion of rising benefit costs. The U.S. rate of net national savings, though rising sharply during the late 1990s due to the closing of the federal budget deficit, averaged less than 6 percent of GDP over the entire decade. This was not only lower than that of any other developed economy - it was lower than in any earlier decade in postwar (WWII) U.S. history. The second U.S. disadvantage is the cost of its health care. After decades of rapid growth, U.S. health-care spending is now roughly twice the average for the other developed countries as a share of GDP. This national cost explosion translates directly into a rising fiscal burden."

Sound bites from the trend watchers we watch.

- Technology will touch and transform everything we know today.
- 60 to 70% of jobs that will exist by the end of the first quarter of this century do not exist now.
- Trade with Australasia will dominate our consumer spending.
- People, predominantly women, will move into stronger positions in the U.S. service sector.
- Dramatic new medical advances will continue to lengthen life spans.
- War, poverty and hunger will increase and affect every aspect of our work and lives.
- Education will, in fact, last a lifetime as working professionals struggle to compete.
- Alliances will be built to broaden our reach into project opportunities.
- The rate of change will continue to accelerate, impacting the rate at which organizations respond to new demands.
- Concerns for the environment and the global community will create new opportunities worldwide.
- Boomers will play a large role in reshaping children's social environment and will forge alliances with teachers and parents to influence children in a positive direction.
- We will continue to hire contributors overseas and many other jobs will be sent packing to other nations.

- Some people believe that we will be forced into a new definition of retirement age soon. Government will take the lead in this effort with resistance anticipated from businesses struggling to get out from under benefit costs they associate with older workers.
- Older Boomers will favor buying personal services over manufactured goods and these more modest buying habits will have an inevitable effect on consumer spending in our country.

> *Hidden within every sound bite, worrisome or not - opportunity lurks.*
> *Do you see your opportunity?*

Additional resources.

Do you crave more information on trends for the 21st century?

For the intellectually curious, look up www.cluetrain.com. Read the Cluetrain Manifesto if you want to have a glimpse into the future of web commerce, a future that even as this book is being written, is becoming the past.

For another perspective, that found in the public sector's well-researched book measuring working trends by the U.S. Department of Labor, read its book *Future Work, Trends and Challenges for Work in the 21st Century*. According to their introduction, this is the only book with the complete report taken from the U.S. Department of Labor's website. Interestingly enough, the book does not measure the opportunities for work on behalf of Boomers. However, amongst other data, they report that America's birthrate is barely at replacement level and the generation immediately behind us is comprised of literally half as many people as our group.

Opportunity knocking, or?

They add that the U.S. population is "expected to grow by 50 percent in the next 50 years with two-thirds of the increase from immigration."

Opportunity compromised?

Ponder this.

If other sources, other writers, researchers and subject matter experts expect that the mature population will find new opportunities because the succeeding generation is too small to handle workforce demands, but the government reports that we will sustain growth through immigration – what is the possibility that immigrants will fill many of the jobs our older workers might have held? In other words, will an immigrant workforce replace us? Will this trend seriously impact opportunities for the working poor in America? The educated?

On another note, the U.S. Department of Labor's research states, "a college graduate now earns 71% more than the average high school graduate." They report "19% of job applicants lack the required minimum math and reading skills." Will older workers benefit from this dismaying fact? This important information should be a part of your own trends research. Some of the facts and suggested conclusions by the U.S. Department of Labor are startling in a very obvious way.

Carleen MacKay's top picks for what's next.

Boomers will continue to shop but what will we buy?

Those of us born during the early edge of the boom (now 55 or older) will buy differently than those born later and who are now in their late 40's and early 50's. Remember that age alone changes our buying habits. Longer life spans and modest incomes will have a major impact on what our group will buy as we migrate through our maturity. It is by understanding what we will buy that will affect our choices as to what we produce and sell. Broad hints of new career opportunities are embedded in the list that follows.

CHECK IT OUT:

The older boomers (55 and older) will buy:

- Books and mainstream publications, especially good quality used books.
- Smaller, one-story retirement homes, in communities for those 55 and older.
- Exercise equipment suited to older bodies.
- Pre-paid travel vacations and time-shares.
- Fashion, including quality used fashion that suits the generation.
- Better shoes.
- Products that help us to remain active longer.
- Oral hygiene care.
- Planned hip and knee replacements.
- Easy to use but state-of-the-art and affordable home entertainment.
- Products online, from pharmaceuticals to dog food, delivered directly to the home.
- Nostalgia and home comfort items.
- Home services that allow freedom from heavy-duty work.
- Physical fitness services focused on this age group.
- Roommates (roommate services to link older adults).
- Swimming memberships.
- Late boomer-equipped automobiles with extra features for aging bodies.
- Security products, especially easy-to-use home security systems.
- Services from home health care workers.
- Information that will help us to stay active in the world of work.

The younger boomers (54 and younger) will buy:

- Anti-aging anything, no matter how far-fetched.
- Health foods, vitamins and nutritional supplements.
- Better tasting, lower caloric value foods.
- Prevention services to avoid chronic health problems.
- Financial services.
- Upscale health-focused restaurant meals and quality foods delivered to the home.
- Motorcycles in a rainbow of colors, makes, shapes and sizes.
- Hip, age appropriate fashion — including high-end consignment clothing.
- Small businesses (especially women-owned) and franchises.
- Alternative healthcare services.
- Elective, multiple plastic surgeries.
- Educational TV, online, interactive, accredited higher "distance" learning.
- The latest in TV's and home electronics.
- Boomer topic sites on the Internet and TV.
- Energy foods.
- Adventure travel.
- Security products.
- Whiter teeth.
- Products and services for pampered pets.
- PC's – and we will start purchasing more products online, because patience for shopping will decrease unless shopping itself is entertaining.
- African American, Asian and Latino Boomers will come full center in the buyer's universe…terrific opportunities for work in both the product and service areas exist in these growing communities.
- Coaches, subject matter experts in mature career and life management, to help navigate the confusing, jobless world.
- Information that will help us to stay active in the world of work.

If you know what people will buy, what can you produce or sell to meet their needs?

For another glimpse into what we will buy (and what you might sell) read *Marketing to Leading-Edge Baby Boomers* by Brent Green.

Who is most likely to work in any meaningful way?

It's a new day and a new game. After we overcome certain myths about economic recovery and those stories that set a false expectation about a return to the world of work as it was, those of us who will thrive in this forever changed, largely jobless world of the mature worker will:

Continue to develop and focus our expertise. This focused expertise will enable us to thrive in a largely de-jobbed U.S. world of work. **Think of us as the Sages.**

Start our own businesses now, on the perceived early edge of change and forget seeking employers as the panacea for our false source of security. **Think of us as the Hardy Pioneers.**

Follow the trends avidly – paying good attention to broad-based change and relating that change to our own work lives. **Think of us as the Keen Observers.**

Always have a Plan "B" – never resting on our laurels from the past. Plan "B" will include continued formal education and skills development over our lifetimes. The online classroom will prove to be the leap forward in providing skills/education to the older worker, and we will move quickly towards this form of formalized learning. Furthermore, we will be the generation that will change the way our colleges and universities teach and, ultimately, change the cost of advanced learning. **Think of us as the Swift Learners.**

Sustain our marriages or form alliances with other mature folks to share financial burdens and allow more freedom from the need to work in endless drudgery. Later stage marriages or alliances will allow us to remain independent and self-sustaining. **Think of us as the Brave Hearts.**

In summary, the people who will thrive are the *Sages, Hardy Pioneers, Keen Observers, Swift Learners and the Brave Hearted*. But, then, aren't these the same qualities you have noted in people who have triumphed throughout your lifetime? Dare we imply that we simply need to re-discover the best in ourselves?

Ah…. so that is, in some part, what this book is about. Our journey is to re-discover the person we were meant to be! That person who is smart enough, swift enough, courageous enough, curious enough and connected enough will have the best chance to succeed. Come along, brave souls, it is the moment to look at the world intuitively, observe the big picture, make a few good guesses at its implications and then process the information logically, analyzing your ideas until you understand where it is that you are headed.

Come down from the clouds – Discover your marketplace opportunities.

You have read the section of our shared workplace journey and the events that shaped our "past." You have looked at the ideas today's youth thinks will shape the near future. You have explored some of the ideas proposed by mature individuals, like you, as well as by scientists, futurists and economists. You have glanced at a few observations made by the authors. Throughout, you have been asked to make notes — to identify ideas that might interest you.

What ideas for your future work, if any, did you take away from reading about the past?
_____
_____

What ideas for your future work, if any, did you gather from the trends according to our youth or the mature population?
_____
_____

Do you think you may need some additional education? If so, what do the trends suggest?
_____
_____

What narrow, deep expertise do you have, if any, that you believe you can use in your future work?
_____
_____

What ideas for future work, if any, did you glean from the trends in your traditional workplace?
_____
_____

Were any work ideas suggested by the scientists, futurists or economists of interest?
_____
_____

Did any of the ideas about what our generation will be buying suggest a new work adventure to you?
_____
_____

Pull your thoughts together and list 2 to 3 possibilities for your future work below:

(1) _____
(2) _____
(3) _____

Reflect.

Take a time out.
Reflect on the work you have done so far in the first three steps of your journey.

First of all, you looked inward.

Do you need to do more work here?

If so, go to any of the many websites offering self-assessment. These personality assessments may be found through Google or any good search engine. Many are free. If you are working with a coach, ask for their recommendations as to assessments that will prove to be most beneficial in your case. Ask your coach to provide a deeper, more comprehensive interpretation of the results than you might have gleaned on your own.

Secondly, you looked at the trends in the marketplace.

Do you need to do more work here?

Additional information may be found in any of the government sites, such as the Bureau of the Census, The Bureau of Labor Statistics and, of course, Ageline through AARP. Goggle.com may be the fastest link to all these sites. You might also consider investigating "Pluck.com." Pluck.com, as the name implies, retrieves news articles from various sources in your areas of interest. Then, of course, there is Info.com. And, by the time you read this book there will be others on the scene. A new source, at least to us, is KeepMedia.com, a subscription service that offers up-to-date archives of over 200 publications.

You are ready to take your next step.

Let's explore some "hot" careers that might meet your goals of new and meaningful work.

NOTES

Step 4

What Careers Are Hot?

This is the fun part.

After a brief, but critically important, introduction about the realities of change and their influence on work in America, this next step introduces you to some of the hot opportunities that exist today.

Oprah Said It Best:

"The future burns so bright, it hurts my eyes."

But, remember that what is "hot" today but may be "not-so-hot" tomorrow.

It is up to you to pay attention to opportunities that may be impacted by revolutionary changes in technology, the globalization of workforces, shifts in the economy, or simply by the realities of marketplace change.

What are the realities of change and their influence on work in America?

Take a few moments to explore some of the realities of change that will affect *"what's hot and what's not."*

Private industry has embraced the concept of outsourcing.

1. As industry continues to divest itself of non-core activities, expect even more outsourcing.

2. As organizations curtail capital spending, we will see more outsourcing to Information Technology (IT) groups, to specific training organizations, such as Six Sigma Black Belt training in Manufacturing, as well as to functional units, such as: Human Resources, Financial Services and Marketing.

3. At the grass roots level, outsourcing will affect the number of critical "core" people an organization needs to employ in order to produce or provide its core products or services.

Do you have a talent that suggests you might look for work in an outsourcing firm or should you start a firm of your own? Do you have a subject matter expertise the marketplace needs? Have you longed to consult, coach or teach? Perhaps you are an outsourced "solution of one." These options are addressed in more detail in Steps 4 and 5 of your planning process.

Ah....but, have you heard of insourcing and shared sourcing?

If you haven't, you will soon.

Briefly, *insourcing* is the practice of using the talents/skills of employees from various parts of an organization in order to meet business demands in other functional units, departments or divisions.

Shared sourcing, on the other hand, is the practice of requiring internal sources to compete with external (outsourced) providers. The theory is that the internal source will have to prove to be better, faster and cheaper if it is to be the sole source of choice by other internal buyers. The practice, while still in its infancy, should make for interesting competition between internal and external providers of services, such as marketing, human resources, information technology and accounting.

Temporary help agencies will continue to proliferate.

1. According to the U.S. Bureau of Labor Statistics, the temporary service industry will account for one of the largest sources of numerical employment growth in the economy over the next 10 years. Included in this temporary help arena are firms that serve all bandwidths of experience, all levels of expertise and, indeed, all organizational needs that might be imagined.

2. Organizations will struggle to remain profitable. Jobs that are important to each organization will be valued based on critical need. Not all positions will require full-time help. When an organization needs a critical skill for a finite period of time or to complete a high-priority project, they will increase their use of Just-in-Time (JIT) help across all hiring platforms. Executives, teams of project specialists, white, blue and gold-collar workers – if you are not needed full-time, it is unlikely you will be hired full-time.

3. Specialty firms that place mature workers will make their mark and they will make their mark soon.

What does this trend mean to you, to your family, to your career?

Do you see opportunity lurking in the shadow of change?

Could it be that this path will offer you more excitement, more fun and more opportunity to learn something new than you might find in a traditional full-time job?

Temporary positions for independent professionals and skilled workers and other free agents are explored in Step 5 of your plan.

More employees will be offered early retirement.

1. As private and public sector businesses struggle to manage their costs, it is anticipated that more and more employees, in both sectors, will experience dramatic changes in their status as continued full-time employees.

2. Early retirement programs are already in evidence. Organizations have made so-called early retirement sound appealing to folks, so much so that people eagerly volunteer to

"retire." Look out — some of the promises made surrounding the continuation of benefits may ring hollow if your firm files for bankruptcy in the future — long after you've left the organization but while you are still counting on the deal promised at the time of your early retirement.

3. Phased retirement is in the planning stages for the few private sector organizations that still offer defined pension plans. In fact, the IRS has extended a helping hand. They have proposed new regulations that would allow employees age 59 1/2, or older, to draw a pro-rata share of their pension if they take part in a formal, voluntary, phased-retirement program.

Today's problems to overcome include:

1. Early retirees' pensions are not likely to last a lifetime for a variety of reasons. From changes in real costs-of-living to survivor benefits not meeting the challenges faced by remaining (often, much younger) spouses, the money will simply not last. For those without pensions, the more than 50% of us who will have only Social Security or personal savings to fall back upon, completely retiring is a bad option.

2. Most people take voluntary, early retirement packages to hedge their bets when struggling organizations offer them the option to leave with their benefits relatively intact. The continued income and benefits afforded by these programs allow these folks to do something else — somewhere else. Some wish to throttle back and work part-time or, occasionally, on-demand. Others prefer to change course to a much less stressful way of working. Still others wish to pursue unrequited dreams in other areas of work. Most do not take early retirement programs in order to golf, day-after-day-after-day-after-day, in a mythological dreamland.

For better or worse, the global workforce is in your future.

1. In addition to the obvious use of the Internet as a recruitment tool in America, this method of recruiting has impacted the number of hires U.S. firms are making in "cyberspace." This tool allows workers from around the world to be recruited at rates favorable to employers. For example, the combination of high-speed data networks, lower wages and high-level educational systems in many countries, such as India and China, allow U.S. employers to get quality work done throughout the world for less than half the cost in the U.S.

2. Take the time to research just which nations are investing heavily in higher education. You need to know about this. The answers affect you today and they will dramatically affect your children and your grandchildren tomorrow. Pick up *Fortune*, *Forbes* and magazines of their ilk. You will not miss the message.

In other words, while cost may be one factor in U.S. firms' migration to a global workforce, it is not the only factor. The best educated people from around the globe, especially in new, high demand areas of expertise, will also be hired at any cost if they can help organizations to succeed.

Watch out – tougher selection processes are the order of the day.

Perhaps you have experienced the difficulty in getting through a selection process even when a bona-fide opening exists for which you are qualified. Behavioral interviewing, psychological testing and assessments are now the norm in many firms' hiring practices. Running the gauntlet through several interviewers is also part of these relatively tougher practices. It is not unusual for a hiring process to take several months following your initial interview. As a mature worker in this youth obsessed land, this process allows even more rejection as people find new ways to reject the so-called "overqualified."

Beware. All that glitters is not gold.

Be wary of the hype from the media that suggests the economy is returning to what it once was.

It is not.

No longer can politicians deliver on the promises of the past.

The world is in motion!

Unemployment is not 6 something %. It is closer to 10%, even in a good economy because:

1. Unemployment statistics do not measure the underemployed.

2. Unemployment statistics do not include those people whose benefits have run out.

3. Unemployment statistics do not count those who do not (or can not) claim benefits for one reason or another.

Stock market prices are struggling up; profit margins are as well — but why? If organizations manage their top-line and variable expenses (people) better than in the past, it stands to reason that profits will go up and the stock market will expand. But surge? Or return to the heyday of the late '90's? Won't happen.

What is happening and what will happen next is something quite different. This different world requires that you find your way through a new maze of choices. Choices exist — they just do not look like the past. That is another reason why this book was written for you.

> Or, as our good friend Brad Tipler put it:
> "Don't seek comfort in your ticket on the last train to the good times.
> The station has already been converted to a hybrid car sales outlet."

And, now, enter the maturing population.

Think about an America where almost half of adult Americans are 50 or older.

Oops.
Would you agree that this makes the mature population particularly vulnerable to global or local outsourcing, where workforces cost a fraction of what we used to demand?

Oops.
Might you agree that certain countries are investing more in research and advanced education than we are and that, it is possible, our older workforce — those who simply went to work in the old world – may not be able to compete with the more recently educated?

Or, are we hot?

Could this be opportunity knocking in a new way because our graying America produced considerably fewer people in the next generation to fill the slots left behind by our age group?

What happens if we seize the moment and backfill the workforce in order to supplement organizations where fewer people will be employed? We do, after all, offer an affordable and experienced alternative to the smaller emergent U.S. workforce.

What about you?

Do you know what there is to do beyond the parameters of your earlier career?
Are you aware as to what third-stage career opportunities have the most potential?
Is there something fun to do that might still offer some income?
Should you buy a small business or a franchise?
What are all your options?
What does it take to get where you want to go?

Steps 4 and 5 in this book will help you to explore more options than you might imagine.

Are you prepared to compete?
Do you know how to overcome objections and to leverage your experience?
Are your marketing tools as up-to-date as you perceive that you are?

Steps 6 will help you to determine if you can meet the challenge of change, overcome barriers and compete locally and globally. Marketing tools are provided for you as examples in Step 8.

What should you do?

Accept that not only will the jobs and opportunities change, but how we work has forever changed and will continue to change at an accelerated rate.

Take a hard look at your current skills and marketability before knocking on traditional re-employment doors that may not be open to you for long. This book will help you to reposition your career no matter how late in your particular game it is. It is a good idea to read it all, each and every page along the way.

For important additional research,

- Refer to the U.S. Bureau of Labor Statistics' article entitled "Tomorrow's Jobs" at bls.gov.
- Research industry trends by specific industry. Goggle it. Pluck it. Info.com it.
- Read books, and research articles, by William Knoke, Watts Wacker, Peter Drucker, Charles Handy and other economists and futurists who will inspire you to believe in a very different future than you might have imagined.
- Add to your research with information from the Institute for the Future in Menlo Park, California.
- Read trend reports by McKinsey, and other research firms, especially as they relate to IT services and back-office services being sent overseas.

What's "hot" according to the Department of Labor?

The top "10" high growth occupations for the early part of this century include:

Occupation	Percent Growth
Computer software engineers, applications	100%
Computer support specialists	97%
Computer software engineers, systems software	90%
Network and computer systems administrators	82%
Network systems and data communications analysts	77%
Desktop publishers	67%
Database administrators	66%
Personal and home care aides	62%
Computer systems analysts	60%
Medical assistants	57%

Many other occupations are projected to grow substantially but the numbers are too many, and the list is too long, to include in this book. Instead, we recommend you visit the U.S. Bureau of Labor Statistics website at bls.gov and scroll down to the Occupational Outlook Handbook.

Note that 8 of the top 10 projected high growth positions are in technology. 9 of the 10 occupations require specific education. The exception is the lower paying personal and home care jobs.

Wait a minute!

Are most of these jobs the very jobs that are being outsourced, insourced or shared sourced?

Ask yourself, if it does not matter to output whether a technician, software guru, informational technology professional or a research engineer sits across the sea or in the next cubicle, would you hire the equally qualified, but far less expensive, individual across town or across the sea? The answer for most U.S. corporations is that they will hire where they can get the best help for the best price. Surprise...surprise... The answer for public sector organizations is that they are trending the same way. These new versions of the old workforce do not constitute "seasonal" trends in hiring — their presence is a basic, underlying change in the new world economy.

These changes affect you.

What other trends are "hot"?

It's a HOT trend to get out of corporate jobs. Wanting to get out of the corporate world may reflect the breach created by corporations that once offered considerably more job security than they provide today. This trend may reflect the volatility of the economy in certain sections of the U.S. Or, it may be that a systemic change in and of itself incorporating new technology, the impact of the global workforce, and the loss of trust in the leaders of our largest organizations have encouraged some of us to look far beyond the career doors that are closing behind us.

It's a HOT trend to study market changes and to hitch career goals to organizations that are anticipated to be good career investments tomorrow. At the end of each calendar year, *Forbes Magazine* ranks the best managed companies of the previous year. This research, while it reflects the magazine's editorial perspective, is one important step to take in targeting your preferred next landing spot. We mine this magazine regularly. *Business Week* is another choice people make when researching information about today's (and tomorrow's) best firms. *WIRED* is a must read magazine for one and all. Other business magazines and trade journals are a matter of personal preference. The point is, for the first time, regardless of the positions you target, you must pay attention to business changes that, in the past, you may have ignored. KeepMedia.com will mine 200 publications at a time on your behalf.

It's a HOT trend to leave jobs voluntarily when you know that the hot business niche you labored in is no longer hot.

What's HOT today — right now in creative career alternatives and in the new corporate world? Keep in mind that what is hot today may not be hot for long. And, remember, for Internet access, type: http://www. followed by the web address.

Biotechnology

Amazing new discoveries that will impact our health and longevity are in late stage research and development. You might say — with confidence — that they are poised and ready to lengthen our life spans once again.

While this industry is hot — it continues to receive the majority of Venture Capital backed investments, most career opportunities in biotechnology require specific skills and competencies during funded startup.

Unless you plan to return to school or wish to seek one of the relatively few administrative or non-technical slots in this industry, it is unlikely that you will be able to jump on-board the early-market biotech boom train.

Boomer Retail Market (especially for women)

A market that is barely tapped is the Boomer women's clothing stores. From business clothes to sports wear and shoes, look for a huge boom here. (Thank you, in some measure, to Diane Keaton for her sexy, interesting portrayal of a mature woman whose age fits this market segment to a "T.")

But, remember that in retail there is a big difference buying between the ages of 50 and 60 years and buying over the age of 70 or 75. The younger group is far more involved in buying products while the older group is likely to be more interested in buying services. Aim for the under 70 market.

Business Network Organizers

With frequent job changes setting a trend, the need to develop and sustain business-to-business (B2B) and "people" networks throughout our working lifetimes has increased. This early stage "hot" business is likely to grow. The pay isn't high – but you can charge for organizing events and for running local networks and, as the organizer, you will gain the advantage of raising your own profile. This high visibility will help to ensure that your own connections get hot and stay hot!

Child Care and Child Development

This is a fast emerging field of interest to Boomers, many of whom have become disenchanted with how our children and grandchildren are being raised today.

Paid tutoring, especially in the old-fashioned 3R's, will continue to be in great demand.

For volunteer opportunities (which can lead to paid tutoring gigs), check out Future Possibilities™, a non-profit organization that delivers life skill coaching for children ages 7-12. At Future Possibilities, trained volunteer coaches, called "KidCoaches", help children to build character and develop healthy life skills.

Founded in 1997, America's Promise™ is a collaborative network that offers volunteer opportunities to help children grow into productive maturity. Long after government leadership is behind him, the founding chairman, former Secretary of State, Colin Powell, will leave a legacy that will outlive his political high profile.

Consignment Store Sales

The trend will continue in the real and virtual sales venues.

People are bringing their quality used items, from clothing to dining room suites, to consignment stores. The growing reluctance to allow strangers into our homes and garages is the motivation for sellers. More people are buying quality items on consignment. Buyer or seller, look around — you'll see new stores in your neighborhood.

Quality toys and next-to-new children's clothing are always good sellers. There may be interesting opportunities selling these types of items within the fast-growing retirement community centers. Of course, you will continue to see more highly specialized consignment stores on the Internet. Could you soon be buying consignment items from other parts of the world?

Crafts — Jewelry Making and Comfort Items

If you like to work with your hands for fun and profit, consider jewelry making. Approach your local merchants or art museums for information. Hand made jewelry is usually sold at Craft Fairs and/or on the Internet. If you are really good at this craft, museums of art may carry your merchandise. For research suggestions, refer to the Home Based Business and Pieceworkers sections in this book.

Other crafts that are hot include "comfort" goods – those goods that may make us feel safe and secure. Quilts come to mind. Legacy gifts, such as handmade items intended for future generations, are a big item today.

Defense Industry and Homeland Security

An active secret clearance is the winning ticket into today's hot defense industry. Even if your clearance is inactive, it is worth investigating opportunities in this sector. Defense industry jobs are not usually a worthwhile pursuit for most of the rest of us.

However, Homeland Security positions, while requiring background checks, are available to citizens with a variety of talent, from retired public safety officers and other personnel to hardworking folks whose backgrounds bear the scrutiny these positions demand.

Ethics Officers

Corporations are at the point where it has become prudent to engage subject matter experts to ensure that ethical standards will be met. This area of opportunity should continue to grow as a few more organizations get their hands seriously slapped by regulatory agencies. At the end of 2003, *Business Week* reported that 27% of large companies hold ethics training sessions for director level employees. Watch this stat continue to climb!

Flexible Workforce Management Experts

As the next, smaller generation meets the larger boomer generation in the workplace, and as organizations struggle to stay as small as they can, subject matter experts and consultants will be brought in by firms and institutions seeking to manage a multigenerational, flexible, resilient workforce made up of full-time, part-time and just-in-time contributors.

Franchises

You will read more about this in the section dedicated to this method of doing business. Even the Franchise world is migrating into the Internet world. Certain franchises are hot and getting hotter and you can check out new franchises at franchisehandbook.com.

Healthcare

It is not too late to change direction into a career that offers the ultimate in flexibility.

Consider nursing. Nurses are in such demand that some hospitals are easing their nursing shortages by bidding for their services. Here is how the revolutionary bidding system works. Nurses scan posted openings and reply with the hourly wage they are willing to accept! One of the innovators of the auction modality is St. Peter's Hospital in Albany, New York. St. Peter's hopes to license "auction" software nationwide very soon.

If you are not up for career re-direction that involves such an extensive investment in learning, Licensed Vocational Nurses are also in hot demand today.

Physical and Occupational Therapists offer additional opportunities in healthcare career re-direction.

Medical Devices

In second place, relative to receiving the lion's share of Venture Capital funding, is the medical device industry. Medical devices are hot today and expected to stay hot in the foreseeable future because of new devices and implants that are ready – or almost ready – for the healthcare market.

If you have held positions in manufacturing firms that have suffered from loss of jobs to overseas competitors or to new technologies, you may wish to use your skills to meet the growing needs for technical talent in this industry.

Nanotechnology

How many angels can dance on the head of a pin? We are about to find out. When particles are reduced to nanometer size, nanotechnologists are working with atoms and molecules.

One amazing result is that they will be able to miniaturize technology to build computers that are as small as the head of that pin we mentioned. According to Josh Wolfe, Editor of *Forbes*/Wolfe Nanotech Report (forbeswolfe.com), firms will manufacture toothpaste that will "not only resist tooth decay but reverse it by rebuilding tooth enamel." Watch out for the international footrace here. America is investing in nanotechnology but we are not the forerunners in the investment race.

New medical devices, new drugs to kill cancer cells and new implants to help patients regain the use of limbs are but a few of the expected results. This technological revolution will redefine how we will live and work and it is predicted to create a market size in the trillions by 2015.

Catching the wave of this technology may mean returning to school for advanced technical training or integrating your existing administrative or non-technical talent in many ways with the firms that are chasing this technology now. It may mean working part-time while building your competencies in this miniaturized world. Get in if you can and if you want to be a part of the next technology revolution.

Personnel Supply Services

We've said it before and we'll say it again. According to the Bureau of Labor Statistics, temporary and interim employment agencies are projected to be the largest source of numerical growth in the economy. Experienced recruiters and business developers are a few of the positions the temporary agencies themselves need in order to build future capacity.

Pet Sitting and other Pet Services

This is a multimillion-dollar industry that caters to our love affair with pets.

There's a growing need for pet sitters (and for other animal related services) and a great deal of fun to be found in this line of business as well. Consider buying the book, *Pet Sitting for Profit*, by Patti Moran.

Startpetsitting.com offers a guide to making money in this line of business. Petsit.com offers another site that connects you with an "international" organization of pet sitters.

Pharmaceutical Sales

Because of the extraordinary increase in medical technology, pharmaceutical sales may offer a great place to make a bet on continued career opportunities. In fact, careers in sales are growing fast as we scramble to outdistance competition from abroad.

The U.S. is the number one pharmaceutical market in the world and you may expect startling new drugs to add continuously to the market precisely because our population is aging.

New drugs are just around the corner for hypertension and adult-onset diabetes, to name but two of the diseases associated with aging.

All of America is anxiously awaiting new drugs to control startling increases in obesity in our affluent nation.

Some Americans are beginning to wonder about our quick fix mentality that enriches the manufacturers.

Watch the trends carefully here. A backfire may be heard from this overcrowded highway of drugs.

Private Investigators (shades of Humphrey Bogart)

White-collar crime has increased and created a demand for PI's. Look up Ed Pankau on the Internet at pankau.com. Ed Pankau is a best selling author, and an investigator in his own right. His books include *Check It Out, How to Make $100,000 a Year as a Private Eye.*

Real Estate Home Appraisers

This is a lucrative business but there are important legal requirements to meet before entering the profession. Any major real estate firm will advise you as to the best path to success in this area of work. Using the Internet, look up the American Association of Appraisers and scroll down to Real Property on their menu. While you're there, take a look at additional appraisal opportunities the site suggests.

Real Estate — Mortgage Brokers

Like the real estate market itself, mortgage brokers are hot when the market is booming and this field is still pretty hot at the moment. Signs are that it is cooling down in some U.S. markets and, with the exception of certain areas, it will definitely cool down in direct relation to rising interest rates.

Will communities in areas where prices have grown beyond the reasonable reach of most buyers, places like Boston and most major cities in California, be impacted first by cooling when the interest rates begin to rise? Or, are there just so many people in these markets that housing starts in these cities will continue to grow? Or, will we see the majority of growth in high-density housing or in the fast-growing retirement community niche?

Place your bets. There is money to be made and lost.

Residential Real Estate — Buying New Properties and Foreclosures

Of course, this is a dynamic and cyclical business. At the time this is being written, mortgage rates remain low, housing prices are high, and people are buying.

However, this is also the precise moment in time when foreclosures are about as high as they have ever been in the history of the U.S. Foreclosures are expected to continue to grow as the workplace continues to operate as small as they can with fewer people in traditional roles and as people "overbuy" during the low interest rate market.

A recent book, *Investing in Real Estate, Fourth Edition* by Andrew McLean and Gary Eldred is a worthwhile reading experience.

Recycling Specialists

From designing consumer products that can be disassembled to the re-assembling of these products, engineers and other technical specialists will find new meaning and new profits in this work that will benefit the environment.

Security Services and Products

Emergency and disaster training in corporations, water purification systems (guarding against pollution or perceived threat by terrorists) and all manners of security devices and systems are expected to flood the market over the next few years.

Senior Services

Is there is anything hotter than senior services? With the population anticipating ever-longer life spans — 90-95 years is now achievable and will be the average by 2050, according to the National Institute on Aging — new services for maturity will be hot. Several services and products were discussed earlier in the book in terms of what seniors will buy.

Tourism/Hospitality — Cruise Lines

Tourism in America will continue to boom as Americans and international visitors enjoy vacationing in different locales.

The Bed and Breakfast industry will benefit greatly from this continued boom as well as from our increased yearning for the security and comfort of, what feels like, home.

The cruise business is one area of tourism that is growing very fast. It is anticipated by some experts that the industry will grow between 50,000 and 100,000 new jobs over the next 5 years. Literally dozens of new ships are under construction. If you are interested in the cruise industry, you may wish to read the *Worldwide Cruise Ship and Yachting Career Guide* by Elizabeth Kirkcaldy Hatton. Published by Innovative Ideas Ltd., this book is especially designed to assist prospective applicants to investigate this exciting industry. You may preview (or buy) the book through any online or mall bookstore.

From full-time positions to short-term gigs, such as Bridge Masters, Beauticians, Baby Sitters, Auctioneers, Guest Lecturers, Fitness Instructors to Gentlemen Hosts, there are dozens of options to explore in the world of sea-going resorts.

Travel Writers and Other Writers

Read Rick Steves' story for a hefty dose of inspiration. Unlike Rick, who is wildly successful, most travel writers do not receive high pay — but if travel is your "gig" — some travel subsidy may pay enough for you to have some fun. For a reference to Rick's publications, you may also wish to visit Rick's website at ricksteves.com.

How about other writing gigs? How hot are they?

In the late 1950's, the average high school senior's vocabulary was 25,000 words. What do you think it is today? More? Less? Here's the painful truth. The average U.S. high school senior's vocabulary, by many accounts, is now less than half that number. Other than simply viewing this as a disgraceful fact, you may see this as opportunity knocking. Simply stated, gigs for writers are growing – although the full-time world of writers may be contracting.

Grant writing pays well.

Sites for freelance writing opportunities include freelancecentral.net, freelancingformoney.com, and bloggingnetwork.com. Of course, Monster.com usually lists thousands of freelance writing jobs.

The bible of the writer's market is a thick book entitled *Writer's Market*. Their website is writersdigest.com. The book offers information on specific editorial needs and submission guidelines for consumer and trade magazines, book publishers, and script buyers.

A recent paperback by Jeff Herman, his *Guide to Book Editors, Publishers and Literary Agents 2005*, is receiving rave reviews.

Web Merchants

Can you get your product or service in front of millions of visitors? If so, you will find that there is money to be made on the Internet. But, watch out – the Internet is addictive!

If you are serious about creating an e-business, take a class through any one of several local area classrooms – from the community college to The Learning Annex – choices abound.

Consider selling books through Amazon or selling merchandise through *e*Bay. Both sites will guide you to this easy and fun way of selling on the Internet without investing in a business or obtaining licenses, patents or copyright protection. *e*Bay auction formats include ascending-price auctions, auctions with/without reserves, the "Dutch" auction and "Yankee" auctions amongst other ways to sell or buy at auction. Dennis Prince's book *How to Sell Anything on eBay...and make a Fortune* will tell you more about these auction formats and offer you additional insight to *e*Bay.

More serious sellers can host "storefronts" on the web, or on *e*Bay itself, thus entering the virtual sales world on a full-time, all-out, store owner basis.

Wi-Fi

Long lines of technological advancements have impacted the American economy. The phone, TV, computer, PC, fax, laptop, cell phone, and GPS are but some of the advances you have experienced.

The "next big thing" is connectivity and Wi-Fi is the rising star. Short for Wireless Fidelity, Wi-Fi is a generic reference to any type of 802.11(a, b, dual-band, etc.) wireless network or communications device/service. Central to the technology is "Wi-Fi Certification" that facilitates interoperability — essentially providing common "access points" with any other brand of client that is also Wi-Fi Certified.

Confused?

In plain English, when you use Wi-Fi technology you can carry one computer from work to home to the airport or to Starbucks and always reach your data or your audience — without wires. If you don't think this is happening now, hop a plane or drive on over to your local Starbucks.

Soon, Wi-Fi will offer much more than simple access to data and people.

It is the foundational infrastructure for the future "smart highway" where the technology will keep you in constant communication with your on-board automobile computer to determine and control things like distance between vehicles, road conditions, traffic flow, alternate routes, weather alerts, and so forth. Can "smart cities" be far behind in this wireless world?

Will Wi-Fi wipe out the phone service? Will our computer savvy nation use our laptops' microphones to call each other?

Hmm...

Technology calling. What will that mean in the long term? Will jobs be lost, as well as gained, once this new technology is applied in many settings?

For updates on trends to watch, go to ratraceremedies.com, fastcompany.com or entrepreneur.com.

What's "hot" in your opinion?

We gave you food for thought. Now, it is your turn to circle any of the "hot" opportunities presented that are of initial interest to you:

- Biotechnology
- Boomer products
- Business network organizers
- Childcare and child development
- Consignment store sales
- Crafts
- Defense and Homeland Security
- Ethics officers
- Flexible workforce management experts
- Franchises
- Healthcare
- Medical devices
- Nanotechnology
- Personnel supply services
- Pet-sitting and other pet services
- Pharmaceutical sales
- Private investigators
- Real estate home appraisers
- Real estate mortgage brokers
- Residential real estate
- Recycling specialists
- Security services and products
- Senior services
- Tourism/hospitality – Cruise lines
- Travel writers and other writers
- Web merchants
- Wi-Fi

Or, add your own thoughts here:

_____
_____
_____
_____

Get ready for Step 5!
The fun of discovery continues!

Step 5

Your Career Options

> *"The best way to predict the future is to create it."*
>
> *... Peter Drucker, Writer, Management Consultant, and Professor*
>
> *Take the advice of someone who continued building a successful career into his 90's.*
>
> This 5th step is where you connect
> **who you are with the new ways to work**
> that are right in front of you.

But first, a few words about research.

DO IT...

You have begun your research, step by step, throughout the first sections of this book, by looking inward, studying trends and taking a quick look at some of the "hot" opportunities available today.

When you continue your study of the material in this book, when you investigate the recommended websites we have listed, and read the books we suggest, you will benefit from all the underlying, easy to understand information you need to start your journey into your future. The recommended subject matter experts' books offer added value because people, whose career focus is well established, have done much of the time-consuming research for you.

BELIEVE IT...
CURRENT KNOWLEDGE IS POWER

When you add up-to-date perspectives by reading periodicals and magazines such as *The Wall Street Journal*, *WIRED*, your local area newspaper (the business section — not the classifieds), and magazines or trade journals that support your areas of interest, you will cement your knowledge about each area of work available to you. Continue to use the Internet extensively as new sites are added every few seconds. The Internet provides some of the best current research you need for any adventure into the future.

VALIDATE IT...
DEPTH OF KNOWLEDGE IS CLARITY

Once you have surveyed "the lay of the land" through hard or soft data research, your single best source of continued research is through information gathered from people who share your interest. People buy your products or services. People hire or engage people. People particularly like to buy from, hire or engage people who know what they want, who are comfortable and facile in articulating their needs and who are clear as to how to connect their interests with those of the prospective opportunity, employer or buyer. *In the world of work, the combination of people, passion, purpose and principled action rule!* You will find a responsive audience when you add people to the mix of research.

Copy and Clip

> *A note for your refrigerator.*
>
> *The world of work is not changing,*
> *it has changed and it will never return to what it once was.*
> *If you want to continue to work, you will need a new strategy in your maturity.*
> *You must play by new rules in a very different game."   ...Carleen MacKay*

And, just a few more thoughts on new strategies for maturity.

If you do not plan to retire soon, and if you agree with the trends and data that clearly suggest most Boomers do not, here are a few of the new rules for winners in this different game:

1. **Realize and accept that work itself has changed.**
   You can't go back – you can only go forward.

2. **Face the fact that you are changing.**
   You are older or growing older, and you must find new strategies that suit your maturity. Eager-eyed, slim-waisted youth will not serve you now.

3. **Abandon fear. Embrace courage.**
   Develop a mantra that speaks to you of courage. For example, reflect on the following words and take courage from the words that others have spoken on your behalf.

   "There will be a time when you think everything is finished.
   That will be the beginning."   ...Louis L'Amour, Writer/Author

   "The future belongs to those who believe
   in the beauty of their dreams."   ...Eleanor Roosevelt

   "One man scorned and covered with scars still strove with his last ounce of
   courage to reach the unreachable stars; and the world will be better for this."
   ...Miguel de Cervantes

   "This country was founded and built by people with great dreams and
   the courage to take great risks."   ...Ronald Reagan

Or, write your own words about courage and repeat these words aloud to yourself as you begin each new day.

Write them down now:

_____

_____

_____

4. ***Become a trend watcher.***

   Entertain the idea that the unexplored world may offer new work opportunities — opportunities beyond your wildest imagination! There is information presented in this book about these new opportunities that will surprise you.

   KeepMedia.com is an Internet subscription service that "grants you access to up-to-date archives of over 200 publications."

5. ***Pick yourself up and get back in the game as fast as you are rejected.***

   Remind yourself that it is "never too late to be what you might have been or to do what you might have done."

   Read Marc Freedman's book *Prime Time* for stories about people who have made a difference throughout their lifetimes, especially in their mature years. Marc is founder and president of Civic Ventures, a nonprofit organization dedicated to expanding the contribution of older Americans to our society. His book will offer countless ideas to those of you who want to give something back to your community. Check out his website at www.civicventures.org.

6. ***Commit to learning and exploring.***

   Now, plunge in and explore the fun and profit that exists in so many of the career options that lie ahead.

7. ***Act.***

   Go on.

   What's the worse thing that can happen if you act?

   What will happen if you don't act?

Angel Investors

Who are they?

It is fair to say that almost everybody wishes for an angel now and again. In this book's context, "angels" are high net worth individuals who specialize in the private placement of funds to finance small businesses. Angel investors band together and finance businesses by building funds and attracting like investors to financially support the fund.

What you need to know.

If you, like more than 60,000+ others in America, have a net worth (exclusive of your home) in excess of $1 million, you may wish to explore the world of angel investing.

Conversely, if you are an entrepreneur and need financing in an amount that would not be sufficient to interest a Venture Capital firm, you may wish to seek angels to invest in your potentially high-growth firm.

Validate your interest.

Review your responses in Steps 1 and 2.

If you wish to enter the world of angel investing, ask yourself the following questions:

1. Are you satisfied that this venture meets your needs?
2. Is your self-described internal analysis in alignment with this career path?
3. Does your spouse or partner support your interests?
4. Are you willing to thoroughly investigate the angel's world of work?
5. Will you develop relationships with angel investors in your community as part of your due diligence?

On the other hand, if you are seeking angel funding for a startup adventure, ask yourself these questions:

1. Are you fundable? Money goes to people who can prove their expertise far beyond a well-written business plan. Money goes to people the angel investors know. Real entrepreneurs spend many hours building their angel network long in advance of actually asking for financial capital. Money goes to management teams with prior start-up experience.
2. Do you have a proprietary product and can you present experience in related areas?
3. Is your product one with high commercial potential?
4. Are you prepared for a drawn-out process filled with rejection?

Explore the opportunities.

Check out relationships between local area Universities and angel investors. Connect with your board of directors or financial services firm to ask for their advice and counsel regarding this career path. Visit your local investment bank.

Continue your research.

Websites: For Internet access, type: http://www. followed by the web address.

> *Entrepreneur.com*
> Their Angel Search section is, as they proudly boast, "the coolest wealth identification tool ever invented!" This tool will help you to raise capital, find investors or wealthy new customers.
>
> *Nextwavestocks.com/angeldirectory*
> Offers a subscribed membership to angel investors and lists venture capital opportunities.
>
> *Techcoastangels.com*
> Lists West Coast angel investors.
>
> *Vfinance.com*
> They claim that more than one million CEO's, institutional and wealthy investors from around the world visit their site each year.
>
> *Google.com*
> Go to Google's advanced search and enter the following key words: angel investors, small business investors, venture capital, entrepreneurial funding.

Books, magazines and periodicals:

> *Entrepreneur, Fast Company, Inc.* and *WIRED* magazines

Prepare your marketing tools.

For additional information and examples, refer to the Marketing Tools section of the book.

- Business cards
- Business plan (including financial plan and marketing plan, if you are seeking investment)
- Professional biography or highly focused resume
- Written introductions or referrals to angel investors by high net-worth colleagues

Boards of Directors

Who are they?

A Board of Directors is a group of people who are legally charged with the responsibility for governing a corporation. In a for-profit corporation, the board is responsible to their stakeholders. In a non-profit organization, the board is responsible to the charitable organization, or community, they serve.

What you need to know.

If you are a soon-to-be retired CEO or "C" level officer in your firm, an active Chair, President or CEO, or a high profile member of your community, this may be an excellent role for you; a cap, if you will, to your distinguished career.

CEO's are often moved "up" from their current positions upon retirement to board positions in their existing organization or institution. In some instances, members are still working for one firm while maintaining a board position with another, non-competing institution.

The bottom line is that in the rarified world of boards of directors, maturity, high-level experience and strategic connections count!

Board members are hired to select and evaluate chief executives for the organization with whom they are affiliated. They are charged with representing both the organization and the stockholders' points-of-view to the firm's CEO. They are often called upon to seek additional resources for the organization, and they will be tasked with managing these resources honorably and effectively.

Board members have a fiduciary responsibility to stakeholders. In the wake of scandal and serious breaches of ethics in some of our American organizations, the selection process for members of boards of directors is tightening. It is also true that these real life scandals have lessened the interest in board membership by some and it is a serious task to contemplate for all. At the same time, the influence gained by membership on boards of directors, the opportunity to do good and to continue to achieve benefits for your organization and your community often outweigh the reluctance to commit to this type of work.

In the for-profit sector, board members are typically well compensated for their roles. In the non-profit community, compensation may be modest and geared toward covering verifiable expenses for the members of the board. In either situation, members are provided with insurance to cover costs of possible litigation.

Whether you are being considered in a for-profit or non-profit organization, the formality of a written application is required. Upon recommendation by trusted colleagues, members of a search or screening committee usually invite prospective board members to apply.

There are advisory board opportunities for small firms and non-profit organizations that, while rather informal, offer you the opportunity to experience a "Board" situation and help you to expand your own network. These advisors are often paid very small stipends to cover actual expenses and, as one result, do not bear the fiduciary responsibilities of the more formal boards of directors. Typically, advisory board members are invited to participate by the organizations they may benefit.

Spencer Stuart's Board Index suggests that boards in the future will favor, in descending order, financial expertise, diversity, active CEO's, technology expertise and international expertise. These boards are seeking business acumen, demonstrated leadership skills, a collaborative mindset and, as stated previously, squeaky-clean integrity.

Validate your interest.

Review your responses in Steps 1 and 2.

If you wish to be considered for a board-of-directors role, ask yourself the following questions:

1. Are you satisfied that this role meets your needs?
2. Is your self-described internal analysis in alignment with this career path?
3. Do you have verifiable qualifications that would interest a reputable for-profit or non-profit organization?
4. Are you familiar with Sarbanes-Oxley, SEC and NYSE or other important regulations?
5. Is your professional background unblemished? Will it bear the most careful scrutiny?
6. Will your personal ethics and values stand the test of inquiry?

If this role appears to be a good fit for you, you are ready to move ahead and explore the opportunities that support your interest.

Explore the opportunities.

If you are still working, interview your firm's board members and arrange introductions to venture capitalists, angel investors and others. Do not approach prospective organizations on your own because a third party introduction will serve you much more powerfully than will a direct approach. Attend events through your local university, interview friends who sit on boards, participate actively in non-profit organizations as a volunteer, and continue to research additional angel investing groups and venture capital firms.

Consider board governance training through major Schools of Business, such as: The Wharton School of Business, Stanford, Northwestern, University of Chicago and UCLA's Anderson School.

Continue your research.

Websites: For Internet access, type: http://www. followed by the web address

BoardSeat.com
Provides general information regarding for-profit boards.

Nacdonline.org
The National Association of Corporate Directors tells you what every board member must know.

Boardsource.org
Provides information on non-profit boards.

Google.com
Go to Google's advanced search and enter the following key words: board-of-directors, for-profit boards-of-directors, non-profit (and not-for-profit) boards-of-directors.

Pluck.com and Info.com
Additional search engine services

Books, magazines, periodicals and an association:

How Corporate Boards Create Competitive Advantage a recent book by Ram Charan.

Directors and Boards Magazine

The Association for Corporate Growth (ACG) has a presence in all major U.S. cities.

Prepare your marketing tools.

For information and examples, refer to the Marketing Tools section of this book.

Business cards	Portfolio (optional)
Professional biography	Website (optional)

Across America – Real people, real stories...Ben Goodwin

I've never really thought about retirement because I love my work and enjoy staying active. Throughout my corporate career I've emphasized sales and marketing, and I enjoy the challenges that those functions entail. I'm currently President of the Public Safety, Security and Industrial Systems Group of SYS Technologies, which provides real-time information technology solutions and wireless communication systems for the Department of Defense, Department of Homeland Security and industrial markets. I also serve as Senior Vice President of Sales and Marketing for the corporation.

As I joined the senior executive ranks, I had the opportunity to serve on the Boards of Directors of both private sector firms and nonprofit organizations. Most recently I served on the Board of Aonix, a global supplier of software solutions for mission-critical and safety-critical applications for the avionics, defense, telecom, medical and other industries. I had joined Aonix as President, COO in 2003, and this was my second tenure with the company. I had joined a predecessor firm in 1990 which merged with another company to form Aonix in 1996. I left in early 2000 to develop a buy-out fund, but the burst of the Internet bubble in 2001 sealed that venture's fate. After consulting for a year I joined a software development firm and headed up sales and marketing for a year and a half. Then Aonix contacted me about returning to the firm. It was in a turn-around mode, and I would have the opportunity to rebuild its sales organization and contribute to the growth of the company.

My first stint on a private sector Board was with Template Graphics. I gained a lot of experience with mergers and acquisitions with that organization when it was sold to another company, but my role was eliminated when that firm turned it into a division and disbanded the Board. One can expect a small retainer and some equity in a company when asked to serve on its Board. I highly recommend that you look critically at the financial health of the organization before committing. You also must understand the details of the indemnification agreement between directors and the company, and you must insist on receiving a D & O (Directors' & Officers') Insurance policy paid by the company.

Congress and the Securities and Exchange Commission have imposed higher standards regulating corporate governance and the behavior of business leaders. With the increased scrutiny on Boards in the post-Enron and Worldcom financial world, individuals must be very careful with their due diligence prior to making a decision to accept a Board position and need to continue to make sure that all the dealings of the Board and its company are on the up and up.

Questions that an individual needs to ask himself or herself to be sure that a Board role is right for them include:

- Can I truly make a contribution based on my talents and experience to the success of this company?
- Do I have the time and energy to go the extra mile to commit myself to this undertaking?
- Do I have the sense of independence to speak my mind about any issue and ask the hard questions that need to be brought up?

You must be able to effectively manage confrontation and fight for what you believe to be in the best interests of the organization. There are many challenges to being on the Board of Directors of a company, but the experience is well worth the time and effort.

I have also had experience on the Boards of nonprofit organizations including the YMCA and the Boys and Girls Clubs. Nonprofits can be even more "Political" than private sector Boards, but the opportunity to give back to the community and make a difference in the lives of others is very rewarding. Many nonprofits need the financial expertise of business people, and it's great to have the chance to have a positive influence in the workings of organizations. The ability to influence fundraising is another major component of what it takes to be successful on many nonprofit boards.

Getting on a nonprofit board or even a "Board of Advisors" for a small business is the best way to gain experience and to determine if serving on a Board is right for you. I have appreciated the opportunity to make meaningful contributions to organizations through my Board work, and I look forward to continuing in those roles.

Coaches

Who are they?

Like the great sports coaches of your past, such as Vince Lombardi, you can use your knowledge and your skills gained over time to help others succeed in life and business. Coaches come in many styles and from many backgrounds. Most begin their coaching careers at the bottom of a ladder and build their reputations one satisfied client at a time.

What you need to know.

Coaching is about helping people to achieve peak performance. If your clients usually achieve peak performance because of your part in the process of learning and developing new skills, you're a coach. However, if they don't succeed in their role, you surely will not succeed as a coach.

A few of today's coaching types include:

- *Business coaches*

    In the business world, coaches help executives to validate their decisions, to set strategies and to tackle tactics.

    They help executives to communicate effectively with various constituents, such as: customers, employees, other stakeholders and boards of directors.

    It is past knowledge of the executives' world and the skills to coach that are the entry points to qualify you for this type of role.

    These are the business coaches who specialize in small business coaching, lending breadth and extending the reach of overworked small business leaders by providing them with just-in-time, cost-effective help.

- *Career coaches*

    In the career management world, coaches help people to navigate the different new world in which we live and work. As people change jobs more and more frequently, as life spans lengthen and as technology, globalization and other changes affect employment choices, the career coach helps their clients to stay abreast of marketplace trends and to make necessary adjustments on a timely basis.

    Career coaching is not for the newcomer, but you may be able to learn the game by joining a career management firm on a project basis. The initial pay is decidedly modest but the upside pay is good.

    Certification, an increasingly important credential for career coaches, takes time on the job, a commitment to achieving the necessary credentials, and the testing of your knowledge by a national association.

- *Financial coaches*

    The best of the independent financial managers act as coaches. They help people to process information and make prudent financial decisions as well as to understand the landmines of various investment strategies.

    Hitching your rising star to an established and successful financial manager is usually an easier route into this work than attempting to launch your own practice. Another alternative for the new coach is to join an established, large financial services firm where its reputation has the effect of building your own.

    Licensing is a requirement of the business and it requires considerable study and investment on your part to meet the strict standards of this type of coaching.

- *Life coaches*

    Another growing coaching discipline is "Life Coaching." A life coach helps people to develop personally and, sometimes, professionally. A well-known example of a life coach is Anthony Robbins who has built a mega-empire by helping people to enhance the quality of their lives and, as one result, achieve their (and his) personal goals.

    Life coaching does not require certification but the role usually falls to psychologists, psychiatrists and others whose established credentials reassure clients of their ability to give credible advice.

- *Specialized coaches*

    The coaching profession is replete with specialists. The "in" term is "subject matter experts."

    Spiritual coaches...

    Ethics coaches...

    Communications coaches...

    Sales coaches...

    Public speaking coaches...

    are but a few of the areas where coaches meet new buyers of special interest services.

Validate your interest.

Review your responses in Steps 1 and 2.

Ask yourself the following questions:

1. Are you satisfied that this venture meets your needs?
2. Is your self-described internal analysis in alignment with this career path?
3. Can you command the initial respect of your clients as a result of your past experience and success?
4. Are you confident that your subject matter knowledge is strong and deep?
5. Do you have the finesse and savvy to inspire your clients to do as you recommend? If not, additional lessons in the gentle, but firm, art of coaching are available.

6. Are you a skilled group facilitator? Or, are you willing to invest in learning the skill of group facilitation?

7. Are you comfortable in the art of self-promotion? In addition to working one-on-one, you will have to promote yourself through community and civic presentations.

8. Are you willing to continue to research in your field, to stay abreast of the latest coaching techniques and information?

9. Do you have an underlying passion for a particular area of coaching? Knowledge plus passion equals an unbeatable combination.

If this role appears to be a good fit, you are ready to move ahead and explore the opportunities that support your interest.

Explore the opportunities.

1. First of all, identify your top areas of subject matter expertise. In virtually all cases, coaches are paid for specific, not generalized, knowledge.

2. Interview coaches you know and respect. Ask for their advice and ideas.

3. Research the certifications and credentials you must invest in if you are to be credible with buyers, even if you offer years of experience and a ton of knowledge.

Continue your research.

Websites: For Internet access, type: http://www. followed by the web address.

B-coach.com
A low-cost virtual business-coaching firm that is worth a look.

Mentors.ca/findacoach.html
Business, personal and other coaching services

Passionforbusiness.com
They offer small business "advice and expertise when you need it, motivation and brainstorming when you're stuck, insight to build you and your business to your highest potential."

wabccoaches.com
This site links you to the Worldwide Association of Business Coaches.

Google.com
Go to Google's advanced search and enter the following key words: business coaching, financial coaching, career coaching, life coaching, ethics coaching, mediation coaching, etc.

Pluck.com and Info.com
Additional search engine services

Books, magazines and periodicals:

Coach Anyone About Anything by Germaine Porche and Jed Niederer.

Coaching and Mentoring for Dummies by Marty Brounstein.

Effective Coaching by Marshall Cook.
Executive Coaching with Backbone and Heart by Mary Beth O'Neill.
Mentor Manager/Mentor Parent by Linda Dowling and Cecile Culp Mielenz.

Prepare your marketing tools.

For information and examples, refer to the Marketing Tools section of this book.
- Branding statement
- Business cards
- Business plan
- Portfolio (strongly recommended — hard copy and online versions)
- Professional biography
- Website

Across America – Real people, real stories...Randy Noe

Out of a considerable amount of soul searching, reflection, and a willingness to explore new possibilities for professional and personal growth, a uniquely qualified executive coach emerged. That coach is our friend, Randy Noe and this is his story.

"Throughout my life I have enjoyed learning by observing and listening with an open mind. I have also had a deep desire to connect and share with others. One of my early teaching experiences as a basketball camp counselor for John Wooden instilled discipline and taught me the basics of his Pyramid Of Success: industriousness and enthusiasm at the base, patience and faith at the pinnacle.

My interest in relationships and human behavior led me to pursue a degree in psychology from San Diego State University. I also wanted to learn about business and finance. I obtained an MBA from the University of Southern California, and then studied an additional three years to become a Chartered Financial Analyst (CFA) to further hone my technical analytical skills.

My executive management and financial consulting experience includes leadership roles for large public and private companies. I have been a leader for the Southern California regional Financial Valuation practice of a "Big-5" firm, mergers and acquisitions specialist for a publicly traded software company, senior finance executive for an apparel manufacturing and retail company with over $500 million annual sales, and Vice President for a major regional California bank. During my twenty-year career in corporate finance I analyzed hundreds of companies and worked closely with CEOs, chief financial officers, senior managers and advisors, and actively participated on several transactions for companies with market capitalizations of over a billion dollars in size. I have also helped many smaller emerging growth companies develop and execute business plans to prepare for sale or financing events.

In 1992 I was a casualty of a corporate downsizing and found myself out of work for the first time in my career. After living in the "fast track" of high finance, I had been given a blessing of time to slow down. It was an opportunity to reassess, reset priorities, and create more balance in my life. I started walking in the morning and let my thoughts wander. I looked back at my past to identify the good times, and the bad times. I wanted to identify situations and activities that gave me energy and joy. As part of this process I identified new interests, my strengths and joys, and some personal mission statements. I am a strong believer in the process of reflection and introspection as paths to assessment, discovery and redirection.

In exploring new directions I began serving in my church by designing and facilitating adult education classes and addressing various topics such as forgiveness. I found strengthening my faith by personal sharing to be very fulfilling. In the process, many people who attended my classes have been very supportive and encouraged me to pursue paths to teach and mentor others.

I discovered the world of executive coaching as part of my networking efforts. In exploring this emerging field, I sought out and met with several highly successful master coaches. I found that my interests, strengths and skills aligned with what they do, how they serve their clients, their business models and best practices. My personal and professional goals and values were brought into congruency. All of my career and life experiences, relationships, passions and skills can be contributed and shared to help others.

Being authentic, open and willing to share my "on the ground" experiences with others enables me to make a personal connection and build a strong foundation for my client relationships. I understand how to create business value, identify critical success and risk factors and drivers of performance. I also know the personal challenges, issues and the pressures that confront business leaders. I have been there.

Executive coaching and mentoring can help others improve their lives in many powerful and significant ways. As an executive coach and advisor I enjoy working with my clients to seek clarity, fulfillment and balance in daily life. I engage them in a process, and encourage, stimulate and challenge them to discover and articulate their own fundamental purpose in life. I help them identify their vision, passions, strengths and joys. I facilitate leadership development, positive thinking and growth in career transition, and resolution of ethical dilemmas. I help my clients heighten their awareness to enable them to make better choices for professional and personal growth, with insight, wisdom and integrity."

Consultants

Who are they?

The dictionary's definition of a consultant is "one who gives expert or professional advice." You might justifiably add the words "high-priced" before the word "expert" as part of the classic description of a consultant.

Consultants have come to be thought of in many ways beyond the definition of the term found in the dictionary. Some people, who are out of work and between jobs, attempt to position themselves as actively engaged in the world of work, by misleadingly using the term to lend a cover to their forced time out. Others use this catchall term to describe any work that is not a regular job. For purposes of this section of the book, think of consultants in its classic definition, that of people who give expert advice but who do not perform much, if any, of the actual work.

If a deep fund of knowledge is the guiding light for mature people seeking to continue in their regular, full-time careers, then subject matter expertise, a fair amount of chutzpah and the ability to handsomely charge for advice is the key to consulting success.

High priced consulting is the domain of the few, the experts; the gurus with both depth and breadth of knowledge and, frequently, an established public presence. If you can provide an organization or an institution with high-priced advice that they will value, you are a consultant.

If not, you're probably not a consultant **unless** you fit into one of the unique categories described in the following exceptions:

> *If you fit within the glare of the public spotlight* afforded published authors, retired Chief Executive Officers of Fortune 500 firms and the like, you may be called upon to enter into a consulting career, especially by the brand-name consulting firms, after the bulk of your working lifetime is behind you.
>
> *If you are, or were, a high-profile lawyer,* the model for the ultimate high-priced consultants, some would say, you might position your expertise with organizations as a consultant. Lest, at this point, you demure and think that these consultants actually do the work, they do not. Their associates do the bulk of the work. The top lawyers create the strategy, oversee and advise clients or associates and then stand up and get counted in the win/loss column.
>
> *If you are a medical specialist,* such as a forensic psychologist or physician, you may consult as an expert witness on behalf of police departments and law firms.
>
> *If you have an established reputation as a coach,* you may be called upon as an expert witness or consultant in matters of labor disputes, such as worker's compensation or employment law issues.

What you need to know.

There are several different ways in which to consult.

You may seek to join a recognizable consulting organization, such as one of the large firms of certain fame and established reputation. Their staffs consist of Master Consultants (The Partners), Associate Consultants and overworked apprentices (typically, recent MBA's). People seldom simply pop into these consulting organizations after a lifetime of working elsewhere as they most often "grow their own" consultants from the survivors amongst the apprentices. A note of caution is in order regarding managing your expectations to join the large firms. In recent years, revenues have been somewhat flat in the larger consulting organizations as buyers migrate to specialized, targeted and more affordable consultancies. Another note of caution is to beware of the typically grueling work ethic of virtually all such consulting firms. However, if you offer the firm a big name, the hours and commitment may be minimal as your role is to lend credibility, the master's touch and a very high profile.

A sub-group of highly specialized industry or specialty particular consulting firms are coming into their own. Technology and systems consulting firms and specific consulting niches, such as Human Resources, are growing. These firms may also double as outsourcing firms, meaning that they consult with and then do the work for organizations they support.

If you wish to start your own smaller consultancy, maturity and expertise may work for you but you will want to carefully consider the barriers to entry before plunging ahead into the small, exclusive world of experts.

A few of the high-need/high-value areas of individual consulting include:

- Start-up and strategic growth consulting for small to mid-sized organizations seeking to grow fast or to outdistance their competition.

- Organizational re-design and turnaround consulting for small to mid-sized organizations' leaders who are concerned with issues surrounding repositioning or retrenchment. Opportunities in this area of consulting are also to be found through the banking community and through bankruptcy courts.

- Ethics consulting for organizations struggling with issues related to business. The consultants set the standards. Ethics coaches help organizations understand and commit to staying a difficult new course with integrity and honor.

Financing challenges affect the survival of independent consultancies. It is critical to include a thorough investigation of your finances and marketplace needs before attempting an independent consultancy because this is a business that is built as a result of your commitment to year-after-year development of clients and success stories.

Validate your interest.

Review your responses in Steps 1 and 2.

Ask yourself the following questions:
1. Are you satisfied that this venture meets your needs?
2. Is your self-described internal analysis in alignment with this career path?

3. Is your knowledge current?
4. Are you marketable as a high-priced consultant?
5. Do you have an established reputation for subject-matter expertise?
6. Is your lifestyle flexible enough to chase consulting opportunities wherever they may exist?
7. Are you prepared to sell as well as to deliver your service?

If this role appears to be a good fit for you, you are ready to move ahead and explore the opportunities that support your interest.

Explore the opportunities.

If you are still working, the time to light your consultant's fire is now. Study the consulting firms and connect with consultants in your field of expertise. If you are the employer responsible for paying consultants' bills, hook the targeted consulting firms' principals into wanting to know you while you are still in the driver's seat. Take the time to check out the costs of operating a consultancy as well as the liabilities and financial exposure associated with this career field.

If you are no longer working, your fire had better be burning bright before you explore the lofty realm of the consultant advisors to the public and private sector businesses you seek to support.

Lest you believe that we have unfairly discouraged you from this course of action and you are confident that you have advice that organizations will pay a high price for, take the time to read any, or all, books by Peter Block. See the research section for referral to one of Mr. Block's best books.

Continue your research.

Websites: For Internet access, type: *http://www.* followed by the web address.

> *Designedlearning.com*
> This is the site for The Center for Consulting Competence.
>
> *McKinsey, PricewaterhouseCoopers, Booz Allen Hamilton, Cap Gemini Ernst & Young, etc.*
> All have websites and there is considerable information written about their services in daily publications, such as your local newspaper and the Wall Street Journal.
>
> *Google.com*
> Go to Google's advanced search and enter the following key words: consulting firms, independent consultants, business specific consultancies (such as healthcare and technology).
>
> *Pluck.com and Info.com*
> Additional search engine services

Books, magazines and periodicals:

> *The Consultant's Calling* by Geoffrey Bellman
>
> *The Consultant's Quick Start Guide* by Elaine Biech

Secrets of Flawless Consulting by Peter Block
Consultative Selling (seventh edition) by Mack Hanan

Prepare your marketing tools.

For information and examples, refer to the Marketing Tools section of this book.
Branding statement
Business cards
Business plan, including marketing and financial plans if you intend to solo
Portfolio or brochure
Professional biography or highly focused resume
Website

Across America – Real people, real stories...John Coyne

From police officer to corporate player, John has finely honed his learning experiences and transitioned to the world of the high-priced consultant. This is his story:

"Developing strong problem-solving skills, enjoying a variety of workplace responsibilities and accomplishing a successful track record as a consumer products marketing and sales executive are three of the four cornerstones that I have built to support my entry into the management consulting field. The fourth and most important part of the foundation is my belief that you must be passionate about what you do in order to be successful.

After over 20 years in business, I have come to learn that pursuing high-dollar corporate positions largely for the money typically leads to a situation where you don't enjoy what you are doing. If you're passionate about what you do, you do it well. Then the money will follow. I think I've had it backwards for most of my career; in other words, chase the money, it will make you happy.

After getting a Bachelor's degree, I began my career as a police officer, following my father into the law enforcement profession. Although I enjoyed the field for four years, especially the variety of work it entailed, I went back for my MBA and then joined Oscar Mayer Foods Corporation in product management. I continued in product management, marketing and sales management positions at TreeSweet and Dial. Then I started my own consulting and training organization where I spent three years specializing in brand marketing techniques to improve corporate brand programs. I then joined Daymon Associates, Inc., the world's largest corporate brand sales and marketing company, and supported clients including Bruno's and PetsMart. Following that, I was Executive Vice President and General Manager (West Area) for Information Resources, Inc., a leading marketing research company.

In 2002 I joined a friend and former Dial Corporation colleague in an interim management assignment at Meyer Foods, LLC. Our goal was to turn around this $65MM company that hadn't made a profit in the five years it had been in business. With my friend serving as President and CEO and I serving as Senior Vice President of Sales and Marketing, we accomplished a number of initiatives over a year and a half period, including revising the company's strategic plan, strengthening its operating plan and increasing sales by 65% during fiscal year 2003. This resulted in the first profitable year for the company, and the experience motivated me to start my own consulting practice.

I developed a niche by providing sales and marketing consulting to companies in the "Early stages" of turn-around situations. Most turn-around consulting is done at the "Late stage" when a company is in dire financial straits, and bankers and attorneys direct financial consultants to do major surgery on the company in hopes of reviving it. By coming in early and assessing the company, its management and its operations especially from a sales and marketing perspective, I provide specific deliverables that will have an immediate, positive effect on the organization and lay the groundwork for a successful turn-around. I am developing strategic alliances with other consulting firms to provide an umbrella of support for client companies.

I have established my own consulting practice where I am leveraging my work experience to help companies improve their business results. Enjoying the mental stimulation of problem solving, I thrive on the challenges and variety of work that my consultancy entails. I have developed a strong passion for my work and am reaping the monetary and intrinsic benefits of an excellent career choice based on a number of principle-based decisions."

Entrepreneurs

Who are they?

They are the real-life innovators of the American dream, the risk takers, and the daredevils of the business world.

A note to you and to all would-be entrepreneurs in America.
If you have a dream, a passion to begin your own enterprise, you are not alone.
If you are concerned that it may be too late, it is - if you think it is.
But, if you hear the siren song calling you to innovate,
and you still have the drive,
begin!

What you need to know.

In support of mature entrepreneurs everywhere, remember that older folks have a lower failure rate in entrepreneurial startups than their younger counterparts. Whether you are 40, 49, 59 or older, the only time you have is now. But then, that has always been true, hasn't it?

Legendary entrepreneurs make up the Fortune 500. From Bill Gates at Microsoft and Jeff Bezos at Amazon to the "Yahoo" gang, the "Monster" group and the "Google" bunch, entrepreneurs are, once again, thriving in America. Keep your antenna up for lesser-known entrepreneurs who are on the brink of emerging on the scene from the biotech and medical equipment industries.

There are sizzling products still awaiting discovery. Some are quite simple and may be right in front of you.

From the screw-top cover on wine bottles that replace traditional corks to — you name it — entrepreneurship at every level is alive and well in America.

A simple recipe for setting the stage for entrepreneurial success suggests that you:

1. Take one dream
2. Add two healthy cups of something you already know a lot about
3. Blend the two ingredients with an emerging marketplace need
4. Set aside the first 3 ingredients while you write a plan
5. Add a dose of knowledge about Local, State and Federal ordinances
6. Validate the plan in your test kitchen of trusted colleagues and other entrepreneurs
7. Copyright or patent your ideas as soon as possible

The recipe is the easy part.

Slow down.

Step back and ask yourself some important questions before you take additional action.

Are you someone who can handle the psychological, physical and financial stress of
 no regular paycheck,
  no corporate benefits,
   no paid time off,
    no collegial support,
     no backup when you are ill?

And, can you endure
 many vocal skeptics,
  moments of self-doubt,
   mistakes that only you can correct,
    miserable consequences when you are wrong,
     months of long hours to meet your commitment to the future?

Stop.

If you have a spouse or life-partner, double-check their commitment to your dream.

Anticipate roadblocks.

One challenge for entrepreneurs is evident. Venture Capital is still reeling from their hasty investments of the mid to late 90's and they will not soon part with their money in the same frenzied ways of the past. This doesn't mean that you can't find investors. The roadblock is there for you in any event. Go for it.

Still interested in forging ahead? Take another step.

Look at some of the traits of successful entrepreneurs.

They are:

1. Skilled at written and verbal communications
2. Comfortable selling new ideas to others
3. Willing to work weekends, holidays and long hours
4. Able to laugh at failure and pick themselves up when rejected
5. Independent and can work alone for long periods of time
6. Able to face new and challenging situations while multi-tasking

7. Quick to rethink changing situations and to make adjustments
8. Suited to working well under pressure
9. Capable of riding a financial roller coaster

They have:
1. A written plan, one that they systematically monitor
2. A clearly defined long-range financial goal
3. The support of their spouse or partner
4. A strong networking presence with professional organizations or investment groups

Take one more time-out, please.

Let's talk about $ $ $ (money).

If you are searching for access to large sums of money, talk with angel investors, venture capital firms and investment banking groups who routinely assist entrepreneurs. Angel Investors provide modest capital to entrepreneurs and, of course, the VC firms provide substantial investment. World-class investment banking groups also provide emerging companies with global capital raising services and second rounds of financing. Learn, and commit to memory, their terms and conditions of investment.

While talking with prospective investors, during your quest to find relatively "easy" money, remember 3 basic truths about getting other peoples' money:

1. **There is no "easy" money.**
   If your name is not associated with success, the money will not be forthcoming.

2. **There is no "easy" money.**
   If you do not have a record for creating profits, you will encounter a painful reluctance on the part of investors to invest in your dream.

3. **There is no "easy" money.**
   Even if you are successful in raising money, after all is said and done, you are likely to find that someone else owns your business. This may be the most important entrepreneurial lesson of all.

All in all, in talking about money, if you can demonstrate some early success on your own "nickel" you are far more likely to receive additional funding or "lines of credit" from financial partners.

Validate your interest.

Review your responses in Steps 1 and 2.

Ask yourself the following questions:
1. Are you satisfied that this prospective venture meets your needs?
2. Is your self-described internal analysis in alignment with this career path?
3. Do you share most of the traits reported by successful entrepreneurs?
4. Do you have a Plan "B" for your venture in the event funding is not available?
5. Ask again: Does your partner or spouse support your plans?

If this role appears to be a good fit for you, you are ready to move ahead and explore the opportunities that support your interest.

Explore the opportunities.

Seek advice from financial services firms and other institutions dedicated to helping entrepreneurs financially launch their new businesses.

If you qualify as a "protected class" under the Federal definition, you may wish to explore grants set aside to encourage this segment of the population to realize their business dreams. (Since the Federal Government has defined the age of "40" as protected under age discrimination laws, this is a good time to explore grants. The Feds are apt to catch on soon that more than half the population is older than 40 – when they do, the protected age will be raised.)

Often frustrated because they can't crack that traditional barrier — the "glass ceiling" — in most American corporations, women and minorities are flocking to the entrepreneurial world as well as into opportunities to start or buy small businesses. This is one reason why the numbers of women and minorities seeking funding are representatively high.

If you are still working, fund as much of your project as possible while you have income. Write your business plan during weekends and evenings. You will be working these longer hours soon.

Understand the rules and regulations associated with intellectual property laws. For example, you need to know the difference between types of patents. Remember that patents protect your invention or your ideas and provide you with exclusive rights to making, using and selling the invention in America. And, you need to know all about trademarks. Trademarks are words or symbols that identify your inventions and distinguish them from others products or services. Do you understand copyright laws? If you are a writer, a computer entrepreneur, a musical composer or an artist of any ilk, a copyright protects the manner in which your words or ideas are expressed but not the underlying ideas themselves. Finally, are your aware of the regulations surrounding trade secrets? Trade secrets can protect you from unauthorized disclosure or use of confidential client information.

On another note, you will have to research your options as to the best basis to legally structure your business. There are sole proprietorships, limited and general partnerships, corporations, limited liability firms (LLC) and S-Corporations. Each of these options requires that you understand the pros and cons they present.

Continue your research.

Websites: For Internet access, type: http://www. followed by the web address.

Antiventurecapital.com/angelinvestor.html
This is an interesting site. They promote their Anti-Venture Capital Guide as "akin to spending a week with the founders of successful fast growth companies." They suggest that learning more about raising capital now will relieve you of the prospective mistake of using today's money-raising services where "middle-men" take your money but don't necessarily deliver the deals. They warn you against up-front fees and other mistakes that are costly in terms of time and money.

Businesspartners.com
The site connects you with angel investors and venture capitalists.

Entrepreneurmagazine.com
This is the online version of the well-regarded magazine.

Vfinance.com
Vfinance offers traditional investment banking services, private fundraising and advisory services as well as assistance with business plans. Vfinance.com will send you a free, updated list of VC firms in the U.S. Headquartered in Boca Raton, Florida, they claim offices in 25 cities throughout the U.S. Their VC starter pack includes a business plan template and instructions that guide you through the process of approaching investors.

Google.com
Go to Google's advanced search and enter the following key words: entrepreneurial opportunities, venture capital firms, angel investors, business lending institutions, small business administration, federal grants.

Pluck.com and Info.com
Additional search engine services

Books, magazines and periodicals:

Starting Your Own Business by Jan Norman

Successful Business Planning in 30 Days, 2nd Edition, by Peter Patsula

The Complete Idiot's Guide to Starting Your Own Business, 3rd Edition, by Ed Paulson

The Successful Business Plan: Secrets and Strategies by Rhonda Abrams

The WetFeet Insider Guide to Careers in Venture Capital
   Tells you how venture capital works, the state of venture capital, the major players, the sectors served and how to enter the field yourself.

Prepare your marketing tools.

For information and examples, refer to the Marketing Tools section of the book.

Branding statement

Business cards

Business plan, including financial and marketing strategies

Professional biography or a highly focused resume or portfolio

Across America – Real people, real stories...David Schick

After spending 30 years in the consumer packaged goods industry, David found himself reorganized out of a job at the age of 55. This is the story of dramatic and challenging change.

"During my corporate career I worked in sales and marketing with leading companies including Warner Lambert, RJR Foods, Alliance Corporation, Ocean Spray and Dial Corporation. Dial was my last stop, and I enjoyed nine-year tenure there. Upon leaving Dial I took full advantage of outplacement services, which were provided as a part of my separation benefits.

I developed a personal marketing plan and conducted a strategic job search with the goal of securing a senior sales and marketing position. I made over 130 contacts and interviewed for a number of positions, but I was not successful in securing a new job. Unless you are looking for a CEO, COO or CFO position, it's challenging at age 55 to land another job in a corporate setting.

I did some extensive assessment of my interests and priorities and decided to reinvent myself in an entrepreneurial environment. While there is risk in taking your skill sets to a new venue, finding a niche that fits can be fulfilling and can lead to a successful conclusion. My journey began two years ago when I joined three other executives in purchasing the rights to what we think is the best cognitive skills program in the country. We established Learning Enhancement Corporation with the intent of developing the best training systems available anywhere. We've taken a paper-based program and turned it into a system that is Web-enabled and digital game enhanced.

Starting a business from the ground up has been full of interesting challenges for my partners and me, but we feel great about our accomplishments so far. In creating the initial group of founders, we realized that we needed to develop a team with people possessing different skills from one another since we couldn't afford to overlap. However, one knowledge base that is essential for all the partners to share is finance.

Understanding the financial aspects of an enterprise is crucial for all involved at the start-up, and our firm has progressed at a steady pace because of it. We worked hard at developing a comprehensive business plan and put together a major presentation to effectively attract investors. I feel that another key to our success in developing funding was the pride that we have in wanting to provide a successful venture for investors to make a return on.

All the partners feel a strong burden to produce for ourselves, our employees and the investors. We're not in it for the paycheck; we're in it to develop a strong business that will reward us down the road.

We've also done a lot of due diligence on our competition and have sought the input of potential customers from the start. As a result, we've refined not only our products but our marketing and sales plan extensively. We've gotten a great response from the marketplace thus far.

A major hurdle that my partners and I have overcome is not having a support team to depend upon. We all came out of corner offices at our corporations and had the luxury of an administrative team behind us. Professionals and executives in the Baby Boom generation weren't usually trained with technical and administrative skills. It's important to assess your capabilities in these areas and get the proper training, such as in the use of a computer.

I've learned that taking the time and effort to conduct a comprehensive assessment of one's self is very important. Especially when you lose your job, it's discouraging at first and you can really get down on yourself. But when you review the skills, knowledge and experience you have along with your accomplishments and contributions, you see yourself in a positive light and develop the confidence to take the action steps necessary to continue to achieve career success."

Fancy-Free Workers

Who are they?

Roget's Thesaurus defines "fanciful" as: "Appealing to fancy: fancy, fantastic, fantastical, imaginative, whimsical." Fanciful workers have thrown over the ties that bound them to traditional careers and have stepped off the humdrum highway into the imaginative lane.

At long last, you need not be bound by a traditional view of work. Come along with us and enjoy a peak into the world of the fancy-free workers.

What you need to know.

This section is all about careers that tickle the funny bone, spark the imagination or hint of non-conformity.

Read on.

- *Conduct tours of our National Parks*
  Look up funjobs.com. Yes, this is a real site. If it sounds like fun, and it is fun — why not explore this site even if you have more traditional ambitions?

  Fun Jobs lists everything from tour guides at Yellowstone National Park to fishing guides in Wyoming. Jobs are often seasonal but they are paid and usually offer housing. If it has been your dream to spend a summer in Big Sky Montana or if you are a Yellowstone history buff, the site is worth a look.

  What would inspire you to become a youth counselor? From Maine to Minnesota, the site offers countless ideas. Fun Jobs lists opportunities throughout America that offer your youthful imagination a chance to play again.

  These opportunities may also be found under "stipend" jobs in the section in our book labeled as such. We also suggest a Google search using this noun as reference.

- *Contribute marketing research*
  Companies will pay you to tell them what you think. You can fill out online surveys from your home computer. There are people who claim that they make $150 to $1000 per month in part-time income for this work. You will have to do some research here, but we've included a starting point.

  Go to Getpaid4youropinion.com. This site requires a paid membership but they will give you a free trial membership.

- *Drive away or sail away*
  National car rental and leasing firms engage people to drive expensive cars to and from destinations on behalf of high net worth individuals, corporate executives and entertainers. The fun of this work may be found in driving the Ferrari not in driving the passengers themselves.

These same agencies pay folks to drive the rest of us between car lots and airports. Look up the websites for national car rental agencies or stop by their many offices for information.

So much for driving.

But, did you know that boat owners pay people to sail or motor their boats between their old and new berths or to be ready for the owners' water vacations? Visit your local marina and check with the dock master.

- *For a whimsical non-job, buy a red hat*
  The second line of Jenny Joseph's poem talks about growing old enough to wear a "red hat that doesn't go and doesn't suit me." From that one line a huge society was born. The Red Hat society is a place where there is fun for women after fifty.

  Silliness is the cornerstone of the society. They even refer to themselves as a "disorganization." Underneath the silliness is a bonding experience for women. Aside from the purchase of your own red hat, the group is about almost nothing but fun. Don't have a red hat? You can buy one from them. Just shy of age 50? Don't worry; you may still join The Red Hat Society. Younger members wear a pink hat until they grow up and reach 50! There is no pay, but it's a great non-career if you simply want to have fun.

  Founded by Sue Ellen Cooper of Fullerton, California, The Red Hat Society promises to become a worldwide phenomenon. You can search for a chapter in your area by going to redhatsociety.com.

  In a sense this is work in that you must organize parties if you choose to start a group and you must commit to going to lunch and engaging in activities with other non-members.

- *Guide a tour*
  Are you a museum or an art buff? Or, perhaps you like to hang around convention centers or take people on tours to your local automotive or aircraft museum. From hospitality to hotels, search your local yellow pages as well as websites offered by local attractions. Summon a small dose of courage and take a tour at your local museum and then offer to lead one!

- *Nonconformists SHOULD apply*
  Sandra Gurvis wrote a book in 1999 entitled *Careers for Nonconformists* that lists 75 jobs from tattoo artists to food stylists and many more that appeal to fun and flights of fancy. The book offers tips to get into these fanciful fields and traps to avoid certain pitfalls as you go. Profiles of people who have succeeded in unusual, fun and colorful work are included in the book. If you are a "child of the 60's" and still have a bit of the flower child living within you, this is a worthwhile read. Or, if you are simply ready for a radical, have-some-fun change, Sandra's ideas will inspire you.

- *Tell stories for fun*
  How about story-telling to children? Can you imagine this job as fun? As of this moment, research does not lead us to recommend any paid opportunities doing this important work. But, whether you find paid "gigs" or not for this effort, it still qualifies

as a fun job and belongs in this section. Book stores, hospitals and libraries are good starting points for prospective storytellers. Check with your local Parks and Recreation Department. Mounting evidence suggests that, as time goes by, reading to children and helping them to learn to love to read will offer modest pay through our schools, libraries and various government agencies.

- *Turn your hobby into a business*
You can deduct all sorts of expenses if you want to earn some money from your hobby. For example, if you buy and sell baseball cards, you can "zero-out" your hobby income. To do this you must be a legitimate business. While a business involving your hobby may come under the heading of fanciful careers, please remember that the IRS will weigh the "fun factor" in determining just how much your pleasure is worth! In other words, your hobby turned business may be fun but it needs to look serious.

- *Wilderness Adventures offer fun and physical conditioning*
Described as "located in a magical place filled with towering mesas, long and twisting canyons, and clear mirrors of water" – Lake Powell Resorts and Marinas offers over 1200 jobs during the summer season. From boat instructors to food servers and retail workers, wages are low but the perks are terrific. If you are accepted as a summer employee at Lake Powell, you receive the use of company powerboats and water toys and even a 7-day houseboat vacation. Stamina and energy are the drivers for these jobs — not youth!

- *Work as an "extra"*
Do you love the movies? Would you like to pick up some extra income? Is it your idea of fun to hang around the theatrical world?

Extra work is employment as background for scenes in movies, TV shows or commercials. You may be called upon to be part of a crowd, creating the setting for a particular scene. There is neither special talent nor inherent skills required to become an extra. Casting agencies look for all types, ages, sizes and ethnic backgrounds.

Then there are the people who stand-in for principal actors. Called "photo doubles," these people must bear a resemblance in terms of size and structure to the actors but do not need to look like the actors themselves.

"Second team stand-ins" simply stand-in for actors allowing time for the principal actors to rest between takes or during rehearsals.

As long as you have no lines to say, you need not join the actor's union. Pay is low, although there is a hierarchy of pay from minimum wage to slightly better hourly pay.

You will have to register with a casting agency that specializes in engaging extras. Typical registration fees are under $50.00. In return for your fee, the agency will take your picture and vital statistics. We recommend that you visit the website actorschecklist.com for comprehensive information regarding the ins and outs of working as an extra.

Well known casting agencies for extras include: *Central Casting* and *Audience Associates/Big Crowds*, both in Los Angeles. In New York, The Reel People Company is a possible resource. Even if you don't live in Southern California or New York, these agencies, and others, book extras wherever a movie is being shot. For a broader reach, the *American Federation of Television and Radio Artists* has both West Coast and East Coast offices and may be contacted for additional information at aftra.org.

Validate your interest.

Review your responses in Steps 1 and 2.

Ask yourself the following questions:

1. Are you ready for a new adventure?

2. Do you, plain and simply, know that it is time to work *just for the fun of it*?

3. Are you willing to pick up the phone and learn more about these fun-filled opportunities?

> *Go on, have some fun.*
> *You deserve it!*

Explore the opportunities.

It is fun to explore your options in fanciful work. Open your eyes as you shop or drive around town. Call upon friends and ask for their ideas. Visit your Parks and Recreation Department.

Continue your research.

Websites: For Internet access, type: http://www. followed by the web address.

Refer to the websites and recommended reading found in the specific paragraph descriptions. Then, take a look at:

Backdoorjobs.com/outdoor.html

Cr.nps.gov/getinvol.htm

Google.com
Go to Google advanced search and enter the following key words: fun jobs, part-time work, and stress-free work options.

Pluck.com and Info.com
Additional search engine services

Books, magazines and periodicals:

Boom or Bust
Read the sections on stress-free work, hot-jobs, part-time work, stipend opportunities and volunteerism. DON'T prepare your marketing tools – pick up the phone, take a walk through the yellow pages or, explore the Internet for dozens of additional ideas.

Franchisees

Who are they?

Franchisees pay franchise owners a license to use a brand name as well as the proven systems and processes of an existing company. In addition to offering you brand recognition, systems and processes, the franchisers provide training, business savvy, marketing knowledge and on-going support as part of your fee. As a franchisee, you will be required to operate within the rules and standards the franchiser sets.

What you need to know.

There are many franchises beyond the obvious large-scale companies with which you are familiar. While the large franchises are beyond the reach of most investors, smaller franchises' initial investments typically range from $15,000 to $100,000. If these numbers still seem high, be aware that people usually come up with only a fraction of the total franchise cost and they finance the balance of the investment.

Franchise Brokers offer you advice on the opportunity that best suits your need. They guide you in identifying financing options and introduce you to franchise attorneys or others that will help to protect your investment. The franchise companies who seek people for their various businesses pay the brokers.

The Federal government carefully regulates franchises and the government's rules are important to learn as a part of your due diligence before launching into the world of franchise ownership.

While we have included a few examples of franchises in some of the hot areas of franchise opportunities, the examples are not intended as recommendations but simply as starting points for your own research.

Hot franchise areas include:

- Apparel
- Automotive products
- Food services
- Bookkeeping services
- Eldercare and other senior services (among the fastest growing Franchises in 2004-2005)
- Electronics
- Health care items and services
- Home remodeling and repair services
- House cleaning and maid services
- Pet services, such as grooming, apparel and gourmet snacks

- Physical conditioning, such as Curves for women
- Tutoring services, such as the Kumon Math and Reading Center

Certain areas of dynamic growth were recorded in 2003 and in 2004. Foremost among these were the services for elders who live alone at home. From extra help around the house to companionship, you may wish to consider one of these franchises.

Let's explore one such franchise opportunity.

Home Helpers, with corporate offices in Cincinnati, is a franchise that offers home care for seniors. *Success* and *Entrepreneur* magazines have identified this affordable franchise as one of the top franchise opportunities to serve the fastest growing group in America — the elderly. Their brochure describes Home Helpers as a cash business with no accounts receivable and extremely low overhead. At one point in time, they offered financing up to 100% for the initial franchise fee but this incentive may already have changed by the time you read this information. Franchise fees start around $15,000. For more information on Home Helpers, their web address is HomeHelpers.CC.

A close second to high-growth franchises for elders may be found in children's products and services. Parents who want better-educated offspring are interested in engaging tutors and independent learning institutions to help ensure their children's competitiveness in this very new global economy. Take a look at Kumon Math and Reading Centers, one such supplemental educational program. Along the same lines, children's fitness is a national concern and franchises such as Stretch-N-Grow are expanding as a result of this concern.

If you have an interest in fitness, you may want to explore franchise opportunities that offer fitness for us older kids.

Validate your interest.

Review your responses in Steps 1 and 2.

Ask yourself:

1. Are you satisfied that this venture meets your needs?
2. Is your self-described internal analysis in alignment with this career path?
3. What type of franchise business interests you?
4. Can you afford the franchise?
5. What are the total costs you might expect to invest?
6. Do you have your spouse or partner's support for the investment?
7. Should you buy more than one franchise location or territory?
8. Are the territories in which you have an interest the best territories in which to invest?
9. Do you want to go with an established franchise or invest in a new, but promising, franchise?
10. Will you take the time to thoroughly research franchisees and ask the hard questions?
11. Do you understand that the franchise fee is only your initial investment?

If this role appears to be a good fit for you, you are ready to move ahead and explore the opportunities that support your interest.

Explore the opportunities.

Attend one of many Franchise events hosted by local area Franchise Brokers.

Continue your research.

Websites: For Internet access, type: http://www. followed by the web address.

> *Frannet.com*
> A brokerage firm specializing in all levels of franchise opportunities, FranNet offers public seminars on franchising in most major U.S. cities. Franchise brokers, such as FranNet, offer brochures and newsletters to interested buyers.
>
> *i-soldit.com*
> A chain of eBay drop-off stores that makes it easy to sell things on eBay.
>
> Google.com
> Go to Google advanced search and enter the following key words: franchise brokerage firms, U.S. franchises, franchise investments.
>
> *Pluck.com and Info.com*
> Additional search engine services

Books, magazines and periodicals:

> *Tips and Traps When Buying a Franchise* by Mary Tomzack
>
> *Franchising Dreams: The Lure of Entrepreneurship in America* by Peter Birkeland.
>
> *Entrepreneur Magazine,* online and hard copy versions.

Prepare your marketing tools.

You will be asked to complete questionnaires to pre-qualify you to buy certain franchises.

Across America – Real people, real stories... John Cookson

This is the story of an electronics engineer who, after 9/11 found that he was moved sideways and down in his company and came to realize that his firm's requirements no longer matched his talents or interests.

"Upon separating from my company I received outplacement services, and I found the assessment phase to be very enlightening. After a lot of introspection and research, I came to the conclusion that I did not want to stay in a corporation and chose to explore franchise opportunities.

I initially looked at high technology based franchises, but most of those offered a sales role.

I wanted a franchise where I could utilize the management skills that I had developed, and I was open to a variety of fields.

I did extensive research and decided to purchase a Navis Pack & Ship Centers franchise in the custom shipping industry. Navis specializes in packaging and shipping special items including those that are fragile, large, awkward and/or valuable.

When investigating the purchase of a franchise, I recommend talking to as many current franchisees as possible. While the franchiser and franchise consultants can offer a great deal of information about the company, talking with the owners of the individual business units is crucial to doing effective due diligence. Gain a strong understanding of the competition as well to determine if the company and its industry are the right place for you to be.

One issue that I extensively investigated was how long it would take to turn a profit in a new business unit. While a specific formula can't apply to every location, by talking with a number of current franchise holders you can get a feel for the time span. While most franchise firms say one year, I would advise to be prepared to go 18 months to two years before expecting to turn a profit. Often the costs associated with setting up and running a business unit are more than originally thought.

During my due diligence with Navis, I interviewed a franchisee in Phoenix who was interested in selling his location. I explored the current status of his business and found that the marketing process and procedures were especially well established including a strong clientele. The financials showed a very good cash flow, and I liked his location in a growing area. We struck a deal in early 2004, and I took over the business in April.

While a few surprises cropped up after I came on board, I was pleased that the extensive research I had done paid off. I am enjoying my new role as business owner immensely.

While it is challenging to wear all the "hats" as a small business owner, I am utilizing many of the skills and knowledge I gained as a project manager in the corporate world. I took the first three months to learn the business from the inside and didn't make any initial changes since the operations were running fairly smoothly. I'm starting to make improvements, especially in optimizing the use of assets, such as better scheduling of crews and trucks to maximize their utilization.

It's a lot of hard work and long hours, but the payoff is worth it. While some franchises, especially retail, support their units with a lot of advertising, don't expect the franchise to do too much for you. Be prepared to operate your franchise as your own business and to work hard and smart to develop the resources necessary for your own success."

Government Workers

Who are they?

These are the folks who, until recently, enjoyed the last bastion of secure, regular, full-time work.

Look out!

This fortress of security is about to be tumbled and this may be to your advantage. Part-time and term-limited opportunities are likely to expand as the government, like the rest of the U.S. world of work, struggles to remain – dare we say it – solvent?

What you need to know about Federal jobs.

Federal jobs still offer some hot opportunities for citizens from many backgrounds. Applying for Federal Government jobs is different than applying for jobs elsewhere and it is important to understand the criteria they demand. Many, if not most, require citizenship. Take a look at some of the opportunities we have investigated.

- Homeland Security and the Bureau of Citizenship and Immigration Services.
  Foremost among recent opportunities are jobs in Homeland Security and the Bureau of Citizenship and Immigration Services. Likewise, bilingual applicants (especially Spanish/English) will be afforded some interesting opportunities not available to others in several areas of government work.

- The Bureau of Prisons.
  Unfortunately, the Bureau of Prisons in the Federal government is always looking for help, although there are youthful age restrictions imposed unless you have previous law enforcement experience.

- The Veterans' Health Administration.
  Like all U.S. healthcare systems, the V.A. is really anxious for help and they will readily work with any qualified healthcare professionals who want full-time or part-time roles.

- The Department of Veterans' Affairs.
  There are disabled veterans affirmative action opportunities set aside for people who might otherwise struggle to work in the Department of Veterans Affairs. VetGuide, a comprehensive website and publication, offers information to all veterans.

- The White House.
  For those of us interested in appointed jobs in the White House, there are ways to serve our country at the home of our President and the first family. Anyone seeking employment in the White House will, of course, undergo tremendous scrutiny. Full background checks are de rigueur for those seeking these positions. Go to whitehouse.gov/appointments/ if you are interested in exploring this further.

- The Environmental Protection Agency.
  An example of an Agency that is making use of workers aged 55 and older is the Senior Environmental Program funded by the Environmental Protection Agency. One-year renewable agreements benefit both the retiree and the agency.

- Remember the Peace Corps.
  Were you inspired by this organization in your youth? Why not now? According to their online brochure, you can help "build a library in Ghana, sponsor computer literacy in Mongolia" – and the Peace Corps is excited about working with healthy citizens of good reputation who offer specific knowledge that will benefit the world.

The following are a few of the Peace Corps' worldwide opportunities that await those with an adventurous spirit.

a. Business development volunteers to work in education, private business and public arenas.

b. Environment volunteers to teach environmental awareness.

c. Agricultural volunteers to work with farmers.

d. Health volunteers to work with issues surrounding nutrition and diseases that affect our world.

e. Information technology volunteers to help organizations and countries come into the new age of technology.

While the positions are voluntary, the Government covers your living expenses, including healthcare, while you are on assignment.

Finally, a few important words to Federal workers expecting to retire soon.

Many of you have expertise that is important to your community and to America. You should know that the Private Sector Council has recommended to Congress that government retirees in critical occupations, or with critical skills, should be candidates for part-time or flexible re-employment. The Private Sector Council suggests that the Federal Emergency Management Agency, the Homeland Security Department and the Centers for Disease Control and Prevention are good candidates for using the retiree workforce. It is a good idea to stay connected with these agencies and to continue to look for opportunities that may suit your mature career.

What you need to know about State, County and Municipal jobs.

Each State, County and City offers opportunities to mature workers but you will have to look up information the old-fashioned way — by research and through networking. For State, County and City programs, research each specific target location.

Continue to research.

Websites: For Internet access, type: http://www. followed by the web address.

Bls.gov
Covers virtually all information about the labor market (from the Government's point-of-view). If you click on the Occupational Outlook Handbook (under occupations), you will view the government's perspective of careers. Scroll to Employment Projections to see the 2000-2010 forecasts.

Ced.org/projects/older.htm
The Committee for Economic Development particularly targets opportunities for older workers on this site.

Wdsc.doleta.gov/seniors/
Senior Community Service Employment Program – U.S. Department of Labor

Experienceworks.org/index.html or *experienceworks.org/staffing.htm*
A directory and information resource for mature workers

Google.com
Go to Google's Advanced Search and type in key words, such as older worker services and identify the State or County in which you have an interest.

Pluck.com and Info.com
Additional search engine services

Across America – Real people, real stories...John Graham

After spending over 25 years in the private sector, first in operations and then in a variety of human resources positions, John accepted a job with Yuma (Arizona) County as its Director of Human Resources. This dramatic change in direction also included a cross-country relocation. A fair amount of change, wouldn't you agree? This is John's story.

"I began my career in the insurance industry where I worked in claims and operations for 11 years. I then accepted a human resources position with Discover Card, the consumer finance division of Sears. Healthcare was my next industry, and I spent a total of 8 years with two hospitals as Director of HR and Vice President of HR. I then switched to the transportation field and headed up HR for a trucking company for one year. I transitioned to a high tech firm for one year prior to hanging out my own shingle as an HR consultant.

A common thread that wove throughout my tenure in HR in the private sector was the opportunity to work with companies that wanted to make significant changes in the role of their HR departments. I sought out senior executives who knew the value of a progressive HR department, one that could serve as a strategic business partner with top management instead of simply playing a maintenance role. I worked hard at tying compensation and benefits to performance in order to show an HR department's value to an organization. I also developed an expertise in the development and management of self-insured health plans which, when administered effectively, represent a significant value to both employee and employer as a component of the company's total compensation program.

After growing up and working in the Midwest, I considered a move to the Southwest. My family and I had visited Arizona on a college trip for our oldest daughter, and we liked the region very much. Yuma County was looking for a HR Director who had experience in self-insured health plan design since it had just converted from an HMO model. The county also wanted to redesign its performance management program, compensation plan, HR policies, and implement a new HR system.

I prepared for my interview with the County like I would with any other organization. In addition to the information in the position description, I gathered as much information about the organization in terms of its history, current structure and, most importantly, its culture. As in the private sector companies I joined, I wanted to make sure that this organization shared the values that I possessed with regard to how it treats employees. I always look for answers to a three part question: Why are they doing what they're doing the way they are doing it? I was pleased with what I found, and the County Administrator was pleased with my technical expertise and the rapport that was quickly established with his interview team.

The position is a great fit for me. Yuma County has developed a culture where all employees are treated with respect and are recognized for their contribution to the organization. The greatest challenge that a new employee faces, especially one who comes from a different industry or field, is to gain the confidence and respect from their peers. As a change agent, I need to validate the reason for making changes and fit the change within the evolving culture of the organization, not just changing for change's sake. The Board of Supervisors of Yuma County, our organization's board of directors, and the County Administrator, my boss, are very supportive of progressive change for the enrichment of the employees and the residents of the County. Though the five Supervisors are all up for election this fall, and changes in the Board could certainly mean changes in the culture and focus of our organization, that's not much different from when a change in leadership takes place in the private sector.

My boss brought me on board to institute changes in the organization, and I've worked hard at developing and maintaining rapport with other department managers, who are my internal clients, in order to be effective in that role."

Home-Based Business Owners

Who are they?

These are people, maybe just like you, who prefer to run their business out of their home. The business itself, such as those run by Bed and Breakfast Innkeepers, may require working from the home. Or, for some, home is simply the place they would rather be!

There is a reason that one of the top ten quotes in America continues to be:

"There's no place like home"

— from the Wizard of Oz.

What you need to know.

According to Paul and Sarah Edwards in the 3rd edition of their book, *The Best Home Businesses for the 21st Century*, the following home businesses have great potential right now.

Bed and breakfast innkeepers	*Financial advisors*
Bookkeepers and bill paying services	*Fitness trainers*
Business plan writers	*Gift basket sales/service providers*
Caterers and personal chefs	*Home inspectors*
Copywriters	*Independent computer consultants*
Desktop publishers	*Newsletter publishers*
Douala services (mother's helpers)	*Proposal and grant writers*
Editorial professionals	*Security specialists*
Elder services	*Translators and interpreters*
Errand services	*Tutor*

Virtual home businesses are growing fast due to the rapid growth of sales over the Internet. Several of the aforementioned businesses lend themselves to the virtual world of technology. Refer to the web-based career section for more ideas regarding virtual home-based businesses.

Validate your interest.

Review your responses in Steps 1 and 2.

Ask yourself:

1. Are you satisfied that this venture meets your needs?
2. Is your self-described internal analysis in alignment with this career path?
3. Do you know which of the "hot" opportunities appeals to you?
4. Are you willing to take the time to make objective, not purely emotional, decisions?

5. Can you work independently?
6. Can you handle all aspects of the business through the sales cycle?
7. Do you have a family member that can help in some way or another?

If this role appears to be a good fit for you, you are ready to move ahead and explore the opportunities that support your interest.

Explore the opportunities.

The Learning Annex, one of many such organizations that teach new ways to work via the classroom or online, includes fast and budget friendly courses in many subjects. Some examples follow:

> *How to Start a Fashion Line.* If you have been thinking about getting into the fashion business, Kelly Gray, the CEO and creative force behind St. John's Knits — one of the most successful fashion brands in the U.S. today, personally leads this course. Home-based fashion lines include ordering, storing and delivering products from home. Sales may include in-home parties at your home or at the homes of prospective clients.

> *How to Be Your Own Detective and How to Make $100,000 a Year (or More!) as a Private Eye* are two courses being offered by Ed Pankau, one of the nation's top private investigators. Mr. Pankau has been profiled in the *New York Times* and *The Wall Street Journal* and he has appeared on *20/20, Inside Edition* and *America's Most Wanted.*

> *Intro to Jewelry Making.* Julia Armfield helps you get started, come up with ideas, master design basics and launch your career in this career niche.

> *How to Write, Illustrate and Sell Children's Books* is a fun-filled, informative workshop that helps you to pursue your interest in writing original works for children. If this work intrigues you, investigate The National Society of Children's Book Writers and Illustrators.

The point is that highly affordable workshops are available, with most priced at fewer than fifty dollars, and they are among the hot businesses we have previously identified for you. While workshops are not the final steps for getting into these lines of business, they will help you to overcome your fears and uncertainties and launch you in the right direction.

Of course, interview people who are in the business of home-based businesses.

Continue your research.

Websites: For Internet access, type: http://www. followed by the web address.

> *Aahbb.org*
> The American Association of Home-Based Businesses.

> *Bbonline.com*
> Links to a Bed and Breakfast site.

Errandservicesportal.com
Site for business that provides errand services.

Homebusiness.com
The American Home Business Association.

Learningannex.com
The site for The Learning Annex Bulletin.

Newsletteraccess.com
Links to Newsletter Publishers.

Google.com
Go to Google's advanced search and enter the following key words: home-based business, virtual or online businesses, home workers.

Pluck.com and Info.com
Additional search engine services

Please note that we have not investigated the businesses the websites represent. The information offered is intended to inform rather than to serve as an endorsement of any particular business.

Books, magazines and periodicals:

Boom or Bust is filled with ideas for profitable home businesses.

Successful Business Planning in 30 Days (2nd Edition) by Peter Patsula

The Best Home Businesses for the 21st Century (3rd Edition) by Paul and Sarah Edwards

Prepare your marketing tools.

For information and examples, refer to the Marketing Tools section of the book.

Business cards

Brochure

Website
(note that there are website developers whose designs permit you to "plug" your information into their master design. Check out www.BigBlackBag.com as one example of this affordable solution.

Written business plan, including financial plan and marketing plan

Across America — Real people, real stories...Tom Welch

Pulling the plug on past experience, Tom bravely faced an uncertain new world and endured the challenges of startup. This is what he has to say about his home business and the challenges he has faced in this new venture.

"Like many professional members of the Baby Boom generation, I would characterize my job changes during my early career as "When I lost a job, I'd just walk across the street to get another one."

I had developed a lot of confidence as I rose through the ranks of the advertising world from stat boy to creative director. I thrived in the advertising agency field, using my degree from The Art Institute of Boston as an educational foundation to advance my career, first in the Boston area, later in San Diego.

I loved the cutthroat world of advertising. Even though it can be a cruel environment characterized by long hours, tremendous pressure and burnout, I felt a great sense of accomplishment in completing a successful project and then moving on to the next one. I learned early on about organizational politics, especially when my bosses got all the glory for successful campaigns to which I had contributed a great deal. I had to balance being a team player with making sure that my contributions stood out, and I realized quickly that I had to blow my own horn.

After spending over two decades in the agency business, I had an opportunity to move to an in-house role as Art Department Manager at Intuit. I started with this leading software development firm as an independent contractor and was then offered the full time position. Initially I was apprehensive about taking it. The ad agency perspective of an in-house position was that it was a demotion. But I liked the management role and the opportunity to build the art department, and I received formal management training and developed strong coaching and team-building skills. All in all, Intuit offered me a terrific experience — while it lasted. After 4 years at Intuit, my position was eliminated when new management decided to centralize the art and design function and outsource a lot of the production work. Intuit was a great place to work, and I walked away with a great sense of accomplishment.

With a wealth of experience in supporting the corporate marketing function both externally and internally, I made the decision to start my own creative business and work out of my home. I am providing production and design work for a number of clients, and one project for a paper company has turned into a part-time marketing director position. While I enjoy the flexibility and independence of running my own business, I'm faced with a number of challenges.

I've had to develop the self-discipline and time management skills needed to get projects done and juggle the needs of multiple clients. Space issues and being at home a lot made for some tense times at first, but my family and I have adjusted to the change. I admit that financial management is not my first love, and the up and down cash flow along with the lack of benefits can be challenging at times.

The lack of comrades continues to be a concern. I've joined the Communicating Arts Group, a professional association where I can meet with others in the field to share ideas and network. I'm also getting out more often to other business and community groups to network and prospect for new clients.

Despite the challenges of owning a home-based business, I see my initial successes as strong motivators for me to continue to develop clients and grow the business. Will it grow to the point of moving to outside office space? It's a strong possibility. But for now, I'm enjoying my short commute as I walk down the hallway to work!"

Independent Professionals

Who are they?

Not to be confused with Consultants who offer high priced advice, members of the independent workforce may offer advice but they always roll up their sleeves to do the work.

As one of the fastest growing segments of the workforce, thousands of people are declaring their independence and striking out on their own. This venue is emerging as the domain of the mature professional who has invested in his or her career by contributing highly experienced brainpower not youthful back power.

You will hear many terms describing the independent professional. Contractors, Free Agents, Contingent Professionals, and Interim Executives are terms that are often used interchangeably.

A favorite author, Daniel Pink has this to say about the future of working for yourself:

> *"In 1999, one third of California's workforce held a traditional job — that is, a single, full-time, year-round, permanent (sic) position with one employer; leaving for work in the morning and returning at night. Two-thirds of state workers held so-called non-traditional positions — independent contractors, self-employed professionals, part-timers and so on. In other words, two out of three California workers did not have the employment arrangement on which nearly all American laws, taxes, and social assumptions are based.*
>
> *As goes California, so goes America. And California is going free agent."*

Daniel Pink's book, *Free Agent Nation* is one book you can't afford to overlook if you are seriously considering free agency (independent) work. Check out his website at the end of this chapter.

What you need to know.

One of the reasons for rapid growth of the independent workforce is global outsourcing. While the shift overseas is significant, one result is that private and public sector organizations are under tremendous pressure to lower costs in our own country. Hence, opportunity is knocking very loudly for the independent professional who can help increase the global competitiveness of U.S. firms at an affordable price.

It is projected that well over 3 million additional technology jobs will leave America by 2015. Heavily impacted by this shift, the U.S. technology worker is a prime example of a group that has been affected by the global economy. If you are a technologist and wish to compete head-on with the world at large, you may need to alter your course to include plans for an independent career.

If you work in the computer and electronic product manufacturing industry in any capacity, you should know that regular, full-time employment is expected to decline an additional 12%

by 2012, according to the Department of Labor.

In spite of, and perhaps because of, the projected decrease in employment, there is a new technological revolution afoot where the independent worker, who has remained competitive, will find many opportunities to contribute.

Knock...knock...opportunity knocking.

Your task is to pay attention to the trends and to continue to reposition yourself on the cutting-edge of your profession.

Ask yourself the following questions:

1. *Should you strike your own Declaration of Independence?*
   The answer is a resounding "yes" if you have specific experience to offer.

   Double the "yes" vote if you are a mature worker with current skills and experience that is well positioned to meet current workplace needs.

   Triple your "yes" vote if you recognized the potential for this type of career early and have begun to research and prepare for this career step.

2. *What are some of the advantages of working independently?*
   Explicit independent agreements, while demanding, are often more exciting than those jobs that involve simply laboring as a member of a regular workforce.

   Work tends to be time-framed, allowing freedom for other activities between "gigs." When an assignment is completed to everyone's satisfaction, expertise is established and, just as importantly, reputation builds. Your phone will start to ring in direct proportion to the reputation you establish.

   The pay is usually very good, often more than what you were making (hour-for-hour) during your years of regular, full-time employment.

   You can stay out of office politics. And, remember, even a bad assignment has a beginning, middle and an end you can look forward to.

3. *Does an independent professional need a contract?*
   Things go wrong because of unexpressed expectations by both the contracting firm and the independent professional. A contract is a safeguard for both parties.

   Treat a contract supplied by a client organization as a discussion document that, after your input, forms the basis of a mutually agreeable contract. A contract need not be complicated but the contracting firm will usually offer a written understanding of the work to be performed and an outline conditions that are important to both parties. Have your contract reviewed by your legal counsel.

   If a firm seems reluctant to offer a contract, a well-crafted letter of agreement, one that you draft yourself, may suffice.

   Examples of some of the content found in typical contracts are included in the Marketing Tools section of the book.

4. *How are fees set?*
   One way to set fees is to bill for time. In this case the client organization pays only for actual time spent on the project. One disadvantage to time based fees, from the client organization's perspective, is that there is no particular incentive for contractor efficiency and there may be a fair amount of client uncertainty as to total costs of the project.

Another way to set fees is to bill for the project. In this case, you both agree in advance of the project on a fixed fee regardless of the time spent. You calculate your project fee by multiplying your billing rate by estimated time and add a cushion to allow for unexpected demands of the project. Some people set project fees by what they think the project is worth or what they know the market will bear. The client organization's advantage is that they know in advance what the project will cost.

Fees are sometimes set based on retainers. In this model, you receive regular monthly payments for your work. The client organization is assured of your availability, often at a preferred rate. On the other hand, there is potential for overuse or nonessential use of your services.

5. *What are the top "tips" to consider before embarking on this career path?*

TOP TIPS FOR INDEPENDENT PROFESSIONALS

- **Understand yourself.**
  You may like the idea of working as an independent professional but may not be suited to the demands of this career path.

- **Research the market.**
  Launching without careful research of marketplace needs ensures poor results. Since change is fast these days, discipline your continued study of the market and follow the trends.

- **Interview successful independent professionals in your field.**
  Ask for their advice and counsel. Listen hard. They will help you to avoid pitfalls.

- **Never work just for the money.**
  Remember that advancing your knowledge and building your reputation are great reasons to accept a project or assignment.

  In a market-driven economy, fees are linked closely to marketplace demand. When the need is "hot" – the money is "hot."

- **Focus your expertise and brand yourself.**
  It's a new day. Like the organization itself, you must now understand the power of creating a core business offering and linking this offering to a "self-brand." If you do one or two things better than others - and you can describe these things well - you'll soon develop a "brand" reputation. Work on your branding statement.

  Paint a "brand" picture using words people can see in their mind's eye, as well as read or hear.

- **Determine if you can market and sell as well as deliver services.**
  If you can't, or won't, sell then investigate people or firms that can market and sell on your behalf.

  As a starting point, make a client out of your current or former employer. This will help you to quickly establish your credentials and reputation.

- **Create alliances with other independent professionals.**
  Soloing is a lonely business and colleagues will help you through rough times as well as provide good sources of new business.

- **Stay out of office politics**
  But — listen hard!

- **Commit to completing all assignments.**
  Never abandon an assignment even if a more exciting opportunity presents itself during a "gig."

- **Set up your next assignment while you are still on assignment.**
  A good way to do this is to set a "come-back" assignment review date (before you complete the current assignment) to validate client satisfaction as well as to tie up any loose ends from their perspective.

- **Remember the I.R.S.**

6. *Who can work as an independent agent?*
   Anyone who has current skills or competencies the marketplace needs. Engineers, technicians, operations professionals, accountants, financial officers, marketing professionals, service industry experts, technology specialists; all can work as independent professionals.

   Two areas of possibility for independent work that you may not have thought of include:

   <u>Sales reps</u>
   Increasingly, firms are looking to leverage their reach into the business community to attract prospective customers. Since selling continues to be, amongst other things, a relationship business, representing firms on commission is one way people are declaring their independence while maintaining their income earning status in a community.

   <u>On-demand project work in the service sector</u>
   Service businesses must play as big as needed when called upon to deliver services anywhere at anytime. Project staff works for hourly or daily rates to ensure that the service firms maintain a competitive advantage in the business community.

Validate your interest.

Review your responses in Steps 1 and 2.

Ask yourself the following questions:
1. Are you satisfied that this venture meets your needs?
2. Is your self-described internal analysis in alignment with this career path?
3. Will you learn to network, even if you don't like the idea of networking?
4. Can you live with the ideas behind our top tips?
5. Can you tolerate the uncertainty between gigs?
6. Have you come to grips with the fact that your old, regular, full-time contributions may not be highly saleable to prospective employers?

If this role appears to be a good fit for you, you are ready to move ahead and explore the opportunities that support your interest.

Explore the opportunities.

If you are currently employed, there may be independent professionals working in your firm. Interview them. Ask them for their tips and to tell you stories about the "slips" they have experienced. If your firm has a legal department, interview the individual who is responsible for crafting the contracts your firm uses. If you are close to retirement, you may wish to explore the possibility of arranging a limited continued engagement with your employer when their business needs require extra help.

If you are not working, but you left your last employer on good terms, re-establish your links with former colleagues who are still working in your previous organization. Seek internal coaches. Internal coaches are former colleagues who can help you to navigate the many channels of your old "parent" organization. You may find that they are longing for your help some of the time!

Continue your research.

Websites: For Internet Access, type: http://www. followed by the web address.

Agent.com
Matches independent professionals with projects.

Ants.com
Charges firms modest fees to link independent agents to their needs.

Elance.com
Provides opportunities for independents to bid on short-term projects.

Ework.com
Charges firms, agencies and project seekers for short-term projects.

DanPink.com
Cutting edge ideas and commentary on the changing workplace.

Freelanceworkexchange.com
Membership directory that brings you "hot leads" in every freelance sector.

Guru.com
Matches independents with projects.

Timejobs.com
Helps small businesses find help for short or part-time projects.

Turnaround.org
The website for the Turnaround Management Association, an organization of professionals who assist distressed companies.

Google.com
Go to Google's advanced search and enter the following key words: free agency, independent professionals, contract workers, interim executives.

Pluck.com and Info.com
Additional search engine services

Books, magazines, periodicals and an important association:

> *Boom or Bust!*
> Provides additional ideas for independent workers in sections on part-time work, just-in-time jobs, mentoring and coaching roles. Refer to the marketplace trends section to validate your perception of your ideal fit with marketplace needs.
>
> *Free Agent Nation*
> Daniel Pink's book is a must read.
>
> *Free to Succeed*, by Barbara Reinhold.
> If you like Daniel Pink's book, you'll like this one!
>
> *Teaming Up* by Paul and Sarah Edwards.
> The book details how to achieve success independently by linking with others.
>
> *The Brand You 50* by Tom Peters
> The book makes the case for self-branding. From designing your business card to landing gigs, Tom Peters shows you how to brand yourself.
>
> *The Turnaround Management Association (TMA)*
> TMA serves as a forum for connecting independent turnaround executives and professionals from all disciplines to exchange ideas and knowledge. It also fosters opportunities for these individuals and provides research on the turnaround industry.

Prepare your marketing tools.

For information and examples, refer to the Marketing Tools section of the book.

> Branding statement (use on all marketing tools)
>
> Brochure
>
> Business cards
>
> Business plan
>
> A highly focused, well-branded, market-needs driven biography or resume
>
> Website

Across America – Real people, real stories...Catherine Marsh

After 26 years of corporate life in the retail and financial services industries, Catherine Marsh was anxious to pursue opportunities that would provide her with a better work/life balance. This is her story of change, independence and fulfillment as an "interim executive."

"My early career included 13 years at the May Department Stores which culminated in heading up its credit card business and seeing the number of card holders grow from 12 MM to 23 MM during that tenure. I then progressed in the financial services industry, accepting a position first with Bank of America's credit card division and then with Hong Kong Shanghai Banking Corporation. My last position in banking was President of The Bank of New York's Retail Bank. I left when the bank decided to sell off 70% of its retail business.

By this time I had moved 8 times in 26 years and had been taught to meet the company's needs before considering my own. This career juncture was a real eye-opener for me. I did a lot of thinking during this transition and took the opportunity to do a full career and personal assessment. I did a lot of networking and was advised to become a consultant. With my expertise in electronic customer relationship management and the numerous contacts I had developed in the financial services field, I decided to give interim work a try.

Initially, I took on six small assignments with as many clients in order to determine if this was the right career choice for me. These projects were in a number of functions including marketing, human resources and organizational development, and I did them for free. I found that these assignments let me utilize my skills in management effectiveness, and I enjoyed it very much. Then I was retained by two banks and completed successful assignments with them for fees. I then decided to grow the business, so I brought in two partners and developed a practice that ultimately had 40 consultants. Of all the "Hats" I wore, I found that I liked developing client relationships the best. But as time went on I realized that the constant travel commitment was wearing on me.

I had moved to Phoenix for lifestyle reasons and decided to pursue opportunities that would keep me closer to home. My husband and I were at a point in our lives where we were at the level of independence from finances (i.e. not having to worry about it) and wanted to have greater flexibility in our schedules to enjoy such things as extended vacations.

I had read several articles about interim executives and spoke to several people who had taken on those types of assignments. Interim executive work is different from consulting in that you fill a specific role with the client company rather than just take on a particular project. So the assignment is larger in scope since it entails all aspects of an executive position.

A client company may need an interim executive when one of its management team is on a leave of absence for medical or other reasons. A growing organization may utilize an executive's expertise on a temporary basis before deciding to make that role a full time position. Or a firm may need the assistance of a skilled executive on a part-time basis over an extended period of time. I took the plunge, networked with small to medium sized business owners and executives and took on an initial assignment.

I knew right away that this was an excellent career move for me. I have the flexibility to pick and choose assignments that are interesting to me and that fit my schedule. I transfer knowledge and skills to those I work with, and I get to assist in the recruitment of new staff. I especially enjoy working with small business owners and gain great satisfaction in making an immediate contribution to their companies. As I networked and developed a clientele, I had the opportunity to refer assignments to other executives. So I established my own interim executive business and over a four year period have grown it to where I currently have 12 clients, three of which I am working with and nine that other executives are assisting.

Interim executive work is not for the person looking for full time employment or dollars; the assignments are temporary and don't always immediately follow each other. So there are definitely ups and downs. But if you are looking for flexibility and an opportunity to take on challenging assignments, I highly recommend interim executive work."

Learners

Who are they?

YOU!

It is stating the obvious to repeat that if you are to live longer you will experience much more workplace change than you have imagined.

But, repeat it we will. Changing workplace and marketplace needs will make much of the work you do today obsolete in a few short years.

By investing in learning new skills, and in developing competencies, your chances of staying engaged in some form of work improve dramatically.

Invest in your future now...before it really is too late!

What you need to know.

- Learning is lifework today.
  It is work to learn and, while pay is not usually associated with the task of learning, it is absolutely associated with the results. Lifelong learning is a part of the new rules of the game if you wish to stay engaged in your career.

- Learning is easier today than ever before.
  You may not be aware that, as a 40-50 or 60 (or more) year old student, there is no particular difference between your ability to learn and that of a younger student.

  In fact, according to the University of California, the only difference between older students and the younger students is that we complete what we start much more often than our younger counterparts.

  Refer to other sections of this book for more information that debunks myths about our ability to learn and assimilate knowledge.

- Learning is about benefiting from the experiences of others.
  An online discussion group such as one held with thirdage.com links you to others who are navigating the mature world of work.

- Learning is more accessible today than ever before.
  All U.S. Universities are re-tooling to accommodate mature students.

  Online universities, such as the University of Phoenix, represent the choice of many people in the new economy. Adults often want a good college education fast and at a dramatically lower cost than through a traditional campus experience. The University of Phoenix offers Bachelors and Masters programs on campus or from your home office. If your degree was interrupted, or if you simply wish to change direction, you will be pleasantly surprised at how reasonably priced and easy this method of learning is. At the time this book was drafted, 211,000 people attended the fully accredited University of Phoenix online or in person. It is anticipated that as many as 500,000 students may be enrolled in the University by 2006. The median age of the student population in 2004 was 39.5 years. The point is that you will meet quite a number of gray haired colleagues whose eyesight may be dimming but whose minds are blade sharp.

At the risk of offending a few of the so-called prestigious institutions of learning, the smart ones are taking their lessons from the University of Phoenix and are playing hard at catch-up with Phoenix's innovative, fast response team who are focused on the real needs of the working public today.

Others, not so smart, are simply pricing "real-time" attendance out of the reach of many students. While they may find takers for their high-priced education, they will lose in the long run as those individuals re-tooling for the future seek, and find, both preferred pricing and easier access in the virtual university setting.

Don't forget to check out your alma mater, local universities and community colleges for online learning opportunities and extension courses that meet your interests. All offer excellent choices for the mature working or non-working adult.

Online Learning.
Borderless, placeless, and costs less!

- *Learning is more fun today than ever before.*
  Extension programs, through established and highly regarded universities, want your money. They will make it easy for you to return to school by offering exciting, state-of-the-art curriculum facilitated by interesting professors and adjunct staff.

  Specialized schools, or non-profit organizations, will offer you learning and a vacation rolled into one! You can study to be a chef on vacation in France or Napa Valley. You can study languages "in-country" and enjoy plenty of time off for fun and exploration.

  Are you 55 or older? Elderhostel advertises their learning experiences as "Adventures in Lifelong Learning" and they go on to say that "The World is Our Classroom." A non-profit organization, Elderhostel offers nearly 10,000 programs a year in more than 90 countries. Expert instructors share information through lectures, field trips and cultural excursions. Elderhostel programs are all inclusive and there are no hidden expenses. Accommodations, meals, lectures, field trips, cultural excursions, gratuities and medical coverage are all provided. They take care of the details. An added benefit of Elderhostel is that they offer adventures in learning that you can participate in with your children or grandchildren.

- *Learning new skills and subject matter will help you to feel better.*
  Research, such as reported by the University of California's schools of gerontology, supports the evidence that formal learning actually keeps you feeling younger. It is certainly true that staying engaged in the world fights depression and loneliness, the scourge of many older adults. There is also increasing evidence to support the old saw – "use it or lose it" when it comes to using your body and your brain!

  Your organization may have mentoring programs in place where younger employees mentor up the organization and teach older workers about areas of technology where there may be some gaps. Volunteer to be mentored. It will help you to feel better about your ability to compete.

What else might motivate you to return to your learning self?

- Wage inequality is rising and the undereducated are getting poorer.
According to the Bureau of Labor Statistics, the average college graduate earned 38% more than the average high-school graduate twenty years ago. Today, it is 71% more. Over the past quarter of a century, wage gaps between the educated and those with less education have widened. The fastest growing jobs in the U.S. require advanced education or specific skills training. Technological change places higher-skilled workers at an advantage. Automation is replacing many lower skilled jobs.

- Overseas workers may impact your choice of occupations.
Pay attention to the news. If what you choose to learn for your next stage in your career may be impacted by lower cost, highly educated folks from abroad – you may wish to rethink your re-skilling choices.

Validate your interest.

Review your responses in Steps 1 and 2.

Ask yourself:

1. Are you comfortable with taking on the task of learning something new?
2. Is your self-described internal analysis in alignment with a commitment to additional learning?
3. Are you willing to explore various ways of learning, such as online universities, community workshops as well as higher institutions of learning?
4. If you don't invest in additional skills or competency development, will you be employable?

If new learning is an integral component to remaining employable (not necessarily employed) you are ready to move ahead and explore the learning opportunities that support your interests and marketplace needs.

Explore the opportunities.

If you are currently employed, investigate your firm's educational reimbursement plan. Discuss your options with your employer. Even if there is no educational reimbursement plan, but the education you wish to engage in benefits the employer, they may be willing to subsidize some, or all, of the costs associated with successful completion of the courses that interest you.

Visit your local high schools and explore their continuation programs. Contact your local community college or the extended studies division of your nearby universities.

If you are actively interviewing, consider building in an educational benefit into your negotiation package with a prospective employer. You might suggest trading benefits you may not need for an educational benefit.

Continue your research.

Websites: For Internet access, type: http://www. followed by the web address.

> *uofphx.info*
> Note other sites available as well for the University of Phoenix

> *Elderhostel.org*
> As previously described, Elderhostel offers an exciting website to peruse.

> *Thirdage.com*
> An online chat room where you can go for advice from mature colleagues.

> *Google.com*
> Go to Google's advanced search and enter the following key words: your local university's name, educational opportunities, continuing education, skills training, online universities, distance learning.

> *Pluck.com and Info.com*
> Additional search engine services

Books, magazines and periodicals:

> *Boom or Bust!* provides a comprehensive section on marketplace trends.

> *AARP* magazine

Other:

> Consider researching lifetime learning tax credits for adults as well as investigating penalty-free IRA withdrawals for higher education. You may even be eligible for financial aid through the Department of Education.

Prepare your marketing tools.

Carefully prepare a professional biography and/or resume detailing work experience that is relevant to your educational interests. You may expect to earn college level credit for practical work experience in many accredited institutions.

Dig up your transcripts. If you can't locate them, contact your college or university and request a copy. Most charge a minimal fee. In addition to transcripts, certain institutions may require you to present letters of support and confirmation of your work experience by current or former managers.

Across America – Real people, real stories…Andrea Klein

Andrea Klein, a lifelong learner, tells a story that reflects her philosophy about continuing education throughout life. It is this commitment to learning that has enhanced the clarification of her values, principles, motivations and goals.

"It has been my experience that a voice exists inside each of us — a voice that whispers to us about our individual authentic gifts. Most of the time, due to the pressures and responsibilities of life, we don't listen. Instead, we make choices, especially in our careers, choices are often expedient and, hopefully, profitable IF we are lucky. But the voice persists. Sometimes it whispers softly, to let you know that you have performed a task superbly, and to acknowledge how much you enjoyed doing that particular successful project. The reverse can also be true. At times you know you are in the wrong place at the wrong time with the wrong people. As a result, you may become highly motivated to consider your options and it becomes clear that you are unable to be your authentic self in your present situation. Your awareness of this, and the resulting unhappiness, is creating an opportunity for change.

Almost all of my career changes have manifested because of these whispers. I have learned to listen carefully. Sometimes the push came from an external force….other times I was pushed by some internal force, urging me to embrace change…In looking back, I realize that changes in my life and career have centered upon learning. And, at each transition point, I have sought and relied upon additional educational experiences to provide me with new skills.

I have attended higher education programs to change careers three times, each preparing me to enter a new (but related) field with high hopes of utilizing my talents and values in a position that I would love. This quest has led over the years from a Bachelors Degree in Education, to a Graduate level Paralegal Certificate Program, to a Masters Degree in Counseling. Often, the very educational experience was the best thing — better than the new career.

I also had a growing realization that wherever I went, I was developing my talents because I simply had to. I am one of those people born to counsel others. In each career, from teacher, to paralegal, to legal administrator to Human Resources, I found myself relying more and more on my authentic self, relying on my own sense of purpose as I developed new skills. I developed business skills in combination with a strong emphasis on the people side of business. I was fortunate that the organizations I worked for appreciated my skills.

Each change has been positive, the additional educational experiences very satisfying and I now realize that I loved the learning itself. When I retired from full time employment 18 months ago, it seemed natural therefore for me to think about what I might do next, and what additional training I might need to begin a 'little business". I was clear that I wanted to do a variety of things, none full-time — a portfolio retirement if you will. I was assisted in this process by Carleen MacKay of Spherion, who became an inspiration and mentor. By now, I was certain that my choices would involve the use of my counseling training and education as well as my career development background.

This introspection did not take very long.

I realized that I was fascinated by this new stage of life. Retirement for me and for others might last as long as some working careers... I reasoned that if I was this excited about the opportunities available to me in retirement that others might be as well. I enrolled in a virtual certification program to learn specifically about the choices that people must make to effectively plan a satisfying retirement. I have become certified to utilize an instrument to guide me in coaching clients planning to retire. I am fascinated by the process — different for each of us, and so rewarding for everyone who participates. The goal, of course, is to fully utilize my own gifts in the service of others — to assist in their identification of their own values, motivations, interests and goals for the future, with a plan and understanding of how their very uniqueness will assist them to better navigate their retirement years in satisfying and rewarding pursuits.

I intend to have a very small consulting practice, finding potential retirees by word of mouth referrals. I am also planning to enroll in yet another educational program to become a certified coach, for my own sense of credibility. I'm still learning after all these years.

This is more than finding something rewarding for myself. In this life stage, it feels very important to do something worthwhile, to help others. I have chosen this path, and hope to continue my own education as a coach and counselor, listening to the whispers that will urge me on to authentic fulfillment."

Mentors

Who are they?

The dictionary defines mentors as "wise teachers renowned for profound wisdom."

One way to understand the difference between a mentor and a coach is to think of a mentor as instructing a protégé in their shared profession. You probably recall a professor who was your mentor in an academic setting. A way to contrast mentors and coaches is to remember that mentors transfer knowledge to others in their shared line of work. Coaches teach subject matters to people from various backgrounds and disciplines.

If you struggled through Homer's Odyssey in high school or college, you will recall that Mentor was the trusted friend of Odysseus. He was left in charge of running the household during Odysseus' lengthy absence. Athena, also disguised as Mentor, helped Odysseus's son, Telemachus, to grow up strong and trustworthy during Odysseus' absence. Two mentors were represented in this novel; one to see that household servants and staff were trustworthy and that they learned to perform their household tasks well. The other mentor, Athena, ensured that Telemachus grew up as Odysseus intended. (This is the model of mother as Mentor figure in epic literature.) Both taught values and principled actions as well as practical ways to run a household or to complete tasks. Both models of "mentor" continue to provide us with a good definition for roles as mentors to people.

What you need to know.

While you might quickly assume that the role of mentor is no different than that of a coach or some of the other independent professionals we have described, we believe that because of ever-faster change and an ever-smaller upcoming U.S. workforce, the role of one who transfers knowledge between generations will take on a new and important meaning in the near future.

Mentors will be closer to Athena and Mentor's models of teaching the younger workers tasks, values and principled action. If you choose this path, you will present yourself specifically as a mentor, not as an independent professional.

Think about positioning your work to help others learn to cope and succeed during times of crisis, high growth or shaky retrenchment.

Think of helping a high potential individual grow into a new role. This practical approach to mentoring helps people to cope with change while engaged in a learning experience.

What better role for maturity? What better legacy to leave behind? What better chance do organizations have to succeed than that afforded by those who can mentor the next generation of workers? What better business idea than for the young to have wise and trusted guides?

Validate your interest.

Review your responses in Steps 1 and 2.

Ask yourself the following questions:

1. Are you satisfied that this venture meets your needs?
2. Is your self-described internal analysis in alignment with this career path?
3. What knowledge do you offer that needs to be transferred to the younger generation?
4. What business acumen do you offer that needs to be transferred to organizations?
5. Do you have the patience to help people self-discover what you know?
6. Have you tutored or taught in the past?

If this role appears to be a good fit for you, you are ready to move ahead and explore the opportunities that support your interest.

Explore the opportunities.

1. Float the idea of your contribution as a mentor to organizations, large and small.
2. Define your contribution and role early.
3. Brand yourself accordingly.
4. Study everything you can find on the profession so that you might "walk the walk" and "talk the talk" of the mentor.

Continue your research.

Websites: For Internet access, type: http://www. followed by the web address.

adultmentor.com
Richard Haid's website. Read his story following this section.

mentoringgroup.com
Provides information about how to mentor as well as how to be a good protégé.

Google.com
Go to Google's advanced search and enter the following key words: adult mentors, mentor associations.

Pluck.com and Info.com
Additional search engine services

Books, magazines and periodicals:

This may be one time that books, and the depth of knowledge they provide, will overtake websites as your preferred research tool.

Coaching, Mentoring and Managing by William Henricks.

Mentoring for Exceptional Performance by Harold Johnson.

Mentoring Greatness by Harold Johnson.

Mentoring: How to Develop Successful Mentor Behaviors, A Crisp Publications 50-minute book.

Prepare your marketing tools.

For information and examples, refer to the Marketing Tools section of the book.

Branding statement

Business cards

Brochure

Letters of recommendation by others whom you have mentored

Website

Written plan

Across America – Real people, real stories...Dick Haid

This is a terrific story because Dick received his Medicare card and his Doctoral Degree within two years of each other. It was after both events that Dick came to realize the richness of his life and career.

Dick's work is about "helping to guide persons into the abundance of the third-quarter of life."

He has touched countless lives and, you may be certain, his legacy is assured. This is his story.

> "I used to be an insurance agency owner and financial planner, but my client's lives became much more important to me than their money. Wealth couldn't buy all that they wanted. Many were captives of their material possessions. Some had far more money than they would ever need, but they couldn't create dreams of a better world that could be empowered by their wealth and leadership. They had been holding onto their money and their lives and their current ways of living for too long.
>
> Then I had a question of meaning in my life, as Peggy Lee sings in her song, "Is That All There Is?" Although I had received awards for the "outstanding this or that" in my business and community life, the question that kept coming up was "Is there something more in my life" in which I could use the unique gifts that I suspected I had? Was there something more calling me? I had the same wife, children, and home, but there had been a shift within me and I was in transition. To test the waters, a part-time internship for five months was arranged with an outplacement firm where I found I could help its clients discover their special talents and passions.
>
> To follow my 'calling' I fired myself by selling my 115 year-old business and set off to invent a new chapter in my life. I experienced a sense of loss because I was no longer a president, missed my co-workers, didn't have an office, and I hadn't typed in over 30 years. I also experienced a faith journey in spiritual development. I started leading pre-retirement planning workshops, which were more about the participants' lives than their money and possessions. I found that the workshop participants planned to rearrange their lives, but they didn't plan to expand them. However, I wanted them to have more because I know that later in life most people have the capacity to achieve more satisfying lives than they believe they can.
>
> I also had a thirst for new learning and to integrate my new knowledge and skills into my prior experience. Twenty years earlier I had considered a Ph.D. program with the Union Institute and University. I was not ready then, but now I had the experience and maturity to design my own program in adult development, which emphasized the Third Quarter of Life. My doctoral research about family business owners stepping down from their businesses became a book; *There is Life After Family Business*.
>
> My coaching training has been through the Hudson Institute, Coach University, and the International Coach Federation (ICF). I was recently re-certified as a Professional Certified Coach (PCC) by the ICF, after having been part of the first group of coaches it certified. The ICF's certification process, using rigorous standards, is based on training, experience, the coach's contributions to the field, and client evaluations. I call myself an Adult Mentor/Coach and emphasize the mentor aspect. It is an ongoing partnership

that helps clients produce fulfilling results in their personal and professional lives as they deepen their learning, improve their performance, and enhance the quality of their lives. They may also explore questions of mission, legacy and "call."

Because of my interest in the Third Quarter, I have developed a niche with persons who want to enter or already are in their Third Quarter. These clients are business owners, executives, and professionals. Because I have stepped down from a business and developed a new life, my clients find this reassuring as I have made this journey myself. I meet perspective clients in the workshops I lead and the classes I teach and from referrals. I do in-person assessment with them to start the process. Many of my clients live far from me and we have weekly telephone meetings with occasional in-person visits. Clients have wonderful experiences as they create new futures.

I have developed deeper and more appreciative relationships with my wife, family, friends, colleagues, and with myself. My spiritual development is accelerating as I mentor Doctor of Ministry students to help these senior pastors become spiritual coaches for their congregations. I am also the learner as I gain insight from my students as well as from people that I meet at conferences and through tele-discussions.

And, I am discovering even more of my gifts. I have a Third-Quarter life which is much more abundant than I could have imagined. This is the very best time of my life."

adultmentor.com
Richard Haid's Website.

Non-Profit, Foundation and Philanthropic Contributors

Who are they?

They are the people who responded to President John Kennedy's inaugural speech when he challenged America by saying: *"Ask not what your country can do for you; ask what you can do for your country."* For those of us who were here in the 60's during the "Camelot" years, we know that these were the words that changed the landscape of non-profits, foundations and philanthropies forever.

Whether your calling is to help your community, America, or the world, this is a good time to focus your work and life on a higher cause!

What you need to know about non-profits.

Non-profits are tax-exempt organizations that provide services to charitable causes.

Some of the better-known non-profit organizations are: The American Red Cross, Habitat for Humanity, World Vision, The World Wild Life Federation and The Special Olympics.

The U.S. government offers free information and advice on financial and tax matters for non-profits as well as information on starting and managing a non-profit. It is important to look at all government links as well as at the government grant site throughout every step of your research. You can also learn a great deal about the non-profit community on the Internet. Beware, the Internet is also a place where questionable organizations dwell.

You can seek to start your own non-profit, become a board member or committee member of an established non-profit, or you can be hired as a paid staff member or engaged as a volunteer in the organization of your choice.

Starting your own non-profit organization begins with having a clear-cut mission as to your intended service, a specific idea as to who or what your service supports, and why it is in the public's interest to have such a non-profit at all.

If you qualify as a tax-exempt non-profit organization, you will enjoy many advantages beyond tax exemption.

The downside is that your record keeping and reporting requirements will be formidable. Each state in the union has its own laws and regulations surrounding incorporation. The advice of an attorney is important to safeguarding your interests, speeding the process of incorporation, protecting intellectual property and eliminating possible barriers.

If your objective is to land a paid leadership position with a non-profit board and you have been a leader in a for-profit organization, your verifiable credentials in business planning, budget preparation, financial reporting, strategic and tactical planning will help you to qualify for such a role. As a former financial executive, accounting professional, or sales guru, your chances for paid employment are better than for most people transitioning from other careers.

Are you concerned that the salary gap between your last leadership position and that of a leader in a non-profit is too wide? The fact is that salary gaps between comparable positions in profit and non-profit organizations have lessened over the years. Other benefits, such as bonuses and incentive-based pay are likely to lag considerably behind the for-profit institutions.

An active role as a volunteer improves your opportunity to be offered a paid staff position. In other words, the shortest distance between two points — you and your desire to become a paid staff member — is not necessarily the obvious one. Beginning the journey as an unpaid volunteer has many advantages, not the least of which is that volunteers are often first in line for paid staff positions. If your background includes administrative work and your skills are current, the transition is usually relatively easy, especially if you are willing to be flexible in the weekly hours you can work (+/- 40).

Whatever your role with a non-profit, fund raising is usually included. Even the volunteers are recruited to raise funds. Your candidacy for a non-profit will be greatly enhanced if you demonstrate that you have the courage to ask for money from philanthropists or organizations. It may seem easy to ask for money, but it is the single most daunting task most folks face.

What you need to know about Foundations and Philanthropies.

Foundations and philanthropies are investments that provide return for the wealthy as well as for organizations and, most importantly, they offer a way to benefit community and society. Donations to foundations bring hope to the world and create a legacy for philanthropists. Donations are tax deductible. If you wish to establish a foundation or give gifts to the community, you do not need this book to tell you how to give away assets. Your financial advisor will provide direction.

Foundations may be private, such as family or independent foundations, or public, such as community foundations. A private foundation is a non-governmental, non-profit organization that is funded by an endowment and managed by trustees. This type of foundation makes grants to non-profit organizations and to individuals who meet their criteria. According to the Council on Foundations, there are more than 63,000 private and community foundations in the U.S. and that number is growing. Most, but not all, private funding is awarded to non-profit organizations.

Foundation grants to individuals may be researched online once you have the name of the foundation that meets your interest. The types of grants made by foundations vary but include grants for education and for certain small businesses that are aligned with each foundation's stated purpose. Individual grant seekers will encounter tough competition from non-profit organizations seeking their slice of the grant pie.

You can arrange foundation or philanthropic scholarships on the advice of your financial planner or estate lawyer.

Validate your interest.

Review your responses in Steps 1 and 2.

Ask yourself the following questions:

    1. Are you satisfied that this venture meets your needs?

    2. Is your self-described internal analysis in alignment with this career path?

    3. Do you have a passion for, and a purposeful mission for, a certain area of service?

    4. Is it time to "give back" something to your country or your community?

    5. Does your partner, or spouse, support your plans?

If one of these roles appears to be a good fit for you, you are ready to move ahead and explore the opportunities that support your interest.

Explore the opportunities.

Interview people who are working in non-profits or with Foundations, especially those whose careers support your similar interests.

Research the several government sites that will help you to understand the process you will face in order to move forward.

Consider volunteering in a non-profit organization and learn the ropes from the inside.

Continue your research:

Websites: For Internet access, type: http://www. followed by the web address.

    charitywatch.org
    Lists the top-rated charities.

    Give.org
    The way to check if the charity meets the Better Business Bureau's standards.

    cof.org/index.cfrm
    Extensive information is available online about foundations and philanthropies through The Council on Foundations.

    Marketingsource.com
    Directory of 35,000 associations and non-profit organizations.

    T-tlaw.com
    Source of non-profit attorneys.

    Google.com
    Go to Google's advanced search and enter the following key words: non-profit organizations, not-for-profit, community foundations.

Pluck.com and Info.com
Additional search engine services

Books, magazines and periodicals:

How to Form a Nonprofit Corporation, 5th Edition by Anthony Mancuso.

Managing a Nonprofit Organization in the Twenty-First Century by Thomas Wolf and Barbara Carter.

Nonprofit Kit for Dummies by Stan Hutton and Frances Phillips.

Opportunities in Fund-Raising Careers by Mark Rowe and Joan Suchorski.

Across America – Real people, real stories - Gregg Goodman

Life touches work in many ways. For folks in the non-profit world, life often begins with pain and this experience influences career choices in the world of not-for-profits and foundations. This is Gregg's story.

"After spending over 20 years in the restaurant industry, I established The Therapy Zone, Inc., a non-profit organization that presents a unique approach to providing therapy to disabled children. Making a transition from the corporate world to the non-profit sector can be challenging, but I was ready to take on such an assignment.

I had spent my entire corporate career with Ruby Tuesday, Inc., a leader in the casual dining industry. Beginning as a management trainee right out of college, I became a restaurant manager, initially in the firm's cafeteria restaurant division and then in the fine dining division. I went on to create a new concept restaurant for the company and gained valuable experience in all aspects of restaurant development and management, including site selection, construction, culinary development and management training. After becoming Director of one of the firm's five divisions, I helped establish Ruby Tuesday's new franchising division and served as National Director of Franchising.

Wanting to get back to the southwestern U.S. where I had grown up and, since my mother was in ill health, I initiated a transfer and became Director of Franchising for the Southwest region. Although this was a great job for me and I loved the company, the on-going travel commitment started to take its toll. We had started a family, and I realized that I was missing a lot by not being home to experience more of my daughters' development. When a new restaurant was being built, I'd be away for as much as six weeks in a row. I knew I had to look for a new job in a different field.

My wife Jan is a physical therapist, and we began discussing the idea of starting an organization that provided a variety of therapies to support the development of disabled children. I have a Masters in Medical Microbiology and had considered a career as a physician, so a transition to the healthcare field was of interest to me. I was also motivated to consider this field due to a traumatic experience I had in childhood. When I was six years old it was determined that my knees were not developing properly. I was in a body cast and then wore braces for a year and a half. Even though the treatment was successful, I remember how people, especially other children, reacted when they saw me during that time period.

Jan and I developed a business plan for the organization, which we initially planned to start while I was still working for Ruby Tuesday. Then once it was established, I would quit the company to join Jan full time in our non-profit venture.

Just as we were getting the final permits to open our facility in Mesa, Arizona, my boss told me that I was being transferred to Denver, which would have been my ninth relocation with the company. Management was kind enough to offer me a separation package and I resigned from Ruby Tuesday, Inc. I immediately assumed the position of Executive Director of The Therapy Zone, Inc. (TTZ), which is a 501(c)3 non-profit corporation.

Starting as a provider of physical therapy, TTZ quickly expanded its services to include speech and occupational therapy as well as equine therapy, which, as the name implies, uses horses to aid in providing therapy to disabled children. TTZ reacted to the needs of the children and their parents, who voiced concern over the fact that they had to travel to different facilities to receive the various therapies that had been prescribed. TTZ developed the concept of rehabilitation and learning center, or "Zone", where various therapies could be provided. The permit and regulatory process has been especially challenging. You learn to take it step by step and to keep your sights on the ultimate goal of creating a service model that effectively meets the needs of the client. The experience of building and operating restaurants and meeting all the codes and regulations governing that industry was a transferable skill that benefited my new career.

I continue to bring my desire for growth and a flair for innovation to the non-profit sector of healthcare. The Therapy Zone plans to build three new locations in the greater Phoenix area and also plans to expand its service offerings to include new therapies and learning opportunities incorporating art, music, science and technology."

Across America - Real people, real stories - Marjorie Blanchard

This section would not be complete without the story of the creation of a local chapter of a vitally important Foundation, the Polycystic Kidney Disease (PKD) Foundation.

As one, among many, who have suffered through a life-threatening disease and emerged to find the most meaningful career in a history of good careers, Marjorie Blanchard's story is one of courage and inspiration.

"I have completely changed career direction 3 times during my working life. Most recently, an International Career Management firm was my employer. I spent 10 years coaching people in the art and skill of managing their careers.

In late August 2002, I took a medical leave to have a kidney transplant. Fortunately, my transplant was successful and I returned to work early in 2003. In March 2003, my company reorganized and eliminated numerous positions - including mine. At first I was surprised and upset as no one likes to be laid off; however, I soon saw the "silver lining" in my situation. Although I enjoyed my job, especially working with those who were seeking new careers, I was ready for a change.

This is my story of change from a career I enjoyed to one I love!

In June 2003, my husband retired and we discussed our future work-related plans. We agreed that we could enjoy life better if we did not take another corporate job — so, together, Bob and I started the San Diego Chapter of the PKD Foundation.

What is PKD?

While PKD is not a household word to many folks, it is the most common genetic, life threatening kidney disease affecting more than 600,000 Americans and an estimated 12.5 million people worldwide. In fact, PKD affects more people than cystic fibrosis, muscular dystrophy, hemophilia, Down syndrome and sickle cell anemia — combined.

Why PKD?

My interest, like others drawn to this world of work, stemmed from my family's genetic link to Polycystic Kidney Disease (PKD).

I first became aware of PKD when I was in 7th grade. My father had been ill for some time and, after testing, we were told that he had PKD and there was nothing that could be done for him. He died in 1958 leaving a wife, 4 young children, a married daughter, and two grandchildren. The loss of Dad, at an early age, had enormous emotional and financial implications for all members of our struggling family.

Time went by.

The 4 children grew up and, for a while, we forgot about the genetic aspects of the disease. More children were welcomed into our rapidly expanding family.

In my early 30's, I visited a Nephrologist and learned PKD was in my future. By my early 50's, the disease had started to show itself - mildly at first! By January of 2000, I was told I had lost significant kidney function and was now in "End Stage Renal

Disease." I was listed on the National Kidney Donation Register and told my wait for a cadaver kidney would take about 5 years. (Approximately 15,000 people die every year waiting for a kidney!) I didn't want to go on dialysis for a number of years so I talked with family and friends and advised them of my need for a kidney.

My niece, Shelley, offered to give me the gift of life and she was my donor because she was a close match and a very willing participant. We had our surgeries and the procedures went extremely well for both of us. My new kidney started functioning even before I came out of anesthesia and Shelley was walking around the block within 2 weeks.

Here is the kicker.

A number of family members have since been diagnosed with the disease. Now they face their own uncertain futures. It is my turn to give back to them and to others who suffer.

My husband and I started the local chapter of PKD. We are responsible for building the chapter and for coordinating fundraisers. My corporate experience dealing with executives, creating promotional materials, public speaking and organizing work teams, are now applied to my role with the Foundation.

I have remained active and continue to develop and learn new skills – all the while helping to find a cure for PKD.

I now know what others meant when they told me that:

**'The greatest rewards for good work
are reaped by the giver not the receiver.'**

Phasers

Who are they?

They are us! The millions of us who are still working and who would prefer to gradually cut down our full-time working commitment by gradually phasing into full-time retirement.

We are the pioneers of the workplace. We know that our experience provides value to our current employers and, at the same time, we realize that time is marching on for us at the same moment the next generation does not have the shear numbers to back fill us as fast as needed.

We are the people who are most likely to have specialized knowledge — knowledge we can leverage to achieve a clear-cut mutual advantage.

What you need to know.

Academic institutions have been offering phased retirement for years. It is easy to envy the tenured professors who enter into such arrangements. They seem to enjoy the best of the world of work as well as the world of leisure.

> Ask yourself:
>
> What could be better than to do what you love while enjoying a little more time, year by year, to develop new interests?
>
> What could be better than having the time to g-r-a-d-u-a-l-l-y adjust to a whole new way of life while keeping a toehold on the familiar past?

Good news.

In the private and public sectors, employers are coming to embrace the idea of phased retirement. In fact, the first rumblings of proposed mega changes, rumblings that will help to facilitate making this a preferred choice for employers and employees alike, are being heard in, of all places, the IRS. The IRS has taken the initiative to propose changes to certain restrictions that penalize both individuals and institutions when phased-retirement is proposed. Look for action from the IRS this year!

Bad news.

For some folks, old-time pension plans are getting in the way of phased retirement. This is because pension benefits are often simply based upon your average compensation during your last several years of employment. If you cut your hours, you cut the pension.

Hopeful news.

Some companies have based their pensions on your highest salary years. In this case, phased retirement may not hurt your pension benefits.

Other firms who simply offer 401k's have flexibility because most such plans have a lower required age (59) in order to receive distributed benefits.

You have a role.

You need to know that it is up to you to make phased retirement a reality. If you are still gainfully employed, enter into conversations about the benefits of phased retirement with your employer now, while your opinions count. Go on. Don't be shy. Speak often about the financial benefits of phased retirement with the leaders of your organization. They will listen with both a business ear as well as with a self-serving ear as most of these folks are Boomers themselves.

> Write to your Representatives.
>
> Join AARP, the American Society on Aging (ASA) or the National Society on Aging (NSA) and let your voice be heard.
>
> Lobby your employer directly.
> Your employer can go through the process of amending its pension plan to lower the so-called (but obsolete) retirement age from 65 to a lower chronological number.

This is one area where you will soon feel the power of maturity because phased retirement will be beneficial to your employer as well as to you. It will happen soon. Why shouldn't it happen for you?

Validate your interest and qualifications for phased retirement.

This is new territory.

Ask yourself the following questions:

- *Are you ready to cut your workweek by one day, just one day?*
  If so, many of your benefits should remain intact as most insurance policies are written to cover workforces who regularly contribute, at least, 32 hours of time each week.

- *What do you have to sell and what do they want to buy?*
  Get very clear about the level of contribution that is aligned with your experience and their needs. Put your ideas in writing.

- *Along the same lines, can you quantify the benefit for your employer?*
  When value is established based on results, corporate savings talk.

- *If you are eligible for Social Security, are you familiar with the regulations, the benefits and the possible downsides of such an arrangement?*
  Start early. Social Security offices are very busy.

- *If you have a financial advisor or an accountant, will you take the time to discuss the benefits as well as the possible downsides of such an arrangement relative to pensions and certain investments?*
  If you don't have an advisor, consider getting one for this purpose.

If this role appears to be a good fit for you, you are ready to move ahead and explore the opportunities that support your interests.

Explore the opportunities.

Start your dialogue now with anyone and everyone who will listen.

Continue your research.

Websites: For Internet access, type: http://www. followed by the web address.

> *Google.com*
> Go to Google's advanced search and enter the following key words: phased retirement.
>
> *Pluck.com and Info.com*
> Additional search engine services

Across America...Real people, real stories...Carleen MacKay

"By co-authoring the book and doing the careful research to support the references I have suggested throughout its pages, I established an identity in our firm. In straightforward terms, I became the subject-matter expert on the topic of 3rd careers.

By speaking publicly, at high visibility professional events about the issues and challenges a maturing America faces, I cemented the idea in a broad range of folks' minds that I was one of the experts.

By lobbying my employer (with firm data) for a new service dedicated to 3rd careers, they suggested a new role for me as practice leader for this aspect of our career management, career transition, career development and workforce realignment consulting services.

By patiently pressing the importance of the service instead of insisting on clear and concise definitions to suit my own self-serving arrangements, they made an offer that was (and is) better than the one I would have proposed.

I am ready to do the most important work of my career and I am eager to enjoy a four-day workweek for the balance of 2006.

And, just in case you want a dose of inspiration, you should know that I was born in the 1930's and feel, each and every day, as if I am just getting started. The renewed energy I feel by working a somewhat shorter workweek devoted to an important cause, is beyond my ability to describe. The opportunity to have some more fun, do some more good and make some more money is exhilarating.

How about you?

Is your most important work ahead of you and, at the same time, are you ready for a shorter workweek?

Do you see your future as a phaser?

If so, remember these words... *specialize...specialize...specialize.*"

Pieceworkers

Who are they?

Long years ago, people produced and were paid by the items they completed rather than by the time it took to produce them. This was how the garment industry began. Bib-overalls were among the popular items produced in this manner.

Then...
Along came "blue jeans."

It was either James Dean or Marlon Brando who made blue jeans a national costume. Take your choice between these rebels of the 50's and credit either, or both, with creating enormous demand for a product once produced, and paid for, by the piece. As sales soared, production moved into factories to satisfy a population hungry for comfort, affordability and a unique American style. Record-breaking sales of blue jeans continue to this very moment. And, whether you call them blue jeans, Levi's or dungarees, most everyone – worldwide – will know just what you are talking about.

Now...
What's old is new again.

Piecework — literally work paid for by the piece — is making a dramatic return after a relatively quiet era as a cottage industry.

What you need to know.

For the mature worker, with time on their hands, this is still a good way to work. You may work very long hours creating your work but you price your work by the piece or by a certain limited number of items. When bought by the piece, the work itself is often a highly original item that attracts selected buyers.

One modern form of piecework is freelance writing. Providing articles, columns and other forms of written materials can be a creative way of exercising your intellect for profit. Opportunities abound to provide content to local, regional and national publications; and the internet has opened up a whole new medium with a high demand for written content.

Another example of where you might contribute piecework may be found in the Arts and Crafts industry. When you produce original crafts in quantity, you will find a large buying public at seasonal boutiques, such as those found during holiday time. If you choose to work this way, your job is to provide a boutique with items for sale and they, in turn, will attempt to sell these items on consignment. You will be paid only when each item has been sold. Likewise, you may choose to place your items in galleries and other retail outlets. If you are a new craftsperson, or artisan, and your work is not yet known, there is little risk to the galleries and retail outlets as they do not pay for items until they are sold.

Other ways to present your arts and crafts include:

- *Museum shops*
  High quality items, especially those that provide interesting links to the past or to certain special interest groups, are often sold to museum gift shops.

- *Mail-order industry*
  Americraft Gift Brokers are an excellent source for selling your crafts to the mail-order industry.

- *Corporations, hospitals, restaurants or other public places*
  So-called "fine art" has the effect of decorating the walls of these organizations as well as introducing the artist to prospective buyers.

- *The Internet*
  From e-Bay to your own website, items move through the world at warp-speed. By far the fastest emerging point-of-sale for craft items, computer images can provide prospective buyers with "fly-around" views of your arts/crafts.

- *Private showing*
  An elegant way of showing your art is through private showings. You must be willing to handle all the details of this type of selling.

Validate your interest.

Review your responses in Steps 1 and 2.

Ask yourself:

1. Are you satisfied that this venture meets your needs?
2. Is your self-described internal analysis in alignment with this career path?
3. Are your products unique in some important way?
4. Do you know how to price your products?
5. If not, will you complete the due diligence to learn how to set your prices?

If this role appears to be a good fit for you, you are ready to move ahead and explore the opportunities that support your interests.

Explore the opportunities.

Do your research now and practice your craft. Join a group of artisans, a co-op or a guild.

Note that special interest groups exist for the physically challenged, for women, and for ethnic artists to explore. In point of fact, as America's population continues to diversify, artisans from every conceivable ethnicity will find their markets. It is happening now.

Local senior-citizen organizations, hobby stores and Chambers of Commerce are excellent starting points for your research. And, along the way, remember that nostalgia items are "hot."

Continue your research.

Websites: For Internet access, type: http://www. followed by the web address.

> *Writersdigest.com & writersmarket.com*
> The definitive websites on writing opportunities
>
> *Worldwidefreelance.com*
> A great resource on how to get started in freelance writing
>
> *Freelanceworkexchange.com*
> Identify and seek out writing opportunities
>
> *Artsandcrafts.about.com/library/weekly/aa011300.htm.*
> Share ideas with other crafters.
>
> *CraftLister.com*
> Online listing of art and craft shows, promoters and crafters.
>
> *Craftmaster.com*
> Features street fairs, festivals, arts and crafts fairs in the West.
>
> *Eventcrazy.com*
> 600+ pages of great events.
>
> *Festival.net.com*
> Features 14,000+ crafts shows, art fairs, festivals and other events
>
> *Google.com*
> Go to Google advanced search and enter the following key words:
> For Writing: freelance, writing, and add specific categories such as business writing.
> For Crafts: craft sales, craft show, arts and crafts organizations, add specific crafts areas of interest, such as jewelry, dolls, etc.
>
> *Pluck.com and Info.com*
> Additional search engine services

Books and Periodicals

> *Writer's Digest* – monthly magazine on the writing field
>
> *Writer's Market* – companion book to Writer's Digest. Purchase it and get a free subscription to its website.
>
> *Crafts and Crafts Shows: How to Make Money* by Phil Kadubec.
>
> *How to Make Money Selling Arts and Crafts on the Internet* by Phil Kadubec.
>
> *Marketing Your Arts and Crafts* by Janice West.
>
> *The Crafts Business Answer Book and Resource Guide* by Barbara Braebec.
>
> *Sunshine Artist* magazine

Prepare your marketing tools.

For information and examples, refer to the Marketing Tools section of the book.
- Business card
- Business plan, including financial plan and marketing plan
- Brochure
- Portfolio
- Website

Across America – Real people, real stories...Gayla Doucet

Gayla describes herself as the modern equivalent of the pieceworker, a person who takes on jobs that produce products on demand. This is her story of love, fun and growing profitability!

"While the traditional view of a pieceworker might be the seamstress working from home to sew articles of clothing for a garment manufacturer, I'm a knowledge pieceworker who produces custom writing, workshops and a variety of other solutions for a number of businesses.

My early career was spent in several positions including French teacher, Xerox copier salesperson, Junior Achievement program director and manager of a temporary employment agency. I then spent 10 years with IBM as a systems engineer, marketing representative, information center manager and customer service manager. I transitioned into technology training with several firms and then branched out into human performance training with TTI Performance Systems, Ltd. My last position with TTI was manager of distributor relations and communications where I managed the delivery of product support for over 3,600 individual distributors throughout North America.

I left TTI in mid 2004 and started People Powered Solutions, LLC. Now I create business solutions, and I still utilize TTI's human performance diagnostics, among others. I'm developing a number of solutions to assist business owners in effectively developing their human capital and to assist individuals in managing their careers.

I've always enjoyed writing and have developed strong communication skills in the variety of jobs I've had throughout my career. I decided to put this strength to good use by offering my writing services to companies. I create articles, workshops and specialized content in workplace performance for websites. One niche that I've developed is selling my services on a subscription basis to companies who need to constantly contact their customers with something new. As an example, I write a new article every other month for a number of firms that subscribe to my services. I currently have 3 client companies that retain me to update their website content on a regular basis.

This 'Piecework' provides me the creativity and income to continue to develop my human performance business. I research related areas for my writing, so I'm able to stay on top of trends that affect the human behavior and workplace performance fields. Having to meet deadlines and produce articles on a continuous basis is challenging, but I'm used to this responsibility and thrive on meeting deadlines. Plus, I'm getting paid for doing what I love; and that's the best reward."

Portfolio Career Jugglers

Who are they?

These are the people who appreciate the value of not putting all their "career eggs in one basket." They believe that the diversified work portfolio, over time, increases their probability of realizing financial success, improves their sense of control and boosts their feelings of security.

What you need to know.

The first person who opened our eyes to this way of thinking about work was the well-known author, Charles Handy. His book, *The Age of Unreason*, changed the course of a lifetime of thinking about work.

In brief, Mr. Handy compared work to managing a stock portfolio.

> Some investments, he proposed, are initially risky but
> they offer a high degree of probability for future growth.
>
> Other investments, such as long-term growth stocks,
> provide a steady and relatively certain climb over time.
>
> Diversifying the portfolio between stocks representing different industries
> increases the probability of financial return on your investment.
>
> In other words, smart investment strategies are usually balanced
> between high risk and reasonable certainty, between long and short-term growth.

Think of portfolio work in this light. If this strategy makes sense to you, you will be one among many others who have diversified their portfolios and created their own working models.

Pretend for a few moments that your work has been that of a career management specialist. Within the scope of that profession you have done many things. You have helped mature workers to navigate a confusing new world. You have helped the person who is returning to work after many years at home raising a family. You are published in your area of career management expertise. You are leaving, or have left, your regular, full-time job. Rather than seeking work with one employer, you choose to create a work portfolio that will allow you the greatest time flexibility in order to continue to develop your writing skills.

The thought process of balancing this example of a portfolio career goes like this:

- From a perspective of the marketplace, there is no doubt that the needs for the mature worker are high and good fees for this type of service are well established.

- Helping people to re-enter the workforce after a long hiatus is also a high need. However, this type of service is reasonably well staked out by a variety of government agencies and private service firms. A review of the market suggests that opportunities may be sporadic and fees will be modest. However, because of your credentials in this area, this service belongs in the portfolio.

- A third investment, as a writer, offers an undetermined financial return. It is likely to provide a modest, consistent income stream over time. This investment provides an opportunity to continue to work well into late life.
- A final investment is your continued development of related skills. A formal course in desktop publishing, and a commitment to learning the art and skills of self-publishing, will provide you with an effective way to leverage your abiding interest in writing and publishing.

A visual representation of the amount of investment in each segment of this portfolio looks like:

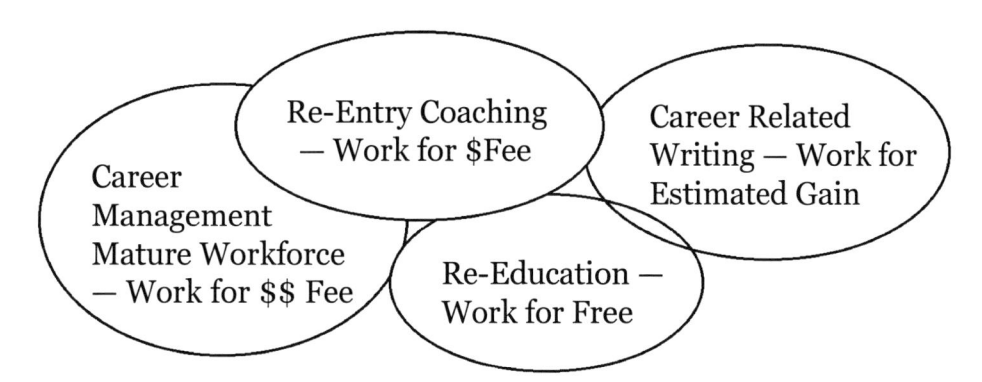

- Career Management Mature Workforce — Work for $$ Fee
- Re-Entry Coaching — Work for $Fee
- Re-Education — Work for Free
- Career Related Writing — Work for Estimated Gain

Note that this example of a portfolio career is balanced with the largest investment of time and effort allocated to the area of highest gain. The smallest, yet very important long-term investment is allocated to learning new skills and it is work for free.

The point is that work is work, whether or not it is compensated.

What does your portfolio look like today?

List a few possible options that might work for you:

Why are you considering a portfolio career?

Check all answers that apply:

_____ Rapidly changing technologies require that I take time to learn new skills if I am to remain employable.

_____ I believe that organizations will continue to downsize, and I do not want to find myself layed-off or terminated at some point in the future. In other words, I'll take my chances on creating a portfolio career now rather than later.

_____ I have a good partner and we have decided to balance work and home life - an option not available to us in the regular, full-time world.

_____ My values are shifting. I want a simpler life – one that allows me more time for other things.

_____ My work "purpose" has changed. I am looking for more from work than just pay and I intend to invest in, and develop, additional competencies.

_____ I see work as a business. "Me, Inc." demands a different business strategy for my own career if I am to remain employable.

If you have checked any of these reasons for pursuing a portfolio career, you are among the increasing numbers of people who are seeing this option as interesting, fun and profitable.

Finally, remind yourself of the advantages of managing a balanced portfolio.

- You will enjoy income from a variety of sources.
- When one income source is "hot" and one is "not" – you will still be in business of making some money.
- You will expand your knowledge about the present and future market.
- You will deepen your reputation as a subject matter expert.
- You will balance your energy between the various components of your portfolio.
- You will be able to shift emphasis as evolving marketplace needs drive change.
- You are likely to have more fun and, over time, realize more financial returns.

Validate your interest.

Review your responses in Steps 1 and 2.

Ask yourself the following questions:

1. Are you satisfied that this venture meets your needs?
2. Is your self-described internal analysis in alignment with this career path?
3. Were you able to identify two or three career options where you are likely to find "portfolio" success?
4. Is your spouse or partner supportive of your portfolio career?

If this role appears to be a good fit for you, you are ready to move ahead and explore the opportunities that support your interest.

Explore the opportunities.

If you are still working, now is the time to identify your interests and deepen your knowledge in the areas of portfolio management that appeal to you. You can go back to school, volunteer for assignments that will raise your profile and take other means to expand your knowledge in your areas of interest. Rebuild your network.

If you are close to retirement, you can begin to plant the seeds with your present employer that you would like to maintain a limited business arrangement with them in a specific area of your expertise after your departure.

Working or not, invest in improving your knowledge in the areas of portfolio management that appeal to you.

- Rebuild your network.
- Go back to school as needed to ensure that your current knowledge is, indeed, marketplace current.
- Investigate firms that market and deliver similar services.
- Meet other experts in your fields of interest.
- Start collecting brochures, business cards and other marketing tools as models for your own.

Continue your research.

Websites: For Internet access, type: http://www. followed by the web address.

> *Creativekeys.net*
> Offers additional information as to how to handle a portfolio career.

> *Google.com*
> Go to Google advanced search and enter the following key words: portfolio careers.

> *Pluck.com* and *Info.com*
> Additional search engine services

Books, magazines and periodicals:

> *Half-Time: Changing Your Game Plan From Success to Significance* by Bob Buford.

> *The Age of Unreason* by Charles Handy.

> *The Elephant and the Flea* by Charles Handy.

> Read the section in *Boom or Bust* entitled "Hot Careers."

Prepare your marketing tools.

For information and examples, refer to the Marketing Tools section of the book.

    Branding statement(s)

    Business card

    Business plan including financial plan and marketing plan

    Brochure (hard copy and online version)

    Professional biography

    Website

Across America – Real people, real stories...Ron McIntire

After 30 years in the Corporate World, Ron McIntire confronted the loss of opportunities in the manufacturing sector – full-time opportunities he had once counted upon were drying up faster than he could apply! This is Ron's story of struggle, adaptation and the continuing changes he faces.

> "In my late 40's, I was the product of years in the manufacturing industry and of my own upbringing as a Midwesterner steeped in Midwestern values that taught me to believe that finding a job in a corporate setting was the order of the day. I also believed that, in order to achieve security, I would have to work long and hard for one employer. I went so far as to join an Asian owned firm for the benefit of having a lifetime job.
>
> I've endured consolidations, restructurings and my own job loss.
>
> I have come to realize that with more than 30 years of work under my belt, and 20 or 30 working years ahead, I must look at other options that contrast with my long held beliefs.
>
> Also, as a single parent, my job of raising my daughters is almost at an end and it is time for me to take a different direction and do some "restructuring" of my own.
>
> I began the process of redirection by asking myself the following questions:
>
> - What matters most to me?
> - Why have I hesitated to pursue a real life and to do things that truly matter?
> - Am I here to live to work or to work to live? '
>
> It wasn't long before I put the thought of one lifetime job in one company in my past. I paid attention to a number of friends who already have businesses of their own. I went to them for their advice and recommendations relative to new ways to work. I studied the trends in the world with an open and inquiring mind. I accepted the system of work as it really is today. It gradually became clear to me that managing a portfolio of opportunities would be my key to achieving my own security.
>
> I am currently developing a portfolio in several areas of work. I have aligned myself with organizations that train and develop people to improve business outcomes. I took my certification in ISO9000 and related subject matters, such as QS9000, ISO/TS16949 and Six Sigma Tools and added certifications in Lean Management and Manufacturing. Armed with this array of training certifications, I have prepared myself to bring this knowledge to organizations in need. I am also developing a small business to serve the needs of the legal industry. Finally, I have pursued and obtained my commission as a notary public and became a Certified Notary Signing Agent. I am exploring ways to capitalize in the world of eCommerce.
>
> Some people wondered at my motivation.
>
> Did I seek to get rich?
>
> This was, and is, not my case. I sought an interesting life pursuing work that mattered to me and that was marketable to business. I took my lesson from the stock market about diversifying your stock portfolio.

Will I succeed?

I am in the beginning stages of this adventure. It has been an enormous struggle. Only time will tell but I have made a good start with some training "gigs" booked over the next months, a few contracts for notary work under my belt, and relationships with two well-known training organizations that, hopefully, will promote my services.

I am diligent in continuing to pursue my goals of new and meaningful work and to achieving a 'real life' that is more about living than about just living to work."

Across America – Real people, real stories...Brad Taft

Courageous friend, whirling dervish and co-author of "*Boom or Bust!*" — Brad is living the challenges of startup. However, he has a unique talent – he is a master juggler and he is enormously organized.

"Co-authoring *Boom or Bust!* is one of several career activities that I am undertaking at this time. My portfolio also includes outplacement, individual career consulting, and marketing and sales for human resources services companies. Add on volunteer leadership positions with two professional organizations and two alumni groups, and I am definitely not wanting for things to do!

After receiving a B.A. in Communications and an M.B.A. from the University of Southern California, I began my career in the executive recruiting field with Korn/Ferry International. I enjoyed the opportunity to assist companies in identifying and selecting managerial and professional talent, and the project orientation of the work was challenging and provided me with a strong sense of accomplishment. I launched my own recruiting practice at the age of 27, and a year later started a graphics design firm with two artists. During this initial entrepreneurial phase of my career, I gained valuable experience in starting up and managing two small businesses at the same time. It allowed me to hone my project management skills even further, and I became proficient at multi-tasking, even though that word hadn't been invented yet.

I moved on to a full time position in the outplacement industry with a small firm in Los Angeles, and over the next four years had the opportunity to take on increasing responsibilities in the management consulting field including general management, marketing, sales and the delivery of outplacement services. Then the entrepreneurial bug hit me again. With a partner, I co-founded Career Transition Group, an outplacement firm that grew to regional status with two offices and nine consultants in a five year period. Wearing all hats as owner of a small business made me realize that I was developing a stronger interest in marketing and sales than the other functions. We sold our company to a national firm, and I ran its Los Angeles office and was also responsible for regional marketing and sales.

That role continued during both an eight year tenure with another national consulting firm and two years with another company. In 2003 I started my own consulting practice in the human resources and career management field. I'm retained by companies to provide outplacement and executive coaching services, and I also provide career transition services to individuals. To supplement my income during the start-up, I took on several projects for other organizations. One that was most interesting was developing corporate sponsorships for the Human Capital Metrics Summit, an annual conference sponsored by Staffing.org, a non-profit organization dedicated to creating standards for performance measurement and effectiveness in the recruiting field. My efforts resulted in generating more funds than expected, and the experience gave me excellent exposure to both the world of nonprofit organizations and to fundraising. It also added to the expertise that I had gained as a volunteer leader of professional and alumni groups over the years and set the stage for developing a new opportunity to add to my career portfolio.

While I never was an accomplished juggler, I learned early on in my career to manage multiple tasks simultaneously with a project orientation. Establishing priorities and following through on details have always been strong suits. My biggest challenge in managing a portfolio of activities is the effective management of time. I'm constantly revising my "To Do" list and determining the best course of action to take to accomplish what needs to be done in an appropriate time frame. Since I am detailed-oriented, I need to critically monitor the time and effort spent on a particular project, and I'm striving to improve my delegation skills.

Another challenge I face is answering the proverbial question "What do you do for a living?" I've learned not to provide a long, complicated answer by listing all of my activities. I usually start with a brief explanation of one of my roles that I feel will be of interest to the person who posed the question. For example, at a meeting of human resources professionals, I will start by mentioning that I am a human resources consultant who specializes in career development and transition. Depending on the age of the individuals I'm speaking with, I'll also mention that I co-authored *Boom or Bust!*

Having a portfolio of career activities is both challenging and rewarding. I strive to achieve little things each day which add up to large accomplishments in the end. I think the best thing about it is the variety of activities in which I'm involved. If I find myself getting tired of something I'm working on, I know there is always another project for me to dive into."

Revolutionary Reinventors

Who are they?

They are the few who have enough guts and passion for something new, or something different, that they will "pay the price" in order to get to the new place. They will step across the chasm of change, fearful or not.

What you need to know.

They are hard to recognize as they come in different sizes, ages, shapes and styles. They do share a common knowledge. They know what their talent is and they recognize they have not been using this talent. Many of these modern revolutionaries will tell you that they have reached the point where they must invest in using their talent, and they will not fall back to using just their learned skills.

One way that I think of these courageous folks is to recall a quote from Katharine Hepburn who said: "As you go through life, you learn that if you don't paddle your own canoe, you don't move." She paddled!

In addition to shared knowledge, they also share common traits and values.

They are:

- Independent thinkers.
- Able to see the relationship between concept and reality.
- Willing to see progress as a process, not an event.
- Concerned with linking their goals and their lives with their careers.
- Clear that doing good work, work that matters to them, counts.
- Lifelong learners.
- Self-challenging.

Does this sound like you?

I can think of no better way for you to validate your answer to this question than to ask you to read the story of Lars Oakeson, a friend and fiercely-determined, kind-hearted client, who dedicated his story to me, his career coach. If the path of revolutionary reinvention is in your future, you will see your courageous self in his story.

Across America – Real people, real stories...A letter from Lars Oakeson

"Dear Carleen,

I was expecting the layoff, so it wasn't a big shock when it happened. After a short while, the reality sank in. I was 51 years old, and I had experience that wasn't very marketable.

My experience, as a manager of electronic repair groups in small companies, afforded me only a small number of possibilities in the new job market. I also had experience as a Technical Planner in a manufacturing firm. Well... how many positions have you seen advertised recently for a Technical Planner?

When I started working with Spherion, the career management firm that my previous company paid to help me with my transition, you and I began talking about writing as a career. I told you that my dream was to write a novel. You started a spark in me by sharing the information that good writers are in great demand, in part because many people in the younger generation read and write at about the eighth or tenth grade level. I knew that I had a talent for writing and I knew that I loved to write. So, after much deliberation, I started thinking that maybe I should take this opportunity (yes, a layoff can be seen as an opportunity) to change my career field. I reflected and remembered that I had written a few technical documents in my previous positions and that I had an extensive technical background. Then, I received the results of an assessment (the Strong Interest Inventory) and it listed "technical writer" as "very strong" on my list of possible career choices. That sold me!

At first, I felt like an impostor calling myself a technical writer, so I only listed technical writing as one of my talents. After joining a writers' networking group at Spherion and taking some software classes that are needed for technical writers, I became increasingly involved in my new career. I started looking only for technical writing positions. I made business cards that stated I was a technical writer and I started introducing myself to others as a technical writer. Ultimately, I programmed myself into believing that I am a technical writer.

It was difficult to find technical writing positions that required very little experience, and many of the positions listed asked for a degree in journalism or some other writing-related credential. Also, being a very strong introvert (which most technical writers are) I made the mistake of not networking enough. Luck was with me, though, because one of the networking contacts I made at Spherion got me in touch with someone who helped me to land a job as a technical writer at a very good company.

There were, of course, certain times when I wondered if I had made the right choice to change careers at my age. I am now very glad that I stuck it out during these times of doubt because my future is much more secure and relevant to marketplace needs than my past work. In particular, I am finally doing something that I really enjoy and I am getting paid well for my efforts.

For those who find themselves in a similar situation, take an inventory of what you're good at and what you truly enjoy. Then, look for a career that matches those two things and take the plunge. If you move ahead with gusto and guts, you can make a bright future for yourself."

Lars has given you his plan for reinvention. You must supply your own courage!

Did you notice that the traits we listed are all embedded in Lars' story?

If you need an added dash of inspiration, read M.S. Peck's book *The Road Less Traveled* and Richard Leider's book *The Power of Purpose: Creating Meaning in Your Life and Work*. These books will inspire the brave hearted!

Still tentative? Engage a career coach to help you bridge the chasm of change.

Small Business Owners

Who are they?

They employ half of the private workforce and they run more than 26 million small businesses. The Small Business Administration (December, 2000) reported that more than 99% of all employers are small business owners. The number of women and minority owned small businesses are growing at warp-speed.

Small business is the heartbeat of America.

What you need to know.

The purchase of an existing small business may offset many of the risks of starting your own business from scratch. Whether you start the business or buy it, there is significant due diligence and hard work involved in making a choice that will work for you.

According to a recent article in Money Magazine about small business success seekers in America, 25% of people who start a small business are under 30, 33% are between 30 and 39, 25% are between 40 and 49 and 12% are between 50 and 59. For those 60 and older the number is 4%. The point is that while age is a factor, it is not the only factor that determines who starts a small business.

What is important to remember is the fact that as people age, they are far more likely to buy an existing business rather than start one from scratch! They are also far more likely to be successful than their younger counterparts because they buy established small businesses that have already beaten the tough odds against new starts where, according to the U.S. Small Business Administration, only half of all start-ups are around after four years.

Mature adults buy small businesses from people they know, often from family members. Others use business brokers who provide them with insight and lists of available companies. (Since the seller pays the broker's commission, there is no need to worry about the cost of working with a reputable broker.) A few people still check out their local newspaper for opportunities.

When you buy an existing business, you will receive current financial information and access to an established customer base. The seller may arrange some, or all, of the financing on your behalf. Be very aware that you also buy a committed lifestyle, one that will take much more of your time than an 8 to 5 traditional job.

Obtaining sound advice from an accountant, an attorney and the Small Business Administration are a few ways that smart buyers protect themselves. Of course, there are business licenses, business taxes, business insurance and many more matters to address than are suggested here.

There are other basic questions to ask yourself before purchasing any existing small business, such as the type of business that interests you and the geographic location of the business.

Validate your interest.

Review your responses in Steps 1 and 2.

Critical questions to ask yourself before embarking on this journey include:

1. Are you satisfied that this venture meets your needs?
2. Is your self-described internal analysis in alignment with this career path?
3. Have you thoroughly researched business trends, such as those found in this book?
4. Can you afford the investment of money and time?
5. Do you have your spouse or life partner's support for the investment of money and time?
6. Will you take the time to thoroughly research your final list of business prospects and ask the tough questions?
7. Can you walk away from your dreams and make an objective decision?

If this role appears to be a good fit, you are ready to move ahead and explore the opportunities that support your interest.

Explore the opportunities.

Interview small business owners. Meet with local bankers that finance small businesses. Take a trip to your local Small Business Administration. Join your local Chamber of Commerce. Re-read the marketing trends section of this book.

Continue your research.

Websites: For Internet access, type: http://www. followed by the web address.

> *Businessnation.com*
>
> *sba.gov/starting_business/startup/guide.html*
> The government's comprehensive site.
>
> *Google.com*
> Go to Google's advanced search and enter the following key words: small business, small business management, entrepreneurship, small business brokers and existing business enterprises.
>
> *Pluck.com and Info.com*
> Additional search engine services

Books, magazines, periodicals and an association:

> *Keys to Starting a Small Business* by Joel G. Siegel and Jae K. Shim
>
> *Small Business for Dummies* by Eric Tyson and Jim Schell
>
> *Entrepreneur, Inc.*
>
> *The Wall Street Journal*

The National Association of Business Brokers

Prepare your marketing tools.

For information and examples, refer to the Marketing Tools section of this book.

Business cards

Business plan (including financial plan and marketing plan)

Brochures

Website

Stipend Workers

Who are they?

Webster's dictionary describes people who work for stipends do so for a "fixed sum of money paid periodically for services or to defray expenses." Some think of stipend work as volunteerism with enough pay to cover costs.

Many, but not all, stipend work is performed by educators, retired government workers, and graduate students.

What you need to know.

A well-kept secret from many of us, stipends provide a modest fee for meaningful work at all stages in a worker's life.

There are staff positions for summer employment as language instructors, program and project coordinators, and advisors to teenagers. Some positions are for conducting "bird" branding in various part of the United States, hosting environmental education workshops, working with at-risk youth, or supporting federal agency management of natural resources in the public lands of the United States.

A growing stipend opportunity is working with State sponsored Youth Corps. People who do this type of stipend work help at-risk urban youth to find new meaning in their lives. Positions are available throughout the year and a modest stipend is provided along with relatively modest housing and simple meals.

Federal and State agencies are undergoing tremendous change as they struggle to maintain costs while supporting thousands of early retirees in the public sector who seek to continue to work.

- In the short term, Congress is expected to sponsor programs that tap into the knowledge of experienced federal workers without impacting the regular, full-time workforce budget.

- In the somewhat longer term, more and more of these openings will be made available to all qualified individuals, regardless of their previous affiliation with the public sector.

Explore two typical stipend opportunities:

1. Abbey Road's overseas programs seek qualified individuals for their summer staff and faculty teams in cultural and language immersion programs. Openings exist for language instructors, program directors, and program coordinators in many countries. Typically, but not exclusively, staff members are university-level instructors, high school teachers and graduate students. Proficient language skills are a must. Their standards are very high and this is not the place to apply if what you are seeking is a free trip abroad. Stipends are modest but lodging is covered and there are discretionary bonus

opportunities for outstanding performance. For more information on Abbey Road, visit their site at goabbeyroad.com.

2. Hawk Watch International offers an interesting site at hawkwatch.org. Recently, Hawk Watch offered stipends for Raptor Migration Counter and Raptor Migration Banders. Their ad stated that applicants must have " good eyesight, be in good physical condition, be able to endure long hours in the field and variable weather, have demonstrated birding and raptor-in-flight I.D. skills and must be able to work well in a team environment." At the time of the advertisement, they paid a nontaxable monthly per diem of up to $1100 per month plus a $150 travel stipend.

Validate your interest.

Review your responses in Steps 1 and 2.

Ask yourself:

1. Are you satisfied that this venture meets your needs?
2. Is your self-described internal analysis in alignment with this career path?
3. Can you afford to make a commitment of time, one that may require long workweeks, albeit for a finite period?
4. Have you the flexibility of lifestyle that allows you to consider living away from home?
5. Do you have a spouse or partner who might enjoy sharing this type of work? Or, if not, would they like you out of the house, now and again?

Explore the opportunities.

Visit the sites suggested above.

Continue your research.

Websites: For Internet access, type: http://www. followed by the web address.

Google.com
Go to Google's advanced search and enter the following key words: stipend jobs and seasonal work.

Pluck.com and Info.com
Additional search engine services

Across America – Real peoples, real stories... Rick Griffith

After working in the private sector his entire career, Rick Griffith was introduced to a temporary opportunity in the nonprofit field as a sponsored executive with the United Way. Here's his story about his experience as a Stipend Worker.

"I've spent the bulk of my career in the manufacturing field. I began by working my way up the ladder in the purchasing function with companies that included Marion Power Shovel, Honda of America, Rockwell International and Monroe Auto Equipment. I then moved into general management, and my most recent position was as EVP & General Manager of an automobile parts manufacturer. After two and a half years in that role, I left that privately-held firm to pursue other opportunities.

At a networking meeting of executives in transition, I met an individual who had experience as a "Loaned Executive" to the United Way of Phoenix. His company had loaned him to the United Way to assist with its fund-raising campaign for a 14 week period the previous year. He continued to receive his full salary and benefits during that time period. He had since retired from his corporate job but was going to repeat his role with United Way and invited me to check out the opportunity for myself.

In addition to "Loaned Executives", the United Way utilizes "Sponsored Executives" in the same role. Individuals are brought on to assist the United Way and are sponsored by companies that donate stipends which the executives receive for the 14 weeks that they spend working on the United Way Campaign. I interviewed for the opportunity, was selected for the role and joined a group of both loaned and sponsored executives in a 2 week training program.

The training program consisted of a comprehensive orientation about the United Way, visits to the agencies that it supports, meetings with community leaders and sales and presentation skills training sessions. United Way employees acquainted us with its structure, philosophy, policies and procedures. Visits to agencies were most enlightening for me since I hadn't had much exposure to the multitude of services provided to those in need. While it was inspiring to learn about the successes that these organizations were achieving in helping people, it was disheartening to realize that so much more needs to be done to fully support those who are truly in need. One interesting statistic I learned was that the average age of a homeless person in the United States is nine years.

I also learned a lot from the sales and presentation skills training sessions. Here we discussed effective ways to present the United Way programs and goals to employee groups, urge them to donate, handle objections and answer questions. I appreciated the role-playing exercises and the opportunity to improve my presentation skills.

After the two-week training program, I was teamed with another executive to manage the campaign with the State of Arizona employees. The State actually has its own fund-raising program that is administered by the United Way. We developed a strategy to inform all the departments in the State's business units of the campaign. We started by identifying liaisons in each department, scheduling employee meetings and distributing brochures.

The employee meetings are called "ASK Meetings" since we are asking individuals to reinvest in their community by making donations. In developing an agenda for these sessions, I would introduce the campaign and its goals, introduce a representative from one of the agencies who would then make a brief presentation about its work in supporting the community, discuss the process for donating funds and then ask for pledges from each employee. By planning and delivering this sales presentation, I gained a lot of professional development.

United Way executives are given a lot of support during the campaign to reach their goals. While we were mainly out in the field, we did have an assigned workstation at the United Way offices and utilized the telephone and email services to communicate with staff and campaign contacts.

The schedule was very flexible, and I could work in meetings of a personal nature between my commitments.

I appreciated the opportunity to work with the United Way staff, the various community agencies and the campaign liaisons at the State of Arizona. These people are all passionate about their work in helping the less fortunate, and an effective environment of teamwork exists throughout the organizations. Luckily for me, I've never had a need for an agency's support. This experience opened my eyes to the real need that exists for community services, and I was proud to make a contribution by managing a campaign that exceeded its goal.

The small stipend I received was eclipsed by what I gained both personally and professionally from this experience. In addition to sales and presentation skills, I gained a lot of self-confidence in leading a successful project. I also appreciated the networking opportunities that I had in meeting a large number of people in leadership roles throughout the community."

Stress-Free Easy-Does-It Workers

Who are they?

These are the people who understand that it is very "in" to continue to work and that it is very "out" to retire completely.

Stress-free by choice,
these workers do not choose to continue to work at a frenetic pace.

They are crystal clear
in their determination to find a role that doesn't cause them to lose sleep over a job.

What you need to know.

There is good news for you. There are many paying jobs that let you manage your time, have some fun, and devote your energy to other aspects of your life. These jobs can help you to rejuvenate and rediscover lost energy.

Take a look at a few of the options we came up with. If you don't find your preferred option in this list, investigate the section on fancy-free and stipend career options.

1. *Cruise Line opportunities*

   For a comprehensive list of the many opportunities, read Elizabeth Hatton's *Worldwide Cruise Ship and Yachting Career Guide.* Many jobs require a full-time commitment for several months at a time. You live aboard and meals are provided. Careers that may interest you include photographers, entertainers, guest lecturers, shore excursion leaders, and port lecturers.

   All types of experts fill short-term, fun positions that allow them to share their expertise. These so-called "enrichment providers" may lecture, teach, or instruct in a variety of roles. They make several presentations while ships are at sea. They spend the rest of their time enjoying the cruise! Some agencies that place these experts include: International Voyager Media in Miami, Lectures International in Tucson, Semester-at-Sea in Pittsburgh (shipboard@sas.ise.pitt.edu).

   We'll bet you already know about the cruise line opportunities for mature male escorts. If you can dance and hold a conversation, you too may qualify as a "gentleman host."

2. *Teaching for a fee*

   The U.S. Parks & Recreation and Libraries Departments offer courses to students of all ages. Subject-matter experts are often invited to teach creative writing, horsemanship, photography, cooking and even retirement life planning. Fees are modest but the teaching itself will elevate your profile and result in opportunities for additional gigs.

Local area high schools and community colleges are wonderful ways to give back knowledge while earning a modest income — to supplement other interests.

An emerging need is to be found in teaching English as a second language and in teaching young people to love reading.

These jobs feel may feel like volunteerism,
but you will be paid
for doing good.

3. *The Fast Food Industry*
McDonald's pioneered the use of mature workers in the fast food business long before it was popular. They know that the very stability, predictability, lower turnover, and conscientiousness of the older worker outstrips the speed and vitality of the younger workers usually found in this industry.

Jack-in-the-Box and other fast-food franchises have been quick to follow suit.

While this job may not qualify as stress-free for some of you, others, especially those who long for non-stop people interaction, may see this work in a friendly light.

4. *Shopping for a Fee*
Companies pay for honest feedback from consumers. You can work during the day, evenings or weekends.

There are even companies that will pay your golf fees for honest feedback about their golf courses.

Other companies that engage shoppers include most major supermarkets, fast food restaurants, and large department stores. One link we explored is shoppingjobshere.com. You may also inquire directly about opportunities with your local supermarket manager. A web resource to explore is shop4fun.com.

5. *The Get Paid Network*
Earn money by taking part in research studies, opinion surveys, clinical research, focus groups, passing out free samples in grocery stores, expressing your opinion in taste testing events.... even getting paid for standing in line for others. For information, go to getpaidnetwork.com.

If you are a Costco or Sam's Club member, inquire about opportunities directly with their respective store managers during your next shopping excursion. Club Demonstration Services, headquartered in San Diego, is uniquely focused on providing customized in-house demonstrations. Their market includes supermarkets and drug chains, mass merchandisers, warehouse clubs, and food service organizations. Their Website is clubdemo.com.

6. *The International Association of Air Travel Couriers*
They offer free airfare and other last-minute special courier fares, a savings on international fares, a bi-monthly travel magazine, a daily courier bulletin of all courier companies, and their schedules. Companies using couriers make different deals with couriers, some involving modest pay in addition to subsidy for all travel

costs. Other firms simply offer greatly reduced airfare (up to 85%) as compensation. The research site we recommend is courier.org/iaatcmembersquestionsanswers.php.

7. Wal-Mart
If ever there was a major chain that "got there first" when it came to hiring older workers, Wal-Mart is that firm. From the greeters outside the front door to the folks who hand you a shopping cart and welcome you to their stores, there is no getting around it, they have seen the future and it is us! And, we're paying them back by driving out of our way to patronize the smart stores that hire our generation. It's easy to apply. Just stop by your local Wal-Mart's customer service counter.

Validate your interest.

Review your responses in Steps 1 and 2.

Ask yourself:

1. Are you satisfied that this venture meets your needs?
2. Is your self-described internal analysis in alignment with this career path?
3. Are you tired of the prolonged stress of a regular, full-time job?
4. Do you find yourself bored and struggling with too much time on your hands?
5. Are you willing to give up trying to keep up with the "Joneses" and simply do what you want to do and what suits your situation?

Continue your research.

Websites: For Internet access, type: http://www. followed by the web address.

Google.com
Go to Google's advanced search and enter the following key words: stress-free work, part-time or seasonal job opportunities.

Pluck.com and Info.com
Additional search engine services

Last words.

You will fill out applications in person or online. Don't worry about marketing tools.

Across America – Real people, real stories…Bob Caskey

This is the story of a man who has made several career changes throughout his life, including one due to a major injury, and has found a "Stress-Free" position that brings him a great amount of satisfaction.

"I began my work life with a seven and a half year stint in the Air Force as a ground power mechanic responsible for repairing generators, air conditioners and other electrical devices. After the military, I became a fire engineer with a local fire department. I really enjoyed that field and developed strong skills and experience over a 13 year period. Then I suffered a career ending injury when I picked up a heavy object and crushed 2 discs in my back. Surgery didn't help my condition, and I had to take a medical retirement at the age of 43.

Although I received disability benefits including pay and health insurance, I wanted to go back to work and had to continue working from a financial standpoint. I accepted a position at an automotive parts store, and for the next 8 years I delivered parts and worked the counter. I enjoyed working with the public and found that my skills as a firefighter dealing with people under duress helped me assist individuals experiencing different levels of stress with their car problems. As time went on I found myself getting tired of working irregular hours, as the retail field requires. Also, I wasn't supposed to lift heavy objects, which some auto parts obviously are. I had an amicable parting with the store and started to search for a new opportunity.

I saw an advertisement for drivers at Enterprise Rent-a-Car. It needed part-time drivers to escort customers from their homes or auto shop to the car rental agency, and I initially was to work only on Saturdays, but that quickly changed to three days a week (Monday, Wednesday & Friday) from 7:30 a.m. to 6:00 p.m. with an occasional 3 hour stint on Saturday.

I am one of four drivers who work at this location. We are all in our 60's to early 70's. What I like most about the job is the opportunity to meet a large number of people as I drive them to and from the agency; most are very nice and talkative. My co-workers and I are making a strong contribution to our unit's Customer Satisfaction Survey results, and our team members get along well. Our manager is much younger than the drivers, but no major generational issues have happened yet.

Communications among co-workers and bosses is vital for a smooth-running business; it's important that everyone understand what their roles are and what's expected of them. My biggest challenge is to dispel the myths and misperceptions that often come up about older workers, and having an effective communications channel to counteract that is important. It's sometimes frustrating when younger workers don't listen to recommendations that would make everyone's job easier, but I'm continuing to improve my powers of persuasion. This position is a great fit for me because it offers a nice working environment and the flexibility I want to have at this stage of my life."

Teachers

Who are they?

Teachers include people who understand that not all educators hold advanced college degrees. They are folks who have leveraged their work experience and talent to help others for pay or for free.

What you need to know.

America needs teaching aids, teaching assistants, and other subject-matter experts. If you have taken an early retirement package from a corporation or, if you wish to do something meaningful that will allow you plenty of time for R&R, full-time or part-time teaching is a good option.

High needs include:

1. Instructors in English as a 2nd Language.

2. Specialists in teaching social and cultural skills, manners, and business ethics.

3. Guest lecturers at local community colleges, state or private universities.

4. Industry experts, such as sales or customer service training for corporations or institutions.

5. Community experts to handle projects for government agencies and provide training in affirmative action, harassment, Sarbanes-Oxley, or other compliance required subject-matters.

6. Instructors at online universities, retail outlets, and computer stores.

7. Teachers to instruct older adults in computer basics and Internet savvy.

8. Art instructors; teaching gigs that provide an outlet for your artistic talent.

9. Trade schools may offer a ticket to teaching success if you are skilled in mechanics or electronics.

10. Children's tutors are increasingly needed as parents struggle to help their children compete.

The point is that you have spent a lifetime learning something.

You have something to teach.

Teaching, while it may involve some "skills training" on your part, is fun, worthwhile, and paid careers abound.

Validate your interest.

Review your responses in Steps 1 and 2.

Ask yourself:

1. Are you satisfied that this venture meets your needs?
2. Is your self-described internal analysis in alignment with this career path?
3. Can you readily identify what you are capable of teaching, right now, today?
4. Is what you are capable of teaching in keeping with marketplace need?

If this role appears to be a good fit for you, you are ready to move ahead and explore the opportunities that support your interest.

Explore the opportunities.

Interview teachers in part-time roles, such as at The University of Phoenix, community colleges, high schools, trade schools, and four-year institutions in your vicinity. Interview people who work in your field and ask them for their opinions about the demand for teachers in your area of expertise.

Continue your research.

Websites: For Internet access, type: http://www. followed by the web address.

> *Google.com*
> Go to advanced search and query by subject matter interest.
>
> *Pluck.com and Info.com*
> Additional search engine services

Read the section of this book that describes fanciful jobs and home businesses.

Prepare your marketing tools

A targeted cover letter and a well-crafted biography will give you an advantage over others seeking this career path. Both will demonstrate your ability to communicate, a critical component to landing teaching positions.

You will need verifiable references as to your character and competency. You should be prepared for a comprehensive background check.

Across America – Real people, real stories... Craig Williamson

Craig Williamson has added the teaching profession to his portfolio of career adventures and finds it to be one of the most rewarding activities he has encountered. Here's his story:

"I have had a varied career beginning with 15 years in international and commercial banking. I then moved into the management consulting field where I have been delivering and marketing human resources consulting services for the past 14 years. I developed strong skills in career planning, job search training and personal and executive coaching. I especially enjoy facilitating outplacement workshops where I support individuals in planning and developing their job search campaigns. This training experience prepared me for taking the plunge into teaching.

I teach on a part-time basis at two universities: University of Phoenix and Western International University. Both are units of The Apollo Group, one of the fastest growing private university systems in the world. I continue to do outplacement consulting and executive coaching, and the flexibility of teaching at the university level is an excellent fit with my current career portfolio. My love of training adults led me to pursue formal teaching positions.

Qualifications to become a teacher vary depending on the type of teaching you do. Working for a school system requires college coursework in a particular discipline, general education courses and, in most schools, student teaching experience. A state teaching credential is also required. While most teaching posts at the elementary and secondary level are full time in nature, part-time opportunities are available including substitute teaching. An advantage to being a substitute is the small amount of time and effort in preparing for a day of teaching, but one must be very flexible in their schedule and be able to respond immediately to a school's need.

Qualifying as a lecturer or a professor at the college and university level typically requires a graduate degree (Master's or PhD) in a particular field. Community college systems usually require a credential, which is relatively easy to qualify for if you have the advanced degree and experience in the field you wish to teach. To round out your preparation, I recommend developing a personal reading regimen that includes books and articles on current educational techniques.

I pursued opportunities with the University of Phoenix (UOP) and Western International University (WIU) because of the flexibility that both provided to me as a full time working professional. Their parent organization, The Apollo Group, is in the forefront of the private university field that specializes in programs for adults, especially working adults. Therefore, the flexibility that UOP and WIU afford their students is also extended to the instructors.

I found the selection process to be very efficient. I submitted my resume and was called in to join five other candidates to meet with a new faculty assessor. Each one of us was told to prepare a ten minute presentation on a subject of our choosing, which we presented to the assessor and the other candidates. I then submitted a written document on adult learning perspectives and had a one-to-one interview with a staff member. The final step in the process was to co-facilitate a course with a professor which began with me observing a couple of class sessions, then co-presenting several others and finally being the sole instructor for the final class sessions.

Preparing to teach courses to adults requires strong facilitation skills. Adult learning methodology shows us that adults need an interactive classroom environment to be taught effectively, unlike the traditional lecture environment when teaching a class of 18 to 22 year-olds in the regular college/university setting. In adult learning, you never assume that you know more than the students. They obviously bring strong skills and knowledge bases to the class. In this regard I find it very challenging to teach adults, and I appreciate the need to stay abreast of the subject matter. With my background in international banking, general management and human resources consulting, I am teaching courses in organizational behavior, human resources, business management, communications and international business.

My advice to anyone thinking of teaching is to decide not only what subjects you have experience in, but those that you have a passion for. Then, research the organizations that provide courses and degree programs in that discipline. Public and private institutions are sprouting up and evolving quickly to meet the increased demand for courses and programs in a wide variety of subject areas. A growing need exists for subject matter experts to teach course offerings ranging from a one session presentation on a particular business issue to graduate degree programs. Decide when and how much you want to teach. Post-secondary adult learning programs emphasize evening and weekend classes, whereas other institutions have a full day time schedule as well.

Develop a clear understanding of the requirements to become "Certified" with a specific institution, and make sure you learn what's expected of a teacher, especially in preparing the curriculum. Some institutions have developed standard lesson plans that include specific tests and PowerPoint presentations. While this doesn't require as much time and effort in preparing to teach a class, it also creates a structured environment that might not be a match with your style. Other institutions are more flexible in allowing the instructor to decide how to teach the material. While they may provide templates of presentations to use, it's up to each teacher to decide how the presentation will be made.

I thoroughly enjoy the stimulating environment of adult learning. It is challenging and tiring at times, especially since I mainly teach during the evenings and on weekends. But it forces me to stay on top of my profession, and I find myself learning a lot from my students while I gain the satisfaction of supporting them as they further their education."

Team Ensemble Players

Who are they?

*In business, as in music,
the ensemble cast
leverages individual contributions
for shared benefit.*

*The single voice is a song.
The collective voice is the Hallelujah Chorus.
It is in teaming
where fun and profit meet.*

Independent professionals who want to build a practice know that pooling their efforts is one of the best ways to work in the increasingly de-jobbed world of the future. Teams include executives who band together to startup or turnaround firms. They include professionals from groups that have been most affected by corporate change, groups such as: Informational Technology, Human Resources and Marketing.

What you need to know.

By banding together, either formally or informally, people of similar, but not identical skill sets, increase their reach into the job market. When team members are accountable to one another as well as to a client, they enhance their early success and the probability of continued success.

For example:

Let us imagine that your expertise is in union negotiation and management. A colleague is an expert non-union advisor to management. Another is a specialist in executive development. A fourth is expert at developing project teams. From the organization's (buyer's) perspective, they can count on deep expertise in any or all of these critical areas.

It is fair to state that organizations' benefit because they:

- Receive just-in-time (JIT) help from reliable, experienced professionals.
- Effectively manage their costs when engaging help to meet specific, temporary needs.
- Can pay for results or time-limited engagements.
- Increase productivity without increasing their payroll.
- Buy services from a "one stop" shop – one with whom they can develop trusted relationships because all members of the team are accountable to one another as well as to the client.

Your team's services, presented collectively, benefit you by:

- Increasing the probability of engagement because of demonstrable, targeted expertise.
- Allowing all members of the team to "play big." This perception will reassure the client.
- Continuing to build your client list at a faster rate than a solo effort might achieve.
- Providing you with collaborative advantages – team members who can help you solve problems.
- Ensuring that you continue to grow your business and make more money with less down time.
- Offsetting the loneliness of working solo without full commitment to a formal partnership.

Some of the times that organizations need additional expert help include:

1. During startup.
2. At times of high growth.
3. During turnaround or restructuring.
4. When there is insufficient knowledge in the core team to tackle a project.
5. When there is not enough staff to handle a sudden upswing in workload.
6. When time demands specialized expertise that should be bought externally, not built internally.
7. At times of cyclical, or seasonal, demand.
8. During times of business crisis.

Certain teams craft relatively formal agreements that outline the terms and conditions of participation. This type of team may agree upon a certain number of new "gigs" each associate must be accountable for bringing to the team within a pre-set timeframe. These teams may split some costs of marketing collateral materials. They will usually formally agree upon values and business standards as well as how they will share prospects and clients.

If your preference is to formalize arrangements, familiarize yourselves with the rules! A few words of caution to "formal" teams.

- You may be entering dangerously unknown waters.
- There may be legal or tax implications of which you are not aware.

Other teams have relatively informal teaming standards basically granting the "right of first refusal" when referring prospects or clients to identified team associates.

There are advantages and disadvantages to both. In either case, some form of understanding will help to manage the expectations of all team members.

Explore the opportunities.

Interview people, and teams of people, actively engaged in your interest areas.

Continue your research.

Websites: For Internet access, type: http://www. followed by the web address.

> *turnaround.org*
> The Turnaround Management Association is the official name of one of the largest organizations that reflect a teaming approach to helping organizations at various stages of change.
>
> *Google.com*
> Go to Google's advanced search and enter the following key words: teaming, team contracting.
>
> *Pluck.com and Info.com*
> Additional search engine services

Books, magazines and periodicals:

> *Teaming*, the best book we have read on the subject by Paul and Sarah Edwards, is a must read for anyone contemplating this exciting way of doing business.
>
> *Consultative Selling*, the latest edition, by Mack Hanan is a second "must read" for prospective teams.

Prepare your marketing tools.

> Biographies of all team members
>
> Branding statement
>
> Brochure(s)
>
> Business cards
>
> Business plan
>
> Contracts
>
> Cover letters, approach letters and other standardized marketing correspondence
>
> Website(s)

Temping

Who are they?

To distinguish "Temps" from other workers in the Independent or Free Agent world, think of this work as the domain of "skilled" workers. Administrators, support personnel, seasonal retail workers, data entry and computer operators are but a few of the people who do well in the world of the temps!

The fastest job market gains in America are in the temporary world. As one result, temporary jobs offer a good refuge in the new economy.

What you need to know.

There are thousands of temporary agencies in America. These agencies place people with a variety of skills in almost any size or type of organization.

The following benefits of working temp jobs are appealing to more and more American workers every day because:

- Using an agency is the easiest way into a temporary position as it does not require that you sell or market your own services directly to prospective employers. The agency markets your services and pays you.

- You can use temporary agencies to obtain work that can turn into traditional full-time employment.

- This is an excellent way to maintain some income with plenty of time off between assignments.

- Some agencies will work with you to improve your skills.

Top Ten Tips for Temps Using Agencies

1. Talk with people who temp and ask them to share their experience with agencies – good and bad.

2. Ask your present or former employer whom they recommend in trusted temporary agencies; then request that they introduce you to an agency with which they have an existing relationship.

3. If you have preferred employers in mind for your temporary assignments, make some calls to check which agencies would make the best fit for your purposes. Most mid-sized to large employers maintain contractual agreements with a few preferred agencies.

4. Register with several temporary agencies to ensure that you receive frequent opportunities to work.

5. Use the agency skills training and computer testing to validate or improve your skills.

6. Treat all agencies with respect. Be available, reliable, and generously competent. They will come through for you time and again.

7. Never leave an assignment without appropriate notice and a compelling reason.

8. In the beginning of your relationship, stay open to new assignments, even those that may require a longer drive than you would prefer. You need to establish a reputation based on reliability, responsiveness, and trust.

9. Always be the first (before the client organization calls) to tell your agency of any problems or issues.

10. At the conclusion of your assignment, write a note to the organization (your agency's client) that expresses your appreciation for their confidence in you. Include the name of your placing agency in the text of the correspondence.

11. Send the placing agency a copy as well.

Typical temp jobs include:

Word processors, administrators, clerical support personnel, secretaries, light and skilled labor, receptionists, call-center operators and so forth.

Typical assignments include:

Vacation or leave-of-absence replacements, "try before you buy" jobs that offer long-term opportunities for regular, full-time employment, and staffing during peak times.

Continue your research.

Websites: For Internet access, type: http://www. followed by the web address.

Craigslist.com
You name it, they list it.

Kellyservices.com
Kelly Services for clerical and administrative support openings.

Manpower.com
Manpower offers everything from blue-collar work to sophisticated technical gigs.

Monster.com and Yahoo.com
Posts a list of temporary agencies that you can use to search by geographical preference.

Spherionstaffingsolutions.com
Fortune Magazine's "Top 5" pick for a broad range of skilled worker openings.

Google.com
Go to Google's advanced search and enter the following key words: temporary agencies, temporary industry, temporary jobs.

Pluck.com and Info.com
Additional search engine services

Prepare your marketing tools.

Chronological resume detailing skills and competencies.

Cover letter outlining specific assignment preferences and geographic limitations.

Letters of recommendation specifically describing your skills, attitude and reliability.

Traditional Re-Employment with a Twist

Once upon a time...

A long, long time ago, in the land of what was "then,"
there were jobs and careers that Americans called "permanent."
Some people still refer to regular, full-time jobs in this way.
They are behind the times.

The word "permanent" passed into history many, many years ago.
If you still use the word — stop.
The word itself sets a false expectation.
"Permanency" in and of itself is a myth!

No job is "permanent."
No organization will promise lifetime employment.
Nothing is "permanent."
Not even us!

The End.

The moral of this story is:
"Don't let misused language lull you into a false sense of security."
Security lives where it always has — inside of you!

Who are the regular, full-time workers?

They are people who work a regularly scheduled workweek, usually 40 hours, and receive the organization's benefits of employment, such as: paid time off, sick leave or personal time, compensation for holidays and, above all, insurance benefits.

What you need to know.

In today's typical organization, both the employer and their employees may leave one another "At Will" for any reason at any time.

Does this sound "permanent" to you?

If you think so, study the lifecycle of the firms you are so eager to join and you will readily observe that it is more likely you will be around in five years than the organization you are targeting will, at least, in its present form.

Mergers, acquisitions, divestitures, business alliances, hirings, firings, outsourcing, insourcing, and shared sourcing – you name it and you can place a strong bet that one of these organizational changes will drive workforce change long before you might voluntarily leave for other opportunities.

And yet, you say you still choose to pursue your next opportunity in what has been your traditional full-time career path?

Do so.

Just don't make permanency a priority.

Don't talk about security. It will scare prospective employers.

Instead, talk about your contribution.

This new way of looking at work should free you up to look at the job itself and the value that you can bring to the organization for however long the relationship should last.

Validate your interest.

Review your responses in Steps 1 and 2.

Ask yourself the following questions:

1. *Do you have a specific fund of knowledge to offer that employers currently need?*

    There are many, many economists, business leaders and futurists who believe that the only way for mature individuals to have any chance of long-term financial success is to develop specific knowledge with which youth cannot compete. Specialized expertise is, in fact, the way of the guru and the sage.

    Your 50's and 60's are the time when your investment in knowledge pays off. Your 40's are when you should be deepening your expertise, even if you are still in a role that requires the talent of the generalist.

    There is a new story being told in a New America.
    The age of the specialist is upon us.
    This is maturity's advantage.

2. *Do you have a verifiable track record of success?*

    "Nothing succeeds like success!"

    In the case of securing re-employment in your traditional career path, this saying still holds absolutely true. Verifiable success is your ticket to continue to work.

For example, when a targeted firm is in trouble, in a state of rapid contraction or expansion – during turnaround or startup, that is your cue to prominently feature your successful record in any of these areas.

In another example, if a targeted firm is introducing new products or services in an area where your experience is solid, you may hold the winning ticket! You, your resume, and your references had better shout, not whisper, this expertise.

Do your homework. Link your record to their needs. Do not be all things to all people, even if the role you are seeking is labeled as a "generalist." There is always a need for unique experience.

3. *Do you have the demonstrable energy and drive that signals to employers you are up for challenges?*

In an era of smaller profits, today's organizations are trying to control costs by staying as small as they can. What this means to you is that more and more core organizations consist of smaller staffs of regular, full-time employees, smaller than ever existed in the past. These core staffs are working harder than ever.

"Older" to some interviewers implies less energy and less ability to cope with the increasing productivity demands in the face of smaller staffs. You have to clearly demonstrate energy, drive, and the capacity to thrive in the new workforce. If you can't, you will likely be passed over. Demonstrating fitness has several dimensions. One is the language you choose, another is the physical stamina, and still another is the perception of the person who is making the decision to hire you.

While it really is fine to be older, you had better look and sound like you are up for the demands of a regular, full-time job. Are you?

4. *Do you have the courage to network and to influence connections rather than relying upon mailing resumes, using agencies, the Internet, and traditional means of re-employment?*

The simple fact is that people hire people. The skill to network and to leverage connections is one that mature workers must rely upon. If you will not learn to network effectively, it is unlikely that you will find many opportunities in a regular, full-time role within an organization. At all but the highest levels of organizations, there is plenty of age-discrimination against 50 year-olds when they barge in through traditional methods of re-employment.

At the highest levels, meaning the "C" levels, you will still find this type of discrimination – only it hits a little later.

Strange isn't it that we don't even think our Presidential candidates hit their stride until their 60's or even their 70's? One of our most admired presidents, Ronald Reagan, managed well into his '70's. The double standards are amazing. We would guess it is fair to conclude that our populace thinks it is more demanding to lead one of our large organizations than it is to lead America itself.

Recruiters in most organizations are young. They may have been trained in the finer aspects of the laws surrounding discriminatory practices, but they are still prey to hidden, youthful prejudice and biases that our generation helped to reinforce a few short years ago. A walk through the recruiters' doors may result in your being screened-out rather than screened-in. Likewise, going in through the Internet can also screen you out, particularly if you have been foolish enough to list all your jobs chronologically back to the days when you first graduated high school or college.

However, most hiring managers have been around for a while. While they may or may not be your age, it is likely that they have reached the point where they perceive advantage in hiring a balanced workforce of both the experienced and inexperienced – Masters, Career Climbers, and Apprentices, i.e., mature, experienced individuals, mid-level careerists, and eager young people in the early stages of their careers.

When you learn to leverage your network so that it earns you entrée and introductions to hiring managers, you greatly increase your chances of being valued for both your experience and your maturity.

5. *Have you continued to stay abreast of workplace changes, especially the routine use of standard business technology?*

   Unless you are selling in-demand expertise that stands alone on its own merit, it is expected that you will be able to use the standard tools available in virtually all offices or places of business today. Routinely using e-mail, maintaining an electronic calendar, and using word processing are the most basic communications tools you will need.

   Before you resist learning these simple lessons, know that the most difficult aspect of using technology is learning how to type. Working or not, take a class. Basic technical knowledge is fun, fast, and painless. Most importantly, it is expected.

6. Do organizations really need your full-time talent?

   Remember that while organizations' bottom lines may improve from time-to-time, the truth is that fluctuating productivity decreases the demand for full-time workers some of the time. Business is producing more with less. In other words, gross domestic earnings may continue to go up, but payroll employment is going down. Furthermore, the technologically driven productivity boom of the '90's that expanded technology globally permitted American organizations to find cheaper but sufficiently talented workers wherever they may be. Furthermore, companies are struggling with out-of-control medical costs and consumers are gradually slowing down their spending.

   You had better be certain of the need for organizations to pay for your full-time talent before you chase traditional re-employment.

   But...here's the important news. If they have a need, and you know that nothing is "permanent" – what's to stop you from offering to come in and help on an interim basis? More often than not, these interim roles have a way of opening up regular, full-time opportunities.

If your answers to all six questions are "yes" – It is probable that you will find opportunities in a traditional career path. Look deeply into the meaning of each question before you try to open a regular, full-time door that may be closing behind you.

Finally, commit to memory the substance behind the words of Alan Murray, Washington Bureau Chief of *The Wall Street Journal* and author of *The Wealth of Choices*, in which he wrote:

> "The workplace is becoming a marketplace. In the old days, pay levels, benefits and promotions within American corporations were determined as much by social convention as by supply and demand...The modern worker faces a ruthless, market-driven world that compensates people according to the market's valuation of their worth. Young employees may earn far more than their older colleagues, if they bring skills or talents in hot demand. Pay disparities in the workplace are frequent and huge."

What do you have to do?

Keep up with marketplace trends!

Now is the time to deepen your subject matter expertise. If you are planning to expand your fund of knowledge, be certain to study the job market and focus your attention on the realities of today's (and tomorrow's) marketplace needs.

Continue to learn!

Now is the time to return to school or to invest in new certifications or earn a vital degree. Accept reality. If you do not have a record of success that meets a prospective employer's needs, you may not be able to leverage your way back into a traditional role. Take heart, advanced education or training is easier and faster to obtain than ever. Workplace credit, extended studies, and government subsidies – all are available to you in a variety of venues. Classrooms are filled with people of all ages.

Step up to the plate!

Now is the time to take an extra course of action if you are still employed. Volunteer to participate in new projects that advance your knowledge. A high-profile role in a trouble spot within your current organization adds a verifiable claim of expertise to your record.

Bump up your networking activity!

Now is the time to increase the reach of your network. Networking is the most effective way to obtain new employment. It accounts, by even conservative estimates, for over 70% of new employment opportunities for mature workers. In the very face of knowing this to be the truth, most people will not network effectively, often resorting to ineffectual approaches rather than risk the rejection they perceive is coming their way.

Since networking is both a skill and an art, it is impossible to cover the subject effectively without ensuring that you learn the skill and practice the art. It is the reluctance to practice the art, not learning the skill that stands in most people's way of reaching their work-related goals.

Finally, remind yourself, when you are dragging your networking feet, that there is solid evidence that supports the need for networking. From the University of Southern California's recent study on the effectiveness of networking for job seekers over the age of fifty-five to AARP's data, the simple truth is that networking is the most favorable way for mature workers to be re-employed.

Focus your goals!

Now is the time to envision your future and focus your new goals. The sooner you write down your goals, the sooner your odds will improve for getting what you want.

Get the facts, engage a coach, and build, or re-build, your self-confidence!

And, this is the place to remind you to engage a coach. You've hired little league coaches, tutors, and personal trainers, haven't you? What could be more important than being able to continue your career and safeguard your income?

Remember these facts; they will increase your self-confidence:

- There will be a labor shortage precisely because the number of people in the next generation, immediately behind the Boomers, will not replace our numbers. For example, did you know that the Employment Policy Foundation projects that as early as 2010 there will be a need for more jobs in the U.S. labor market than the projected workforce will be able to fill?
- The next generation does not necessarily bring all the skills or education essential for jobs.
- And, did you know that women and minority men will make up two-thirds of the American workforce within 20 years?
- Along the same lines, did you know that by 2030 it is projected by the 2004 Corporate Executive Board that the majority of managers and professionals will be women?

Generational forces are upon us.

Diversity forces are upon us.

Companies will have to adjust, just as you must.

Explore the opportunities.

We've told you how. Get going.

Copy and Clip

Refrigerator Note:

Remember that companies will come to realize the benefits of a workforce that includes all qualified individuals.

And, if the only way to get there from here is to accelerate the rejection thrust at you by unenlightened employers, do just that!

Accelerate their rejection — increase your efforts!

Continue your research.

Websites: For Internet access, type: http://www. followed by the web address.

Careerjournal.com, Careers.org and the Jobhuntersbible.com
Good starting points.

Ncoa.org
The National Council on Aging will help you to overcome even more myths about aging. They will help to increase your confidence as time moves on.

Google.com
Go to Google's advanced search and enter the following key words: job boards, professional careers, mid-career opportunities, mature careers, third careers.

Pluck.com and Info.com
Additional search engine services

Books, magazines and periodicals:

Boom or Bust. Read: Real People, Real Stories. For an extra measure of bravery, read ahead to Step 6 for ideas to overcome challenges and barriers to achieving your goal of regular, full-time employment. To maintain your sense of humor, read the section on Humor, Maturity's Advantage. Arm yourself with knowledge and overcome challenges by reading the Debunking the Myths section.

Prepare your marketing tools.

For additional information and examples, refer to the Marketing Tools section of the book.

Branding statement

Business cards

Business plan

Employment agreement (if you are an executive)

Objective statement that links your "brand" with organizational need

Professional biography

Targeted resume– consider a combined format

Written campaign communications for traditional re-employment

Across America – Real people, real stories...Anonymous

The following story of traditional re-employment — with a twist — is a fine example of someone who escaped from the large corporate world into a smaller organization. Our friend decided to remain anonymous, but the story is worth reading if you are seeking a new way to achieve a bit more balance while leveraging your experience.

"After years in corporate life, I transitioned to a small company in order to fulfill a number of lifestyle goals. I gained a lot from my experience in the corporate world, but I was ready for a change.

I grew up in the Midwest, spent four years in the Navy and then started up the corporate ladder with an international steel company. Beginning in sales, I progressed into sales management, then operations. Relocations took my family and me to several Midwestern cities and then to California where I got to start up a communications and marketing function for the firm. I thrived in positions of greater responsibility and was rewarded handsomely for it. After an acquisition, I was offered a post at corporate headquarters and was responsible for corporate services and employee services. So I had a well-rounded career that gave me a lot of room to grow professionally and earn an excellent living to support my family.

As I reached my early fifties, I started to realize that my philosophy toward my work and my life was changing. I was getting tired of striving for more and more, both in terms of responsibility and in acquiring material things. I became interested in eastern philosophy and saw the need to transcend into the "Wisdom" half of life. I realized that I had never completely bought into the corporate lifestyle and the trappings that came with it.

So when my company went through a major reorganization and I was "Downsized", I saw it as an opportunity to investigate other career directions that were a better fit for my interests and me. I received outplacement assistance with a major consulting firm, and I took full advantage of receiving support in assessing where I had been in my career and developing new work and life objectives. I wasn't ready for a major career change, but it was evident that I needed to find an opportunity that provided a better work/life balance. As a result, I decided to return to the Midwest and accept a general manager position with a mid-sized steel company.

After two years with the new company, I realized that I needed another change. I wanted a career opportunity that would keep me energized and passionate about work but that would allow me the time and opportunity to pursue even more personal activities. A former colleague of mine urged me to investigate a firm he had just joined in Arizona. It was the U.S. subsidiary of an Indian company that developed and marketed accounting and financial forecasting software. I accepted a district manager position that required a background in general management as well as sales and marketing.

This job with a small company has given me the opportunity to get more involved in outreach activities in the community, and my wife and I are able to spend a lot more time getting to know our neighbors.

Overall, I feel that my work and personal life are in much better balance than ever before."

Venture Capitalists

Who are they?

Venture Capitalists back global start-ups across town or across the world. VC firms provide large amounts of capital to different industries and to organizations in different stages of development. Firms that fund initial startups and/or first rounds of financing may not fund second and third rounds.

If you are seeking venture capital, getting a venture capitalist to respond to your interests almost always requires a referral by a respected business associate whom they know. If you can gain this level of interest from an individual in a VC firm, you should use him/her as your coach.

People who are attracted to work in this field are investment professionals, high net worth individuals, and high-profile folks who can afford to play!

What you need to know.

According to VentureOne, as reported in *Forbes Magazine* in December 2003, the number of venture-backed IPO's in the first nine months of 2000 reached 184. In the first nine months of 2003, that number was 8.

In early 2004, we began inching back, one venture at a time, but with some remarkable differences from those traditional investments of the past. By mid-year 2004, the venture-backed startups were bouncing back at a slightly faster clip. Looking ahead, there is cause for optimism.

The fewer the venture-backed startups, the fewer the Initial Public Offerings. IPOs in America have remained constrained. VC firms have cautiously backed few startups and still — one sound we have been hearing is the closing of several, well-known VC doors.

Nevertheless, if we can heat up needed technology in high-cost, highly regulated places like Silicon Valley, all bets are off and the VC's will continue to defy the odds by doing business in places like California. Businesses (and careers to support these businesses) will still look very different than in the past. In other words, we may be developing the technologies here for someone else to produce there.

From a career and work perspective, it is important to watch the VC's and their investments if you wish to continue to work in America in the new economy. Watch carefully and you will learn where to invest your existing talent, your commitment to continuing education, and your hard earned dollars.

At the moment, VC funding appears to be focused on the biotech industry, including medical equipment firms that are gearing up for emergent innovations. Although biotech is a darling of the VC's, it is important to remember that these are not the only organizations receiving funding. A sidebar comment suggests that some biotech investments will pay off because of advances in products for an aging population.

A growing trend is that venture-supported small firms are performing a greater share of total U.S. research and development. According to the National Science Foundation, the dollar value of small company R&D rose from $4.4 billion in 1984 to an estimated $40.1 billion in 2003. One conclusion you might jump to is rather obvious: small companies are providing much of the fuel of innovation!

U.S. Venture Capital investment still dominates global investment. Our collective wealth, at this moment in time, is helping to bridge the gap between past VC failures and a future where alliances between former VC firms will accelerate and the smaller firms will close.

Continue your research.

Websites: For Internet access, type: http://www. followed by the web address.

Nvca.org
The National Venture Capital Association will provide you with comprehensive information on Venture Capital.

Google.com
Go to Google's advanced search and enter the following key words: venture capital firms, venture capital, VC's.

Pluck.com and Info.com
Additional search engine services

Books, magazines and periodicals:

Forbes, Money, Inc., Entrepreneur and *VentureOne*, the classic sources of research and knowledge for those who wish to follow work trends as well as investment opportunities.

Volunteers

Who are they?

There is a correlation between growing older and an increased desire to share experience and knowledge with other members of the community. This "need to give something back" is provocative to many people around the age of 50. By the age of 60, the call to "give back" will often become profound.

> ***If you want to leave a legacy,
> volunteering is one way to achieve this goal.***

You may choose to use your passion for one cause or another as leverage into a new world of voluntary service.

Others who have entered the realm of the volunteers, include:

> People who have lost their so-called "permanent" corporate jobs and who are reluctant to start hunting for another job. When they take the time to step back and re-evaluate how they are spending their lives, many people set new goals that include some form of volunteerism.

> Some people who have experienced life's tough challenges. Personal illness, the death of a parent, a child who has failed to thrive and many other life accidents are their motivation to enter volunteerism. These people may be more in touch with their feelings than those of us who have emerged into mid-life scar-free. They have walked a painful path and have a greater than usual appreciation for others who share their common burdens.

> A few lucky folks who are financially independent. They may view volunteerism as an opportunity to retain their spark of commitment and involvement. These people are well suited to the career path of the very active volunteer.

When your answers align with one of these scenarios, you are ready for a serious look at a new strategy, one where people work for the opportunity to meaningfully contribute to the common good and where they often find another chance to reach their full potential.

What you need to know.

As a first step, consider the value of revisiting your introspective work – the self-assessment where you began this journey. Assessment is a process of learning who you are and who you are becoming. This is your opportunity to renew dreams and refresh your life purpose. Most importantly, self-assessment allows you to integrate who you are with what you do, of particular importance in this career field.

Next, the following ideas will help you to find the volunteer group that satisfies your interests.

1. Investigate your hobbies. Is there something you have been doing all along that particularly matters to you?

2. Review your life circumstances. Have you or your loved ones been touched by chronic illness or accidents?

3. Have you met the challenge of caring for an aging parent? Do you want to help others avoid the pitfalls and traps you have experienced?

4. Are you a parent or grandparent with an especially warm spot in your heart for children?

5. Has there been a role model or mentor who has inspired you by their contributions to a certain volunteer organization?

6. Are you vitally concerned about some aspect of our society, so much so that you feel compelled to help in an important way?

People just like you create profound new visions for their future because of circumstances such as those described. By this stage of life, you should have a clear view of areas that interest you.

According to a 2002 survey sponsored by Civic Ventures, a non-profit organization founded by Marc Freedman (author of *Prime Time*), older Americans would "commit to volunteering if they received a small incentive for their service, such as discounts on prescription drugs" or other small stipends to offset the costs associated with volunteering. Civic Venture's spokespersons go on to say that "offering such an incentive could double the current older adult volunteer workforce."

Sidebar: The section on stipend work offers opportunities that offset the costs of doing important work that is very similar to volunteerism.

Explore the opportunities.

The new non-profit communities.

New communities just now emerging onto the scene are worth exploring. Some of these communities will fill the looming needs created by our own changing circumstances such as longer life spans. You can help to re-shape the course of our social, cultural, and economic history.

Schools and recreation centers.

The need is very high. Some of America's children cannot read and write at a level that will help them to realize their potential. You can help them.

Organizations and government agencies.

Did you know that, at any given time, between 5 and 10% of Peace Corps volunteers are older than 50? There are other government agencies to explore as shown in the recommended websites.

Continue your research.

Websites: For Internet access, type: http://www. followed by the web address.

Faithinaction.org
Cares for neighbors with long-term health needs.

Civicventures.org
Non-profit, parent of Experience Corps

Experiencecorps.org and Seniorcorps.org
Use your experience to benefit society.

Globalvolunteers.org
The Peace Corps with a twist.

Peacecorps.gov
Yes, that Peace Corps

Google.com
Go to Google's advanced search and enter key words that match your interest.

Pluck.com and Info.com
Additional search engine services

Books, magazines and periodicals:

Age Power by Ken Dychtwald, Ph.D.

Leading Without Power by Max De Pree

Longevity Revolution by Theodore Roszak

PrimeTime by Mark Freedman

The Creative Age by Gene Cohen, M.D.

Prepare your marketing tools.

Develop a biography linking your interests and qualifications to specific needs of targeted non-profit organizations. Be certain to include a skills section.

Web Merchants and *e*Bay Sales
— Income and Fun —
on the Internet Highway

According to the Department of Labor,
Internet revenues will soon exceed U.S. auto industry sales.
By the time you read this, it may be true.

Part-time seller, or online entrepreneur, the rush to selling on the Web is,
in spite of the huge numbers of users, still in its early years.
Who knows where the excitement will lead?

Who are they?

They are the old, the young, the housebound, the pioneers, the educated, the clever. In other words, the people who use the Internet as a business are just like you!

*e*Bay began as a business for the newly jobless and a few hearty home workers. Today, more than 150,000 people earn a full-time living selling everything from anti-aging creams to automotive aftermarket parts through *e*Bay. This firm has created something so revolutionary that its hub for global commerce is a new economy in and of itself.

What you need to know.

Check out the advantages of selling on *e*Bay:

> It is such big business that there is even an *e*Bay University that will teach you how to sell online.

> There are payment-processing systems that allow your buyers to make secure payments 24/7.

> Products and services are subject to review by the consumer. Quality counts.

> Selling on *e*Bay is an easy way to make a smooth transition to the Web Merchant world.

> *e*Bay is more, much more, than a way to get rid of stuff in your attic.

> You can make a part-time or full-time living off of *e*Bay.

> You can actually start a store on eBay with a virtual "storefront."

One of the best books about eBay is "*eBay for Dummies*" by Marsha Collier. According to Marsha's biography, she started this version of a merchandising business after the birth of her daughter. Since then, she has been featured in *Entrepreneur Magazine*, received the "Small Business of the Year" award in California and has found fun, fame, and fortune for her efforts.

A good way to dunk your toe into this type of business is to start by selling one item at a simple auction.

You may then graduate to new ways of auctioning merchandise. A good example is through Dutch Auctions, suitable for selling multiple items at a discounted price. There are Restricted Access Auctions for adult items and Private Auctions for selling private art collections and other high value items. You can run multiple auctions at one time. You can even buy software from eBay to setup and run these multiple auctions from home. There are many, many safeguards that benefit bidders and sellers, all of which are important to understand.

A few of the trends in this marketplace suggest that while there is no secret formula to success selling online, certain mainstream sales items move faster than others. Perennial favorites, such as books, coins, dolls, entertainment, and sports memorabilia are good merchandise choices.

Web Merchants:

Setting up your own Web Business as a home-based business is the next step in selling goods or services on the Web. This requires significantly more business savvy than using *eBay*'s tools and support. Plus, you will be responsible for your own marketing and other aspects of advertising.

You will need a business license to sell on the Web. You may need a city tax registration certificate as well. And, if you are doing business under a fictitious name, you will have to file a fictitious name statement. Since websites (URL's) may be changed on occasion, check sba.gov/hotlist/license.html for current State-by-State listings. There are restrictions as to what you can sell, business practices and serious issues surrounding the ethics of doing business by this method that are important to know. Otherwise you could receive more than a hand slap for mistakes in judgment.

As you learn more about selling over the Web, you will want to take the time to explore some of the web-based businesses that are proving successful.

A sampling of full-out Web-based businesses includes:
    Automotive parts
    Automobiles
    Books
    Collectibles, such as vintage dolls
    Consignment Items
    Estate Auctions
    Hobbies
    Games

Gift Items

Garage sale items

Retail products that you buy "off-season" and sell "on-season" (such as holiday items)

Validate your interest.

Review your responses in Steps 1 and 2.

Ask yourself:

1. Am I willing to invest a brief time in learning about the many ways to sell on the web?
2. If I choose to start a storefront on eBay, am I prepared to run every aspect of the business, including inventory management, shipping and billing?
3. Do I have a spouse or partner who is willing to pitch-in and help?

Continue your research.

Websites: For Internet access, type: http://www. followed by the web address.

Auctionstealer.com and auctionsniper.com
Offers strategies to buyers and information to sellers.

Ebay.com
Offers information on eBay, on their University as well as a guide to help you learn the basics of selling.

i-soldit.com
A chain of drop off stores that makes it easy for anyone to sell on eBay.

Paypal.com
Offers a secure online money transfer service between buyers and sellers.

Google.com
Go to Google's advanced search and enter the following key words: eBay University, sales training, sales organizations.

Pluck.com and Info.com
Additional search engine services

Books, magazines and periodicals:

The eBay for Dummies book is so comprehensive, so filled with the information you require, that it is recommended as one of only two resources to help get you started. The second is *How to Sell Anything on eBay...and make a Fortune* by Dennis Prince.

Entrepreneur magazine

WIRED magazine

Step 6

Gap Analysis — Challenges and Barriers

> *In the book, Life Launch, Frederic Hudson and Pamela McLean wrote that the most important ability for sixty year olds "is a capacity to vision and dream again, to imagine ways to add value to your life as old overtakes young."*
>
> **Just think...
> Isn't this ability just as important for you
> no matter what chronological age you are today?**

You have journeyed inward, looked at work trends and explored certain realities of the market. Review the opportunities you have explored and the many ways there are to work.

What do your best or most interesting opportunities look like so far?

_____
_____
_____
_____
_____
_____
_____

What stands between you and your best, or most interesting, opportunities?

_____
_____
_____
_____
_____
_____
_____

Time out.

Is what stands between you and your most interesting opportunities one, or more, of the following?

Check ( ) as many of the responses as they apply to you.

_____ 1. I am afraid of the unknown.

_____ 2. I lack self-confidence.

_____ 3. Employers or clients who view me as too old will reject me.

_____ 4. I have made too much money — I will be rejected because I appear too costly.

_____ 5. I am too fat, too skinny, too _____ too _____.

_____ 6. I lack certain skills or education to accomplish my goal.

_____ 7. I don't know how to network.

_____ 8. I haven't interviewed in years.

_____ 9. I don't know how to negotiate.

_____ 10. I am not a "sales" type. It feels like bragging if I talk about my accomplishments.

_____ 11. I don't know how to make my next step happen.

If you have checked any items between 1 and 5, you have identified your **challenges**.

If you have checked any items between 6 and 11, you have identified your **barriers.**

There is a distinct difference between meeting challenges and overcoming barriers.

Challenges.

When you define the word challenge, what comes to mind? Do you think of challenge as gearing up for what lies ahead? Does the word itself suggest possibilities or a blind, terrifying leap into an unknowable abyss?

When it comes to meeting challenges head-on, there is nothing to stop you but the myth and stereotypes that you – yourself – helped to create a few short years ago and, of course, that ugly, four-letter word – fear. Fear causes anxiety and anxiety causes inaction and negative thoughts. Negative fantasies ensure that you won't cope with change but will instead retreat into the familiar, even when clear evidence to the contrary indicates hope for success.

Think of the people whose stories you have read in this book and how the challenges that drove them forward into the future caused them to give up searching for a past that no longer exists.

> They faced their fear of the unknown, met the challenges of maturity, and are doing some of their best work today.
>
> They believed that their longer lives gave them new opportunities and broadened their personal and professional landscapes.
>
> They scoffed at the implication by some that humans are focused solely on survival and made the choice to strike out in a new direction — bravely facing dramatic and daunting change.
>
> They transcended that part of the brain that is solely driven by habit.
>
> They came to a place of absolutely knowing life still held responsibility and fulfillment for them.
>
> They accepted the challenge, invested an ounce of courage, a pound of knowledge, and found new meaning in that part of their lives we have labeled "work."

Get out of your own way.

Meeting your challenges is about taking that step into using the rest of your brainpower to discover your own future. It is about increasing your knowledge about the facts — not the myths — of maturity. It is about tapping into your own redeeming sense of humor and it is about exploring the stories of others who have found the courage to move forward in spite of their own challenges. You stand in your own way when you let challenges, real or perceived, defeat you.

They met some of the challenges by gaining new knowledge about the new workplace. It is your turn to learn.

Yesterday's Workplace

<u>Pay for Longevity and Pay for Performance</u>

You were paid on a so-called "merit" system — that is, as you progressed in the same or similar jobs, your performance and pay were reviewed periodically at a fixed point in time. You received increases in line with your largely time-based, so-called "merit" contributions.

As time went by, new systems emerged that linked pay to the performance of the individual as well as to the performance of the firm. In this system, even if the individual performed well but the firm did not, a pay increase was not an automatic outcome. The workforce consisted largely of regular, full-time employees and a few free agents.

<u>Infrequent Job Changes</u>

You were viewed as a dilettante if you changed jobs more than once or twice in a working lifetime. In large part this was because new skills were introduced slowly and change was incremental.

The New Workplace.

<u>Pay for Contributions and Pay for Results</u>

A growing number of firms are paying for promised results and added value, such as measurable customer satisfaction. Value — not time — is their driving force. Value is quantifiable experience — you can sell the value from the investment in your fund of experience.

The workplace, just like you, is learning to "deal" in this new economy. Firms are figuring out how to manage a flexible, indeed a global workforce and how to effectively hire or engage more and more free agents to meet Just-in-Time needs. By virtue of experience, you can help organizations to move forward into the future.

<u>Frequent Job Changes</u>

Increasingly, employers will engage you for your state-of-the-art skills and competencies. If you stay abreast of changes and learn new skills, you will remain employable regardless of how often you change jobs.

Yesterday's Workplace

Permanent Jobs

So-called permanent jobs were never really that. In fact, the change in traditional organizational language from permanent, full time employment to regular, full-time employment occurred more than 20 years ago.

Where were you? Did you notice?

You should have noticed the change in language from "permanent" to regular.... Say goodbye to permanency and even to the so-called regular workforce.

When the language of employment changed, the systemic change meant that more and more people were let go from regular jobs.

Temporary Jobs

Temporary jobs were largely used to (1) determine your general suitability for "permanent" employment – thus avoiding bad hiring choices and minimizing opportunities for litigation or to (2) supply interim, just-in-time, help when critically needed.

Implicit Agreements

This was the "implied" agreement that, as long as you kept your nose to the grindstone and the company didn't fail — you were safe.

The New Workplace

Employment "At Will"

When permanent jobs went the way of the past you became an "at will" employee.

The organization changed the implied contract with employees to a time where they could let you go for any reason or no reason at all, with minimal concern for inferred promises except for those requirements imposed by State and Federal Laws.

It is not a big step to imagine that At-Will employment can work for you as well as for the organization. You can use this to assure employers that you are comfortable with change and are looking forward to contributing your talent and skills to meet their needs for whatever time may be required.

Contingent Workforce

This is the term for the workforce that works in any way other than "regularly." It is predicted that between 40 and 50% of today's regular workforce will work contingently within the next 10 years. This change is happening now and it is good for all stages of the mature generation.

Explicit Agreements

This is the time for the "art of the deal." Explicit agreements for time, outcomes, and fees are gaining ground — learn how to deal.

Meeting the challenges of change.

Your shifting workplace.

It is important for you to connect the changes in the workplace with what is happening or what has happened to you.

It is your task to make these changes work for you.

How might you use the knowledge you've gained about workplace change to your advantage?

Meeting the challenges of change.

Facts work.

Your challenge is to separate fact from fiction.

> 1. Did you know that Boomers work harder, take less time off, and are less likely to jump ship than younger employees when rough waters threaten to sink the organization?
>
> 2. Did you know that we are able to learn and develop at a comparable rate to our younger counterparts and that we may cost employers less in medical benefits?

Do you think these are myths?

Increase your knowledge with facts about mature workers.

Dispel the myths that you, yourself, during your shortsighted youth, helped to create a few short years ago.

> **Myth:** Older workers can't work as hard as younger workers.
> **Fact:** The U.S. Department of Labor reports that people 50 and older work harder than younger workers.
>
> **Myth:** Older workers are sick more often.
> **Fact:** The American Council of Life Insurance reports that people 45 and older call in sick an average of 3.1 days per year compared with 3.8 days per year for those 44 and under.
>
> **Myth:** Older workers are more likely to jump ship when challenges surface.
> **Fact:** Many studies dispel that myth. For example, The National Association of Working Women reports that women over 45 are 88% less likely to leave voluntarily than their younger counterparts.
>
> **Myth:** We are just not as smart as younger workers.
> **Fact:** Another myth to be debunked. According to a recent Harvard Study, the ability to use an accumulated body of knowledge keeps rising throughout the lifetimes of healthy people.
>
> **Myth:** And, of course, somehow our memories are poor and we can't learn as well as younger folks.
> **Fact:** California State University compared the grades of students 25 and under with those 49 and older. There were no significant differences in the grades. The significant difference was that older people dropped out at a much lower rate.

Myth: Health insurance for mature workers is too costly.
Fact: Health insurance costs less for a 55-year-old employee than for a 35 year old with 2 dependents.

Myth: Older workers are paid too much for what they can contribute or what is valued.
Fact: It is well past the time for employers to realize that the only way for income to go is not "up." In today's competitive environment – income needs to be market-driven at any age if U.S. organizations are to compete. Employers and people alike should be far more concerned with paying for value received instead of for time invested.

How might you use the knowledge you've gained about workplace facts to your advantage?

Meeting the challenges of change.

Humor works.

Humor is maturity's advantage. On a broader scale it is, of course, a lifetime advantage. Humor is an important way to meet the challenges of change.

Whether interviewing for a job or a "gig", you will find some terrific advantages in maturity. You may even wish to make a certain "tongue in cheek" point or two to prospective employers about some of these advantages. At the least, you will find the opportunity to smile at the silly world we have created. Hopefully, you will even laugh a bit at yourself.

Check out the following humorous ways of presenting your advantages and smile.

> *You were educated when people could read AND write.*
> *By many reports, today's average high school senior has a vocabulary of 10,000 words as compared with high school seniors of your generation when your peers (including you) sported an average vocabulary of 25,000 words.*
>
> *You do not begin most sentences with the word "like."*
>
> *Even if you were foreign born, you bothered to learn English.*
>
> *You are confident about your ability to use words in context.*
> *For example, you know when to use the words lie and lay. Allow us to illustrate. You lie to your employer and lay with the customer.*
>
> *You can write a grammatically correct email or business letter.*
>
> *It is within the framework of your experience to automatically follow-up with a thank you note to each potential customer or prospective employer.*
>
> *Your written communications are logically presented in the U.S.'s preferred language – English.*
>
> *You are not tattooed and have not pierced your tongue or any other sensitive body part.*
>
> *You get to work on time each morning because employers can count on the fact that you were not likely to be out partying the night before since you are usually asleep by 9!*
>
> *You have no sick kids at home from whom to catch the measles, mumps or chicken pox.*
>
> *You understand that "business casual" does not mean cutoffs and a torn tee shirt.*
>
> *During a behavioral-type interview you may, at long last, have some credible past behaviors that really will predict future performance.*
>
> *Being overqualified might logically suggest that your prospective employer will get "more for their money" if they hire you.*
>
> *You are clear as to who you are and what you do best and can communicate both to a prospective employer or client.*

You have overcome the need to exaggerate. Your credentials, for better or worse, speak for themselves.

You don't have hidden agendas. The simple truth is that you may need and want to work.

You may have been with one firm for a very long time and some prospective employer may choose to view that as a liability...
.... but your previous employer has been acquired and re-acquired so often that you can legitimately claim you have worked for several companies without ever changing your parking spot.

If you are an older "Boomer" you may help a prospective employer to rest assured that you are not after their job.

It is legitimate to claim that it is far more likely you will be around in 5 years than their company will be... at least in its present state.

You know how to cope...you've already endured death, divorce and disaster. A little trouble at the office is a nit and staying the course during times of organizational stress is a walk in the park.

You can count change.

At long last, you understand company politics AND you know how to keep your mouth shut.

You can smile at many things that used to make you cry, such as an incompetent boss or an irrational customer.

You can deal with rejection and no longer need to take every business action personally.

You do not need to be home at any particular time. You are — finally — free.

You can point out that employers will reduce taxpayers' liability by encouraging older workers to work longer.

If you are old enough, you might suggest that you are more than willing to forgo health insurance since you have Medicare.
> *This works especially well if you also suggest that by working a shorter than standard workweek, the prospective employer's liability for providing you with benefits is NIL.*

Another humorous way of responding to the implication that you are overqualified is to say:
> *"Good news for you Mr./Ms. Employer... While you may perceive me as overqualified, I am proud to tell you that I am a committed underachiever."*

When confronted with an employer's concern that, by taking a job below your qualifications, you will likely move on as soon as something better comes along....you may want to resist responding with:

"If I could find a better job than this, I wouldn't be taking this crummy opportunity."

> *(Thanks to John Arslain for this one!)*

Meeting the challenges of change.

Preparation works.

On a more serious note, when it is suggested that you are overqualified, you should prepare your response long in advance of actually hearing the "charge."

By the time you are in your early '50's, being overqualified is one of the most difficult objections for most of us to deal with. At the same time, it is the most nonsensical and frequent excuse used for not hiring mature workers in the U.S. today.

Being overqualified simply means you are either too costly or too old but employers often hide behind inane excuses such as: *"We are concerned that you will change jobs as soon as something, more in keeping with your outstanding qualifications, comes along."*

Try this:

> Ask your prospective employer who they would rather have operate on them, a master surgeon or a surgical resident?
>
> Or, if the prospective employer is a luxury car buff, ask if they would rather have the master mechanic work on their 500 SL Mercedes, or the apprentice du jour?

First point made. What is wrong with being overqualified especially if they have serious problems for you to help address, such as startup, turnaround, or other organizational crisis.

Follow through with this:

> If you can help people to believe you are clearly committed to the work itself, they may realize your passionate commitment more than compensates for this "barrier."
>
> You may have to reassure them that, while money may always be a consideration since everyone wants to be paid fairly for work, money no longer fuels your career drive at this point. You have been prudent and careful in managing your finances and no longer must take jobs based solely upon position or income. You know what you are good at and that if what you do is what they happen to need – you will both win. In other words, "If you are the right person for this job, then position or income will not be a concern."

When all else fails:

> If you are up for a fight, you may choose to make a cause out of such subtly discriminatory practice. Complain to the CEO — He or she is likely to be older himself or herself!
>
> Go to the Equal Employment Opportunity Commission (EEOC) if you must. While your complaint may or may not help your cause, it may be important to your sense of self-worth. Step out into the fray and help the rest of your contemporaries who are facing the same issues!

You have added to what you know.

You have examined the changes in yesterday and today's workplace.

You have read the facts and the myths about older workers.

You have armed yourself with some humor and tactics.

What else is stopping you?

Meeting the challenges of change.

A GOOD JOLT WORKS!

This is where seemingly insurmountable challenges meet the lightning bolt of reality, and here is proof.

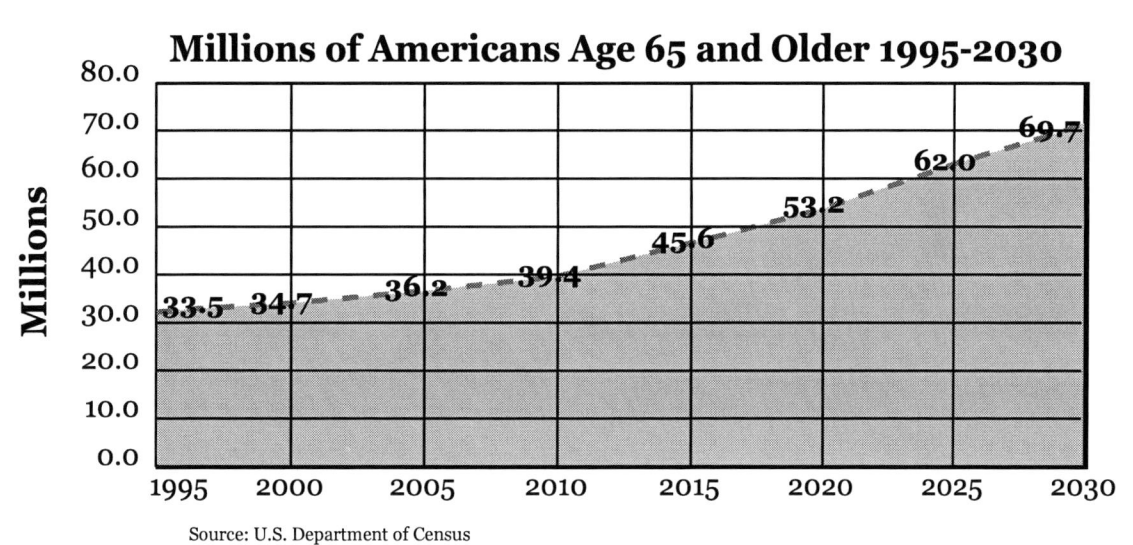

Millions of Americans Age 65 and Older 1995-2030

Year	Millions
1995	33.5
2000	34.7
2005	36.2
2010	39.4
2015	45.6
2020	53.2
2025	62.0
2030	69.7

Source: U.S. Department of Census

Building the courage needed to meet the challenges faced by the mature workforce takes knowledge, humor, planning and a good jolt!

If you are 40, 50, or 60, the odds are that you still have a very long time to live.

If you have 20 to 40 years to live, and you don't work in some capacity, ask yourself:

Will my finances sustain my preferred lifestyle?

Will I continue to be a vital and active member of society?

What are the implications to my emotional, financial, spiritual, physical, or intellectual health if I live 20 to 40 more years without work being some part of my life?

Give up fear – It is holding you back.

Here's another Brad Tipler quote to keep you motivated as you navigate the swirling challenges of change:

"Take the recent hydro dam project approval, and the water rising around your ankles, as clues that your job in local real estate is over.

...Learn to sell boats."

Read, reflect, and respond to the questions on the next few pages.

What are the emotional implications if I live a long life without some form of work as an outlet for my time and energy?

- ...Will I have enough fun?
- ...Will I still feel valued?
- ...Will I even bore myself?

Journal your thoughts and feelings:

_____
_____
_____
_____
_____
_____
_____
_____
_____
_____

What difference might I expect in the quality of my emotional life if I continue to work in some capacity?

- ...Will I find new adventures?
- ...Will I discover the satisfaction of doing something beneficial on behalf of others?
- ...Is it likely that I will be more joyful in my day-to-day life experience?

Journal your thoughts and feelings:

_____
_____
_____
_____
_____
_____
_____
_____
_____
_____

What are the financial implications if I live a long life and some form of work isn't a part of what I do with my time and energy?

...Can I meet my obligations or will I be dependent upon others?

...Will I have to sell my home?

...Will I have enough discretionary income for some extras?

Journal your thoughts and feelings:

What difference might I expect in the quality of my financial life if I continue to work in some capacity?

...Will I take that longed for vacation?

...Will I visit children and grandchildren more frequently than I might under other circumstances?

...Will I create fun and memories for my children that I would, otherwise, not be able to afford?

Journal your thoughts and feelings:

What are the spiritual implications if I live a long life and some form of work isn't a part of what I do with my time and energy?

   …Will I come to terms with why I was here in the first place?

   …Will I find enough value in the experience of aging?

   …Will I be bored and feel disenfranchised compared to others and risk losing ground spiritually?

Journal your thoughts and feelings:

What difference might I expect in the quality of my spiritual life if I continue to work in some capacity?

   …Will I stay connected with people who can help me to continue to develop my spirituality?

   …Will I find that doing good work itself might bring its own spiritual rewards?

   …Will I create new meaning in my own life as well as in the lives of others?

Journal your thoughts and feelings:

What are the physical implications if I live a long life without work as an outlet for my time and energy?

   ...Will I lose energy and become inactive?

   ...Will personal habits (like grooming) suffer if I don't maintain a disciplined routine?

   ...Will I grow old and infirm before my time?

Journal your thoughts and feelings:

_____
_____
_____
_____
_____
_____
_____
_____
_____
_____

What difference might I expect in the quality of my physical life if I continue to work in some capacity?

   ...Will continued working help me to stay committed to my physical well-being?

   ...Will continuing to work motivate me to optimize my health?

   ...Is work itself contributing to continued physical well-being?

Journal your thoughts and feelings:

_____
_____
_____
_____
_____
_____
_____
_____
_____
_____

What are the intellectual implications if I live a long life without work as an outlet for my time and energy?

   …Will my ability to gain new knowledge be impaired?

   …Will I lose my sense of curiosity and wonder?

   …Will I withdraw from opportunities to engage in intellectual discussions?

Journal your thoughts and feelings:

_____
_____
_____
_____
_____
_____
_____
_____
_____

What difference might I expect in the quality of my intellectual life if I continue to work in some capacity?

   …Will I be a more interesting person, from other perspectives, if I continue some form of work?

   …Is it possible that, in a significant way, my intellectual capacity is somehow connected with work?

   …Will I continue to learn and to grow in knowledge?

Journal your thoughts and feelings:

_____
_____
_____
_____
_____
_____
_____
_____
_____

And now, for the big question of the day, ask yourself:

Is it possible that some form of work,

in and of itself,

might lengthen my lifespan?

_____ Yes or No?

Final thoughts about the challenges set by the fear of risk and the risk of fear.

Fear is a four-letter word meaning "I can't" and it is the perfect out for some people because, after all, if they think they can't – they won't.

Risk is a four-letter word meaning "I can't change" and yet the world, even life itself, is about risk and change.

Linda Ellerbee defined her thoughts about risk in a wonderful way when she said: *"To risk change is to believe in tomorrow."* You will meet the future in any event. If you believe in tomorrow, you will have to risk change.

Awaken, you sleepy traveler from the past. Your longer lifespan is a gift of time and opportunity to use more of yourself — your brain, your compassion, your courage, and your contribution to the next generation.

Copy and Clip

A note for the refrigerator of those who are unemployed while reading this!

"So his work there was made possible by his having been unemployed at the right moment.
But that, ... is as good a way as any to be catapulted into world fame."
...Arthur Miller

Barriers.

Unlike the word "challenge" that we defined as reflecting an internal fear to be overcome, or a risk to be avoided, the word "barrier" suggests that some thing, an obstacle, is in the way.

Barriers are usually found in the networking, interviewing, negotiating, or sales process. The obstacle in the way is the limited amount of time you have invested in formally learning these above listed skills.

The good news, and there is only good news, is that removing the barrier is simply a matter of investing the time, now that you know what's required. In most cases, the investment is minor and involves mostly your time!

Without this investment, you will find that your outcomes will continue to be spotty.

With it, you will find dramatic and startling improvement in the results.

Overcoming Barriers.

Skills or educational gaps.

One thing that may get in the way of your success is the lack of an important skill. If you have identified an area of interest and your gap analysis suggests that certain skills are missing from your repertoire, it is easier than ever to bridge this gap. Skills can be learned. But, you have to get out of your comfort zone and commit to learning.

You can't afford to stop learning!

Start learning right away. You can't hope for an employer to train you on the job if the available market suggests that the skill or skills you lack are readily available from others.

Another common barrier is the lack of a formal education. You've heard of Stanford, Harvard, Yale and all the big name schools, but do you know about the fully accredited University of Phoenix? The University serves over 200,000 students both in the classroom and virtually. The median age of these students is 39.5 years. Officials expect UOP to double in size within the next 5 years and they expect the median age to rise as well.

A large number of working adults are engaged in "distance learning" – an experience that is described as the fastest growing segment of higher education in the U.S. for working adults.

Suggestions for exploring the many options available to you range from visiting your local community college, exploring online learning opportunities, taking high school extension courses, to finding mentors and career coaches who, quite literally, will coach you into the future.

The point is that education and advanced learning experiences are easier to obtain than at any previous time in the U.S. There is no reason to crouch behind the excuse that your skills are obsolete or that you need advanced education when the answer to learning is at your fingertips.

Educational gaps can be bridged at any age, but you may have to return to school and earn your degree.

You can succeed without it if you have comparable experience. However, there are degrees of success. Imagine yourself struggling through an open window pried open by experience alone compared to a vision of your waltzing through an open door broadened further by the advantages of education.

Overcoming Barriers.

Networking.

The inability to network is a serious barrier for many. Networking can conjure up several emotions, some good and many bad. Done poorly, networking can result in rejection and, ultimately, action paralysis. Action paralysis is a sure way to lose.

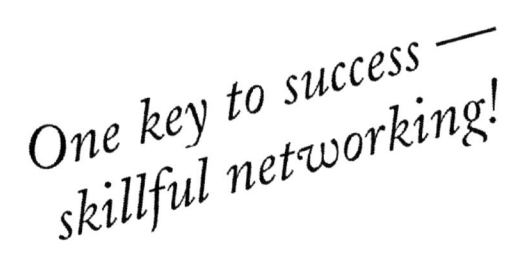

One key to success — skillful networking!

In its classic definition, networking is the process of exchanging ideas, information, or resources for mutual benefit. The key word in the definition is "mutual."

Effective networking, therefore, is the art of giving as much, or more, than you receive from others. In our field of career management, we often say:

"You can have anything you want if you will help others get what they want."

Gaining information, such as probing for a job lead, is one goal of the process of networking.

Not everyone is comfortable seeking information and advice from others. Only you know what your comfort level is today. Are you comfortable calling others and asking for advice and help?

Even if your answer is a resounding "no" — by defining your objective, researching areas of knowledge pertinent to achieving the objective, preparing and practicing your approach, and then developing and implementing an effective strategy, you can gain much of the confidence necessary to network successfully.

Here's the deal:
Networking is a style and a skill, not an inherent talent.

You must develop your skills to fit the style of networking that is right for you. That's the art of networking — when skills meet personal style — you become a net worker!

If you commit to following our recommendations, you will gain many of the networking skills you need.

> *Focus on what you want to gain from contacting others.*
> If you are searching for a new work opportunity, research a number of industries and narrow the types of industries to those fields that you want to investigate.
>
> *Develop questions that you want to ask individuals in those fields, such as:*
> How did you transition into the position you now hold?
> What advice would you have for someone exploring opportunities in your field?
> By asking questions, you are communicating both respect and interest in the other person. It's easy to approach someone when you know what you want to ask. It is the first step in effective networking.
>
> *Continue your research.*
> Identify trends and other targeted information that will assist you in developing additional questions. What you learn will become the ideas and resources you can give to those you contact.

There are numerous sources for doing research, so take the time to investigate the channels of information available. Your cadre of colleagues, current and past co-workers and bosses provide a great place to start. The Internet is more effective for research than as a job-finding tool, so take proper advantage of it. Companies, trade and professional organizations, educational institutions, and a variety of publications offer a wealth of information on their websites. Don't forget that public and university libraries have an abundance of resources. Today's librarian is a database expert who can bring a high level of efficiency to your search for information.

Remember that networking is a competitive sport.

You need to provide value to the people you are contacting. By thoroughly investigating a topic and anticipating what information is of interest to the people you seek to network with, you demonstrate that you are a worthwhile contact.

To many people practice "Turbo-Networking". They think they can be successful at networking by playing the numbers game, contacting everyone they know in rapid succession and asking for leads and information. They are adept at taking but not at giving.

When meeting someone face-to-face, bring along a reprint of an article of interest as a "leave-behind" piece of information.

By developing a strategy, you can maximize your time building relationships with those people who are in the best position to assist you. This is vital. You want to gain immediate information and you want your connections to remember you in the future when they are in a position to refer you to a new opportunity or when they learn of information that they know would interest you.

Prepare and practice.

Preparing and practicing what you plan to say is a vital step in the networking process.

Keeping your objective in mind, develop a list of questions and statements that incorporate the knowledge you've gained from your research.

Practice a crisp and concise opening statement followed by a question to your contact. In any conversation, the questioner is in control of the information flow. You want to command control from the beginning in order to achieve your networking objectives.

In addition to providing information that you feel will be of interest to your contacts, ask if there's anything else that you might research for them. Also, don't ever complete a networking meeting without asking for suggestions of additional people to contact.

Stay with your strategy.

Pull out all the stops in developing an initial list of people to consider contacting. That doesn't mean that you are going to interface with everyone on the list. With your networking objectives in mind, you need to prioritize those contacts in the order of their assumed return benefit to you.

For example, if you are looking for a job (or "gig"), develop the following lists of individuals:

1. Hiring authorities — People potentially in a position to make you an offer.

2. Influencers — those who make recommendations for staffing or connect you with decision-

makers.

3. Knowledge holders — people who can provide information helpful to you, such as consultants or suppliers who deal with a number of companies that you are interested in learning more about.

In addition to knowledge, they offer a good resource for introductions.

A word of caution.
A source of negativity toward networking is that some business people, especially younger workers, equate networking with "Network Marketing", or multi-level sales organizations. You may not want to state that you'd like to "Network" with someone. Remember that networking is sharing information for mutual benefit, so communicate that you'd like to exchange ideas on a topic of mutual interest, and back up the request with a brief amount of information based on the research that you have done.

Investigate something relatively new on the scene - Internet Networks.
The Internet has spawned a new breed of network. The Internet "Social Network" functions in the following way: You register at a website and include information about your background and interests. You also provide a list of email addresses of people you know. These actions generate a broadcast email from the social networking service to your contacts which asks if they'd like to sign up. Then you can send out information requests to anyone on the network and, in turn, receive appeals for information as well.

The theory is that, with all the connections that exist on this network, almost any request for information, including introductions to specific people, such as a vice president at a company you'd like to meet, is possible. The challenge of this process is that it is a technology-enhanced form of Turbo-Networking, and you need to determine if it's worthwhile to answer appeals from people you don't know, especially if they want an introduction to a friend or colleague of yours.

Try one or two of the services to see if they are worthwhile, but stick with the ones that offer their basic service for free instead of those that charge a fee. Examples of network websites include:

LinkedIn.com

Ryze.com

Network for Life.
By consistently applying the networking process in a variety of situations, you will hone an important set of skills that will continue to bring positive results to many aspects of your life.

Hire a coach.
Still intimidated by the thought of networking? Hire a coach who specializes in helping you to marry skills and style — the art of networking. Your investment will be repaid. You'll improve your self-confidence as you improve your techniques, and you will begin to enjoy the many people you meet along the network highway.

Take a class.

There are many, many networking specialists in America. A few of these specialize in coaching groups, i.e., they provide instruction in networking to a relatively large number of clients at a time. This classroom style of learning is worthwhile if it allows for individual practice. Try to find a workshop that limits attendance to less than 15 or 20 people to make certain you receive your share of practice time.

Overcoming Barriers.

Interviewing — an experience that makes grown-ups tremble.

Don't quite know why you would want to feel this way — because, if you are prepared and have practiced for the interview, anxiety will give way to excitement.

The 2nd key to success — preparing and practicing!

Learning as much as possible about the individual(s) you'll be interviewing with, their company and its industry is important in setting a strong foundation for success in the interview process.

While much information can be gleaned from traditional sources including the Internet, trade publications and other periodicals, seeking the perspective of individuals who have had a relationship with the hiring manager, and other company representatives, is priceless.

Develop a list of questions that you anticipate will be directed to you by each interviewer. Create appropriate answers to them, and think of follow-up questions that you can ask to gain information that will help you effectively match your skills, knowledge, and abilities with the responsibilities of the job. By asking questions and discussing trends and issues that affect the job, company and industry, you show an interest and enthusiasm not always shared by other job seekers. Your research will add to your comfort level and will help you exude the confidence and express the content necessary to impress the interviewer with your candidacy.

Know your weak points and prepare yourself for a discussion around these points. They are bound to be discussed.

The informational interview.

This type of interview provides you with important information from people who are in your industry, business niche or career field. The point of the informational interview is to gain needed information and, if possible, obtain referrals to target organizations.

Whether seeking regular, full-time employment or a contractual/consulting opportunity, the informational interview is often the shortest distance between two points. It may appear to slow down the job search process, but the opposite is true. It will speed it up. Why? Because it is still the people to people connection that offers the best results.

This is your informational interviewing checklist:

Prepare carefully in advance of the information interview.

Do as much research as possible to identify the issues, trends, and content areas that you want to discuss.

Formulate questions that will enhance your understanding of the subject matter and to increase your knowledge of the topic and what affects it.

Define your objectives and develop a line of questioning that will lead to attaining your objectives.

Always ask the individual to recommend other people to talk with to gain additional perspectives.

Remember to come to an informational interview armed with data that you can share. By doing as much research as possible before this meeting, you can contribute your thoughts and perspectives to the conversation and make the meeting worthwhile for all involved.

The screening interview.

In the screening interview, a recruiter, internal or external to the company, conducts an initial interview to determine if there is suitable interest on the part of an employer to consider you further. This type of interview may take place in person or over the phone.

Here is a trick to surviving a screening interview:
Stay focused on their needs.

One way to think of getting through this barrier is to realize that the screening interview is there, in some measure, to screen you OUT not just to screen you IN. In other words, you want to say enough to get invited to the next round of interviews but you don't want to say too much that will result in your being screened out.

Know, in advance, how you are going to handle questions about compensation, especially if you are concerned that your salary may be too high.

Successful completion of the screening interview leads to a second interview, or round of interviews, with the hiring manager and/or the hiring team.

In-person interviews.

The Human Resources (HR) interview is the traditional first step when the company is large enough to support an HR Department. At all but the highest positions, the designated HR representative usually meets with you first. They are there to determine your "fit" within the team and the company. It is your challenge to demonstrate your interpersonal and other requisite skills. They will not fully understand all of your capabilities but enough to ensure that you "match" the job description profile. In other words, HR representatives are paid to refer people who fit the culture of the company. They don't want to refer people who are not likely to fit that profile

A common mistake people make is to underestimate the importance of "fit." For example, scientists and engineers often are at a loss during this stage of the interview because their specific knowledge appears to be at odds with the HR individual's knowledge. Don't try to bridge that gap. Very few individuals in the "people" end of any business will be able to talk your language. Concentrate on keeping much of your discussion linked to their interests and to reinforcing the match between their requirements and your skills.

The hiring manager interview.

> This interview may result in a job offer or you may be scheduled to meet with others in the company. Whether you meet one or half a dozen people during the interview process, the hiring manager usually has the ultimate authority to make the decision to hire.

The confirming interview.

> Peers, subordinates, and other team members may be invited to provide input during the hiring or engagement process. These folks wield influence and it is important to address their needs. While they do not have the authority to hire, they can "black-ball" prospective candidates.

The board of directors interview.

> At the highest level of employment, you may be asked to present yourself to the "board." If you are at this level of employment, hire a coach to help prepare you for this intense experience.

Understand the interviewer's perspective.

> Interviewers have four primary areas of interest.
>
> 1. Can you do the job? – Do you possess the competencies needed for success?
> 2. Will you do the job? – Are you motivated to take on these duties and responsibilities?
> 3. Will you fit in? – Are you a match with the company culture and management style?
> 4. Can we afford you? – Are your expectations and the firm's aligned?

A few interviewing reminders.

> The employment interview must be an information exchange where both parties contribute to the conversation.
>
> The interview process can be summarized in a two-part question on the part of the prospective employer:
>
> **"What did you do for them, and what can you do for me?"**
>
> Develop a results-oriented approach to your answers. Be prepared to demonstrate contextual examples of your talents in solving problems, meeting challenges and deadlines, working under difficult conditions, and achieving success for previous organizations. Practice this art of "behavioral interviewing." When the interviewer asks you to recount specific situations, give yourself the opportunity to present your talents in the context of real-life experiences, emphasizing the results of your efforts.
>
> Be prepared to discuss how you would react in hypothetical situations. Interviewers may present a scenario and ask you how you would handle it. Think of what talents and

attributes you want to emphasize in managing their scenario. You can also draw parallels to real-life experience in order to effectively demonstrate your requisite attributes to the interviewer.

Why interviews often fail.

Surveys of recruiters and hiring managers include their reasons for rejecting applicants. The following are the top eight reasons are why candidates receive a failing grade in the interview process:

Lack of clear career direction and objectives

Lack of enthusiasm and vitality

Unprofessional or unkempt personal appearance

Poor eye contact

Criticism of past employers

Poor verbal skills

Limited knowledge of the field of specialization

Little interest in the company and industry

A successful closing formula.

Emphasize your heightened interest in the job (if you are still interested) and ask what the next step will be.

Send a thank you letter and use it as an opportunity to summarize the positive points of the meeting and to bring up items that you want to elaborate on or forgot to mention during the interview.

Maintain control of the follow-up. Acknowledge the interviewer's busy schedule and offer to get back to them within a certain period of time. Our recommendation is that you get back to interviewers as promptly as possible. A drawn-out response time between contacts has the effect of dimming the lights of memory on the part of the interviewer or interviewers.

Even if the position is not of interest to you, tell the interviewer immediately and follow through by sending a thank-you letter, perhaps offering a referral of someone who may be more ideally suited to the position, thus cementing a relationship that may be helpful to you both in the future.

Continue your research.

Read books on interviewing. Take the time to interview where the outcome is not serious – in other words, where you are not anxious to get the job or the opportunity. This real-time practice is valuable. It will decrease your anxiety and increase your self-confidence.

Hire a coach.

Still intimidated? Or, has it been many, many years since you have interviewed and you know that your skills are rusty? Hire a coach who specializes in helping you to marry interviewing skills with personal style. Your investment will be repaid. Your interviewing results will improve dramatically when you practice with an expert.

Reminder:

The lifetime job has vanished into the past.

You will need this skill again and again in the future.

Invest in yourself.

Overcoming Barriers.

Negotiating. There's more to life and work than money.

The 3rd key to success — win-win negotiating!

When you think of negotiating with a prospective employer for full or part-time work, what comes to mind? Do you think principally, and exclusively, about the money? Of course not. Yet, we often trap ourselves in a discussion about money as though other aspects of a negotiation are secondary.

Look inward. What is most important to you?

Check it out!

- _____ The job itself
- _____ The ability to do good work, work that matters to you
- _____ Time freedom
- _____ Work-life balance
- _____ A location close to home
- _____ Significant recognition
- _____ Autonomy and the freedom to set your own goals and schedules
- _____ The opportunity to travel
- _____ Controlling the direction an organization takes
- _____ The opportunity to help others in a direct way
- _____ A chance to learn new skills
- _____ Working with people who have similar values and ethics
- _____ Personal challenge
- _____ Working from home (telecommuting)
- _____ A lot of variety and challenge
- _____ A high level of creative or artistic opportunity

Add your own list:

_____
_____
_____
_____
_____
_____

The point is, some of these items may be more important to you than money at this moment in time.

If you are wondering about what you said about yourself in an earlier chapter, re-visit Step 2 where you defined your interests and your motivations.

Back to money:

Of course, money is important. But, how much money depends upon your personal situation, your marketability and your sense of who you are and what is most important to you at this time of life.

We highly recommend that you hire a negotiation coach if you really want to learn the art and skill of negotiations in several venues. Karras Negotiating Seminars are well regarded by many people who have invested in their in-depth working seminar. There are independent coaches who specialize in teaching the art and skill of negotiating for small business owners, consultants, independent professionals, and others.

A few last words:

There is so much written on negotiating, that it is worth "Googling it." Choose the information that best meets your needs.

Our favorite book, *"Getting to Yes"*, while a bit dated, is a worthwhile reading experience. You can order used copies through many of the online bookstores.

Overcoming Barriers.

Sales. Overcoming the myths of the "natural-born salesperson."

This is an important subject for independent professionals, consultants, and others who seek to sell products, services and, especially, themselves.

The 4th key to success — selling results!

While there may be a few so-called "natural born salespeople," most successful salespeople tell you that it was the skills they learned combined with the qualities of persistence, reliability, and follow-through that were their keys to achieving success. In other words, while there is a sense of self-confidence and extraversion that some salespeople naturally display, these are just qualities that enhance outcomes but do not, in and of themselves, ensure a high degree of success.

There are many services and products you may choose to sell. It is helpful to think of what people sell in terms of two general categories:

Commodity sales or consultative sales.

Commodity sales occur when the product or service is standardized.

Razor blades and toothpaste fit in this model.

Price is often a clear driver in buying this type of item. Costco, Sam's Club, Wal-Mart and other large retailers have the commodity sales methodology down pat. They know that it does not take specific sales training to enter this area of sales. Instead, they invest heavily in customer service training because, given seemingly equal products and prices, it is almost always true that people will buy from people they like. That is why excellent customer service is always an important part of this sales game. When competing on price, take a lesson from this message. Invest in a customer-focused approach. Thank you letters, advance letters, and letters of reference are all part of the sales cycle that will help you to set yourself apart when the appearance of a price-driven sale needs some differentiation.

Consultative sales require understanding of the buyer's situation.

This is where you can separate the talented and experienced salesperson from the commodity salesperson previously described. A consultative sales process requires the salesperson to understand the context of the buyer's situation. They need to understand the "business drivers" of the organization or the individual purchasing the product or service.

The successful salesperson will always do a great deal of homework in order to understand the decision process the buyer will use. This type of salesperson needs to know how to carefully provide a framework for the prospect during the buying process. They need to know how to sell to a committee, a single function business owner, or through a process of competitive bidding.

If you seek to sell consultative based services or products, you will need to take sales training to learn every aspect of the process. If you wish to stand-apart from the competition for a job — you will want to take consultative sales training and learn every aspect of the process.

Read books on selling. Mack Hanan is a terrific author on the subject of value-based (consultative) selling. He has written several books on the process. Look up the books by author and select the books that best fit your situation.

An interesting website to explore is the Sales Training University at: *Sales-training-management-institute.com*

If you want to find a sales expert to help you, try:

Elanceonline.com for freelancers who provide sales training.

Hire a coach. The investment will pay for itself.

Step 7

Goals, Objectives, Brands and Your Written Plan

GOALS set the expectation of what you wish to achieve over time. For example, if you are seeking to reposition your career from a full-time and regular job to the independent workforce, you will set goals that help you to learn more about the independent workforce whether or not you are still engaged in working the old-fashioned way.

To refresh your memory of what you – yourself – wrote in Step 3, review your completed work on the page titled: "Come down from the clouds – Discover your marketplace opportunities."

Goals are your guiding beacon to a future of your choosing.

OBJECTIVES help specific audiences, such as prospective employers, clients, or customers understand what you want or need — today— in terms of linking their interests with your own. Clear-cut, short-term objectives are useful for people in transition. Objectives are the stepping-stones you must achieve in order to attain your goals.

Objectives are stepping-stones on the way to goals.

BRANDS are a unique and succinct way of describing goals and objectives in terms that help your audience to understand and remember you. Brands are much more than logos or catchy sayings. They are instead a way of describing yourself that is both memorable and consistent to a particular audience at a specific moment in time.

To refresh your memory of what you – yourself – wrote at the end of Step 2, review your completed work on the page titled: "Come down from the clouds – Pull together Steps 1 & 2 of your plan."

Brands are a way of describing your objectives or goals in a memorable fashion.

WRITTEN PLANS are the **S**pecific, **M**easurable, **A**ction-oriented, **R**ealistic and **T**ime-framed methodology you intend to follow in order to achieve your immediate objectives as well as your long-range goals. A plan begins by taking certain steps, such as setting your goals, defining your objectives, and branding your identity. It continues by listing what steps you will take and when you will take them. Most plan setters borrow the traditional acronym S.M.A.R.T. to use in the planning process, as highlighted above. We suggest that you use S.M.A.R.T. as your own model for career planning.

Written plans pull together the actions you must take in order to achieve your objectives and goals.

Goals — Your guiding beacon to the future of your choosing!

Power up!
Use what you have learned!

There is huge power in setting specific goals and then chasing them with a vengeance. The process you have engaged in throughout the book has been designed to lead you through a goal-setting exercise that will meet your unique needs.

Check out your work so far:

_____ You have completed the exercise designed to discern what you no longer want to do.

_____ You have listed your values, your preferred work environments, and your motivators.

_____ You have completed both of the "clouds" exercises.

_____ You have investigated the "hot" opportunities that the market offers.

_____ You have read about the opportunities that best suit your interests and talent.

_____ You have reviewed your challenges and barriers and made some plans to address them.

_____ Your vision is clear as to which path, or paths, makes the most sense for you to follow.

If you have skipped a step or two, take a brief moment to complete your work. When you can check all the above items, you will find yourself ready to tackle the relatively simple job ahead.

Now engage in a short, but powerful, exercise to set new goals. There is only one rule. Please finish each step of the exercise before you read or work forward.

First:

From the list of new opportunities you have explored, capture or visualize your career or work interests, advancing from the numerous choices we have given you. For example, you may wish to (1) coach, (2) consult and (3) teach. For purposes of this exercise, the number of goals is limited to your **top 3 choices**.

1. _____

2. _____

3. _____

Next:

Look at your list and force-rank your top 2 interests (order of preference).

1. _____

2. _____

List the ways you would like to work over the next few years.

There are no limitations.

Just list your interests.

For example, you might say that you would like to work 20 hours a week for 9 months of the year. You may say that you prefer to work now and again. Or, you may be ready to start a home business. Refer to your workbook notes.

1. _____

2. _____

3. _____

Review your list and force-rank the top 2 ways you would prefer to work over the next few years.

1. _____

2. _____

NOTE:

The third choices that you have eliminated for now are your fallback positions if your original force-ranked goals are unavailable to you.

STOP:

Look at your four top forced-rank responses and think of these as your guide to setting your goals.

In order for these to qualify as goals, it is important for you to think of them as:

Specific

Measurable

Action-oriented

Realistic

Time-framed.

For example:

Goal #1

Within two years, I want to be in a position to work no more than 20 hours a week in stress-free work that will provide me with some discretionary spending money. I will explore Wal-Mart, a part-time role at my pet's veterinarian's office, and mystery shopping in my local community. I will complete my initial exploration of local opportunities within 3 weeks from today.

Goal #2

A second goal, in the same timeframe, is to explore docent roles, working for free, or simply for expenses, on a casual basis at the Zoo and/or at the Aerospace museum. I will complete my exploration within 3 weeks from today.

When I have concluded the 3 weeks of investigation, I will have a clearer understanding of the demands of either or both positions. I will know if these opportunities are right for me in the long run. I will know if I have to take additional steps in the next couple of years or whether this type of transition is as easy as I hope. I will commit to continuing to stay ahead of marketing trends as they relate to stress-free work in order to be well positioned to make one or another of these roles by the time I reach 60 (2 years from now).

I will then write the balance of my plan.

Your top 2 goals for the future are:

_____
_____
_____
_____
_____
_____
_____
_____
_____
_____
_____
_____
_____
_____

Did you state your goals in positive terms?

Did you eliminate "will-not" statements and concentrate on what you will do?

Let's assume that your long-range goals are more demanding, perhaps more sophisticated, than the seemingly easy goals of the example given. Please list those gaps you will need to fill-in if you are to achieve your goals.

Write down the specific (S.M.A.R.T.) actions you must take in order to prepare yourself to overcome these gaps and achieve your goals.

Once you have identified your goals and have completed the investigation of the market, use an Excel spreadsheet or create a time-line that will serve as your guide to taking the steps to achieve a future of your own choosing. Keep your plan simple and S.M.A.R.T.

If you need additional help, examples of strategic planning documents exist in books and on the web.

It is useful to learn to describe yourself in terms of your immediate objective (what you want to do next) as well as your skills, interests, values and accomplishments. A good objective statement includes all these components and does so as briefly as possible.

Objectives — Your stepping-stones to achieving your goals.

Here's a real-life example:

"I am seeking a CEO position in a small to medium sized software firm. I prefer a company that is in startup or one that is challenged by a business crisis, such as found during a turnaround. I offer such a firm a strong record of transforming and building powerful, team-based organizations that can effectively respond to rapidly changing marketplace demands.

Most recently, while with XYZ Corporation, I led the turnaround from _____to_____, restoring an assured competitive advantage to my employer."

Here's a second, real-life example:

"I want to take my transferable skills from the for-profit corporate world, where I worked in Financial Management for the past 10 years, into the non-profit world where the opportunity to do good matters. In addition to my experience in day-to-day financial management, I was charged with securing several additional rounds of financing in order to support my current employer's objectives. I see this success in fund-raising for-profit as very similar to the challenges of raising funds in the non-profit world.

A lifelong commitment to _____(name of organization)_____as an active volunteer, plus my financial management and fund-raising skills, have prepared me for this next step in my career.

Note that these objective statements may be stated in conversation or, with some modification, written to network connections or prospective employers.

You will, of course, design your own objective statement. It will take rehearsal and editing to hone your message to a desirable form. Practice…. When it seems to reflect your best efforts, try it out on others and see if they respond to your words and meaning the way you want them to. Adjust your message, as necessary, to reach the broadest audience possible.

Try writing your own objective statement here:

_____
_____
_____
_____
_____
_____

Brands — Creating Memorable Impressions.

Clarity of purpose — that self-branding of your goals in a short and memorable fashion — sets you apart from the crowd. Branding, in part, is about creating a memorable impression and a clear-cut identity.

The importance of self-branding cannot be overemphasized. It is one barrier that many people fail to overcome and can carry the unfortunate impact of confusion, or worse, a bored audience.

Allan Murray's book, *The Wealth of Choices*, states that *"brands are the decision-making shortcuts"* that influence buying whether purchasing goods or engaging people. He goes on to write: *"It's time for me – and you – to take a lesson from the big brands, a lesson that's true for anyone who's interested in what it takes to stand out and prosper in the new world of work. Regardless of age, regardless of position, regardless of the business we happen to be in, all of us need to understand the importance of branding. We are the CEO's of our companies: Me, Inc. Our most important job is to be head marketer for the brand called YOU."*

The book, *Be Your Own Brand*, by David McNally and Karl Speak, offers a formula for branding yourself.

Briefly, they make the case that a good branding statement is:

Distinctive – It stands for something – your values or style or ethics.

Relevant – It connects you with the importance others place on what you can do for them.

Consistent – It is reinforced by repeated behaviors and specific language.

And, finally, from the book, *Make a Name for Yourself,* by Robin Fisher Roffer, we offer you excerpts from her formula to help you create your own personal brand strategy for success.

Robin recommends that you "dig deep to unearth who you are." We have helped you to find the language to describe who you are throughout the steps of this book. If you can, create a word picture of who you are and learn to talk about yourself in these terms.

She goes on to recommend that you "define your dreams and put them into action." You have done this in previous exercises. Describe your long-term goal or your short-term objective consistently. Use the same language in almost everything you write, including emails and conversations with friends. It is through consistent, crisp communication that people will begin to remember you for who you are — because you have taken the time to prepare your script!

Robin advises you "to be relentless and to go after your targets with a vengeance" and, if you aren't getting the results you seek, "figure out what is stopping you." Adjust your branding statements to make certain that, for the most part, people will understand and relate to the uniqueness of who you are and what you want.

An important piece of her advice is to "recruit a squad of brand cheerleaders." These are the people who can help get your message out and into the working world.

We add:

1. Keep examining the process.
2. Read the recommended books on branding.
3. Work on your self-confidence.
4. Do whatever it takes to keep you going.
5. Write down your objective(s).
6. Brand yourself in line with your objective(s).
7. Remember that a good brand is short, action-oriented, a bit provocative, linked to the other person's pay-off, and finely tuned through several iterations, (rehearsal and editing).

Try your own branding statement:

_____
_____
_____
_____
_____
_____
_____
_____

Don't solo when you're stuck.

Get help writing your plan.

If you have done the work, this is the easy part. Just pull together what you know.

Copy and Clip

Refrigerator Note!

And, as you struggle to create your brand, because we know you will, remember the words of that world-famous author, James Michener, who said:

"I may be the world's worst writer, but I am the world's best rewriter."

Almost there...
Pull together your written action plan.

Start.

State your long-term goal (if different than your immediate objective). Be specific. Answer the questions:

1. What do I want in the long-term?
2. When do I want it by?

Capture data and incorporate it into your planning process.

List the steps you must take to reach your goals. List the steps or actions you must take in order to achieve your immediate objectives. The more demanding the long-term goal, the more steps you will list.

State your immediate objective.

1. What do I need to do next on the road to achieving my goal?
2. By what deadline must I complete this objective?

State your next objectives.

1. Once I achieve my immediate objective, what is my next one?
2. When is my deadline for this next objective?

And so forth.

Items to consider in objective setting.

<u>Capture your marketplace analysis.</u>
This is the segment of the market (career) you are attempting to reach. Write down what you know about your target market and what you have yet to learn. Incorporate the lessons you have yet to learn on the way to achieving your objectives.

<u>Identify your assets and your "gaps"</u>
List your skills and competencies, your interests and talents. This is your internal analysis.

Gaps are what you need to "fill in" in order to reach your target market. List your challenges and barriers.

Be specific. Include plans to overcome these challenges and barriers in your objectives.

<u>Time-line your action steps and your objectives.</u>
Set your time-line for each action. Include points-in-time when you plan to measure the success of your plan.

There are strategic planning documents in books and on the web. Take a look at a few of these plans – they will help you to fill in the blanks in your own planning process.

Time-out for a S.M.A.R.T. check-up.

Is your plan specific, measurable, action-oriented, realistic and time-framed?

Now... **ACT!**

REVIEW your plan with a coach or someone whose business judgement you trust.

For more examples of business plans, visit Google.

Step 8

Your Marketing Tool Kit

Think of yourself as a writer.

Your job is to communicate to your reader what they need to hear, not just what you have to say.

Use your own voice.

Write as you talk.

Rewrite, rewrite, rewrite.

The words and phrases you use communicate volumes about who you are and how you present yourself. Words express your creativity, your feelings as well as your philosophy of life and work. Words communicate your goals and objectives.

For better or worse, each reader of your marketing materials will make assumptions about who you are by what you wrote to them!

A writer's checklist.

As you write, check yourself periodically by asking the following questions about everything you have written:

> Have you written to the reader or the audience, not just to yourself?
>
> Did you connect with your reader or your audience in your opening line or sentence?
>
> Did you use everyday words and did you use short sentences in favor of long-winded sentences?
>
> Have you used visual phrases made up of words that people can "see" in their mind's eye while reading?
>
> Have you varied the length of your paragraphs in order to capture the attention of the reader?
>
> Did you make your point, stick with your point and reinforce your point? Will your message stick?
>
> Have you made certain that your communication is as short as possible?
>
> Have you maintained control of the follow-up actions you seek?
>
> Has your work been edited by a third party?

A few words about "visual phrases." Words broadcast a visual image as the person reads. They help to create context and clarify the meaning of your message. For example, your mind can actually see and hear the purring of a cat just by reading the words.

To the extent you are able to paint word pictures, you will help your readers to grasp the full intent of your communication. You will stand apart from the ordinary writer and create a stronger impression than you might otherwise.

The following word pictures are examples of phrases that others have used to set visual images:

Chronicle achievements	Principled action
Confer advantage	Seamless service
Courage to care	Spring from sound logic
Drive change	Target of innovation
Fast-track to success	The final frontier
Generate fun-filled excitement	Transform the world
Inner peace	Uncommon sense
Laser-like	Unlock the past
Stop the flow of exiting employees	Warp-speed
Create pathways to the future	Winds of change

Biographies.

Your biography erases the limits of time and the boundaries of space.

Biographies travel at Internet speed around the world

to touch anyone, anywhere at anytime.

What you need to know.

The advantages of using a professional biography are many.
Consider that your biography:

>Quickly tells people who you are.

>Clearly communicates what is important for you to say.

>Links who you are and what is important to you with your targeted audience's keen interest.

>Identifies what it is that makes the reader want to invest the time in getting to know you.

>Is the perfect communications tool for electronic media.

Use a biography if you are currently working.

The potential exists for your biography to increase your personal and professional visibility and it will help the organization's leaders to align your qualifications with their needs. As the electronic media becomes more sophisticated, look for an internal "living" talent pool made up of current biographies (not resumes) as the preferred method of internal introductions.

Warp-speed change created by mergers and acquisitions, corporate redirection, relocation of entire product lines to distant shores, consolidation and restructuring accelerates the need for organizations to quickly identify and re-deploy full-time, part-time and project talent to meet new challenges. When information on talent is instantly available, such as through a self-developed, self-monitored, updated electronic biography, organizations benefit.

Use a biography as an independent professional (AKA – free agent).

If you are part of the fastest growing segment of the working population, the independent professionals, you have joined many others who know that they must clearly communicate their valuable and marketable expertise in line with the prospective client or organization's urgent need. A focused biography, rather than a rambling resume, is the perfect tool for the "just-in-time" independent professional. If you use a biography as an independent, you will raise your profile and improve your success rate by relying on the Internet or a firm's Intranet to link your written qualifications with the organizations' needs. Likewise, you will effectively introduce yourself to all members of your temporary project team and greatly increase the odds of being remembered and recalled when future organizational needs arise.

Use a biography in networking groups and professional organizations.

When you join a networking group or a professional organization, your biography will connect you and your interests with members of either group. It will warm-up your welcome, encourage others to reach out to you and greatly increase the odds of being called upon when your unique qualifications are needed on a committee or for a project. When used by professional groups, biographies even increase membership in the groups themselves as the word spreads about the extraordinary "human" element of the organization.

Use a biography to strengthen your sales results.

As a sales professional, your biography will accelerate the process of establishing trust in you, the seller. It will demonstrate the benefits of working with you, create a marketable difference between your sales proposals and those of the competition and reap unexpected benefits when used as a powerful introductory document to prospects in advance of a first meeting.

Use a biography as an introductory document for group presentations.

It goes without saying that a biography is one way to ensure that you are properly introduced when you have been invited to speak before an audience. When you design your presentation document you create the connection you want with the audience. You will raise their level of interest and excitement in the presentation itself and save yourself the uncomfortable experience of shameless self-promotion when having to introduce yourself if the host does not have the right grasp of your credentials. Finally, your well-written biography will have the subtle effect of increasing your self-confidence before you step up and onto the stage.

Compare a few of the benefits of a well-crafted biography with that other, often confusing and "use" limited marketing tool, the resume.

BENEFIT	BIO	RESUME
Automatically signals that you are "looking for work"	No	Yes
Provides effective introductions for guest "speakers"	Yes	No
Demonstrates focused interests and current expertise	Yes	50/50
Links people to a variety of organizations and institutions	Yes	No
Tells people who you are from a "values" perspective	Yes	No
Ensures current information for organizational re-deployment	Yes	No
Strengthens sales proposals	Yes	No
Facilitates worldwide electronic introductions	Yes	No
Strengthens introductions to new work teams	Yes	No
Instrument of choice for independent professionals	Yes	No
Useful in obtaining funding for your small business	Yes	50/50
Provides an interesting reading experience to the reader	Yes	No

Few good rules exist that were not meant to be broken! Consider the information in this next section to be your guideline to the basics of biographical structure and design.

Context.

Stay focused. Too many messages are confusing. Test for "flow" of your central message. Make your most important point early in the biography and repeat throughout with other supporting examples. Use metaphors or story-telling techniques to attract the reading/listening audience.

Fonts/Type.

Use a 12-point font. Increase to a 14-point font for presentations or stage introductions. Select an easy-to-read type. Times New Roman and Arial are standard choices. Georgia is a personal favorite. Limit changes in font size or design style. Limit the use of italics.

Language.

Remember that typical adult reading skills are often at, or below, the 10th grade level. Use simple, direct language and powerful short sentence structure. Be aware that people usually "scan" before they read. Lead each paragraph with your most important point. Use words that the targeted audience typically uses. Avoid jargon and abbreviations unless you are confident that the targeted audience is in absolute "sync" with your language shortcuts. Be very careful when selecting words. The right words send the right messages. Poor choices mislead and confuse. Use your branding statement in your biography.

Visual Impact.

Design for "eye" and "I" appeal. Use white or off-white paper. Select soft-colored paper for stage presentations. The colored paper will help your host to find your introduction in the excitement of the moment! Always use the best quality of paper you can find. Use "white space" liberally. To borrow a well-known metaphor, remember: "It is the music between the notes that creates the symphony." It is the white space between sentences that attracts the mind's eye. Limit the length of any paragraph to a maximum of 6 or 7 lines, even if you must "break" the usual rules of grammar.

Use words and sentences the target audience can "see" as well as read or hear. (For examples, turn to the section on suggested words and phrases that help the reader to "see" what you are saying.) When using e-mail as your method of written communication, be just as careful with the design of your biography as you would be with any written document.

Length.

Keep it short. 4-5 well-crafted paragraphs are sufficient for most biographies. In all cases, limit your biography to a maximum of one (1) page.

Content.

Keep your biography action-oriented and positive. When you introduce yourself by citing your accomplishments as well as by describing who you are, you satisfy the reader's thirst for information about you (fit) and your abilities (function). It is this combination of writing about *who you are and what you do*, presented in an interesting format, that makes for a compelling read.

Give important credentials high — but limited — visibility or you will bore the reader and audience.

Connecting to who you are:

Take a look at the following life-skills and place a checkmark next to the descriptions that best describe who you are most of the time. Then, remember to describe yourself in terms of these life skills.

Are you especially **creative?** Do others remark on this quality? Are you known for seeing many possibilities to solving problems? If you want to describe yourself as creative,

Check   here _____

Do you describe yourself as **entrepreneurial?** Will you take risks? Would others describe you as an ideal partner for a business venture? If you want to describe yourself as entrepreneurial,

Check   here _____

Are you *future-focused?* When new ways present themselves as solutions to old problems, are you the first to adapt to a new way of doing something? Do you have a good sense of the future? If you want to describe yourself as future-focused,

Check   here _____

Are you driven by **interpersonal relationships?** Is it important to you to be part of a team? If others were asked, would their first inclination be to describe you as someone they would want on their team? If you want to describe yourself in this way,

Check   here _____

Do you bring a strong sense of **organization** when completing projects? Is your ability to efficiently structure project tasks what you are known for by others?

Check   here _____

Do you like to influence others to your way of thinking? Do you like to compete and win? You may wish to describe your natural interest and abilities in **sales** or customer service.

Check   here _____

Can you concentrate for long periods at a time? Do you like to work the kinks out of systems? If so, you may seek to communicate your strong **systems orientation**.

Check here _____

Some people are driven by **social or spiritual values**. If these values are your driving force, you most likely have a strong need to help others and yourself to achieve altruistic goals. If this sounds like you most of the time,

Check here _____

Examples taken from other peoples' biographies illustrate how they used words and phrases to describe both who they were and what they did.

To convey **entrepreneurial accomplishments:**

> "Founded and ran a successful apparel manufacturing firm that catered to a previously underserved buyer – the mature professional. Led the firm from startup through buyout by a large retail conglomerate." Followed by: "Pioneered ways of exploring new opportunities in..."

To convey *future-focus:*

> "Conceptualized, designed and built three technology rich molding plants in an industry that does not readily embrace changes in technology." Followed by: "A key to operating all institutions in the future is learning how to take advantage of technology."

To convey **organizational** strength:

> "Monitored firm's managed care health insurance programs. Obtained and thoroughly reviewed proposals. Conducted a cost/benefit analysis of all proposals and bought the most comprehensive program at the best price available."

To convey **creativity**:

> "Architect of experiential learning concept, model and curriculum for people who must learn to manage their careers in a rapidly changing and exciting new world."

To convey **systems orientation**:

> "Steadfastly used a systems approach to manage the merger of five confectionary businesses." Followed by: "Measured the impact of these new ideas item by item, etc."

To convey **interpersonal skills** or **ability to influence others**:

> "Helped people to change their attitudes of fear and uncertainty to excitement and anticipation about the newly restructured organization."

When you seek words and phrases to describe your talent and skills, borrow ours.

When you choose to describe your **creativity**, consider using versions of the following action words and phrases:

Architect	Innovate
Artist	Inspire
Author	Intuitive
Conceptual	Invent
Create	Original or originate
Imagine	Perceive
Ingenious	Unique

When you choose to describe your **entrepreneurial** talent and skills, consider using versions of the following action words and phrases:

Action-oriented	Influence change
Champion new ideas	Invent
Change	New
Compete	Overcome obstacles
Curious	Passion
Dare	Persuade
Energetic	Pilot
Fast	Produce
First to think of	Risk friendly

When you choose to describe your ***future-focused*** talent and skills, consider using versions of the following action words and phrases:

Adaptable	Future-focused
Big-picture	Insightful
Challenge the past	Look forward
Champion new ideas	Proactive (overused)
Change the world	See patterns and meanings
Envision	Trendsetter
Explore	Visionary

When you choose to describe your *interpersonal* talent and skills, consider using versions of the following action words and phrases:

Collaborative	Liaison
Community	Mediate
Contribute	Mentor
Cultivate	Relate
Develop	Resolve
Empathy	Service orientation
Guide	Synergy
Help	Teach
Inspire	Team developer

When you choose to describe your *investigative* talent and skills, consider using versions of the following action words and phrases:

Concrete evidence	Investigate
Curious	Question
Detect	Research
Discover	Scientific perspective
Explore options	Solve
Feasibility studies	Strategize

When you choose to describe your *leadership* talent and skills, consider using versions of the following action words and phrases:

Accomplish	Lead
Achieve	Long-range
Champion	Produce results
Change agent	Persuade
Creative force	Manage risk
Decide	Maximize return
Delegate	Motivate
Devise	Reduce the threat of risk
Effect	Strategic
Global focus	Structure
Goal driven	Transform
Inspire	Trust
Invigorate	Value
Judge	Vision

When you choose to describe your **organizational** talent and skills, consider using versions of the following action words and phrases:

Accomplish	Integrate
Assemble	Maximize
Check	Methodize
Determine	Meticulous attention
Exact	Organize
Firmly focused	Plan
Infinite care	Precise outcomes
Initiate	Schedule
Install	Support

When you choose to describe your **sales centered** talent and skills, consider using versions of the following action words and phrases:

Assertive	Fearless
Challenge	Quantifiable record of results
Compete	Self-starter (overused)
Confident	Think fast
Disciplined approach	Win

When you choose to describe your **systems oriented** talent and skills, consider using versions of the following action words and phrases:

Accuracy	Logical
Analytical	Objective
Concrete	Process driven
Data oriented	Reflective
Factual	Steadfast approach
Focused follow through	Systematic

When you choose to describe your **value centered** talent and skills, consider using versions of the following action words and phrases:

Authority	Independence
Balanced approach	Life purpose
Belief systems	Passion
Challenge	Philosophy *

Creativity	Principled
Diversity	Recognition
Environment	Self-actualized
Ethics	Self-confident
Flexibility	Social contribution
Helping others	Spirit or spiritual

* If you have a personal philosophy, or well crafted branding statement consider using one or the other in your value-centered biography. For example, Linda Ellerbee wrote: *"Change is one form of hope; to risk change is to believe in tomorrow."* A retiree wrote: *"I wanted to do something to lose sleep over again."* Can you see how, when woven into a biography, these statements — or philosophies — tell the reader something important about the writers?

When you want to create "mind-pictures" for the reader – words and phrases they can see in their minds' eye, consider using versions of the following action words and phrases:

Believe passionately	Principled action
Better (not more)	Purposeful life
Bigger view	Ratchet-up
Capture imagination	Reach for the stars
Chronicle achievements	Reward innovation
Confer advantage	Scientific proof
Courage to care	Seamless service
Drive change	Set the stage for learning
Eye on the future	Show (not tell) you
Fast-track path to success	Spring from sound logic
Foundation for the future	Stimulate ideas
Full steam ahead	Strategic focus
Generate excitement and fun	Success story
Guided by values	Target of innovation
Guiding principles	Tear down walls
Inner peace	The final frontier
Invest in	Transform the world

Editing.

Don't edit your own work. Typos are glaringly noticeable to everyone **<u>btu</u>** the writer.

How will you know when you have written a great biography?

When you have written a creative and truthful document that *demonstrates who you are* in a compelling format that intrigues the audience to want to know more, you'll have met one test of a great biography.

When your biography helps you to *stay focused on the central theme* of your unique career and your career's purposeful journey, you'll have met the second test of a great biography.

When your biography clearly demonstrates the wonderful gifts you bring to others, *from their perspective*, you'll have met the final test of a great biography.

Where can you find examples of biographies to give you food for thought?

Some of the very best biographies are the shortest.

1. Look on the cover of books on your bookshelf. You will find some terrific bios from the dusty books lining your bookshelves in your living or family rooms.

    For example.

    "Kevin Cashman is Founder and CEO of LeaderSource, an international leadership development and executive coaching consultancy with offices across the U.S. For more than twenty years, he and his organization have coached thousands of executives and teams to enhance performance. His clients span a variety of Fortune 500 and fast-growth companies in the consumer products, healthcare, medical products, high technology, manufacturing, service, and food industries.

    Cashman is author of *Leadership from the Inside Out*, the #1 best selling business book of 2000 and named one of the top twenty best selling business books of the decade by CEO-READ. He is a contributing editor to *Executive Excellence* magazine and has been featured in *The Wall Street Journal, Chief Executive, Human Resource Executive, Fast Company, Strategy and Leadership, Oprah, CNN*, and other media.

    A believer in dynamic life balance, he has participated in more than fifty triathlons and has practiced and taught meditation for over four decades."

    Simple, to the point, gets the message across and touches on who he is as well as what he has done!

2. Look in your current stack of magazines. There is almost always a biography or two to use as models for your own. *Fast Company* magazine regularly publishes biographies that meet the test of good reading combined with substantive information.

3. If you have access to sales proposals, look at the biographies that support the proposals. Did they accomplish their purpose? Did they substantially link the sales professionals or delivery professionals' experience with organizational need?

4. A 45 second search through Google that listed just the key words "Professional Biographies" turned up more than 2 million possible sources. In other words, if examples are your motivation to write your own biography, there are plenty of models available.

5. Collect and save examples of biographies that appeal to you.

Branding statements (one more time).

It is useful to learn to use the spoken word effectively. To do this, you must first write down what you want to say and commit the words to memory — to brand, if you will, your message in the eyes and minds of clients and prospective employers.

This is the moment to look again at the branding statement you prepared in Step 6 of the process. Are there any last minute "fixes" such as better language choices you would like to make? If so, do this now. Rewrite your branding statement and commit your branding statement to memory:

As needed, try one last fix on your own branding statement below.

Stand apart.

Brand yourself as though you were a product.

Brochures.

A brochure is an ad that captures the essence of your product or service offering and lends credibility to your business venture, whatever it may be.

What you need to know.

Effective brochures are simply designed. Some of the best are written on tri-fold, landscape oriented, standard sized paper that may be used as a direct mailer or inserted into a #10 envelope and mailed traditionally.

Brochures may also be created electronically for Internet mailings, and there are many design sites available on the Internet. Sites to explore include: theprintguide.com, surefireadvertising.com and vistaprint.com. Take a look at digitalebrochures.com for e-brochures.

A basic design example of a typical hard copy, tri-fold brochure follows:

Cover

Presents the name of your organization or service.

Includes your branding statement, or an encapsulated version of your branding statement.

Displays contact information.

Inside first page

Describes your customer range, or the range of industries your service or products support.

Inside center section

Describes the services or products your organization provides.

Inside last page

This is your endorsement page. Brief quotes from satisfied clients, with their company names, appear on this page.

The outside back cover

Details who you are and why you are qualified to provide the help you claim to offer. It is also where you might list any colleagues or associates who are aligned with you in your service or product offering.

Good examples of brochures are at your fingertips.

Visit printing companies, office supply stores, and even your local supermarkets or coffee houses for examples. Collect a number of brochures and use these as models for your own efforts.

Business cards.

The "personalized" business card is back in force.

Unless you are employed full-time in one role for one organization, you need your own, customized business card.

Your business card is your first opportunity to make a first impression.

Design it carefully.

Looks count.

What you need to know.

At its minimalist best, a business card includes your name, title (if any), your business name, business address, phone, cell phone and e-mail. The back of this type of card is blank.

A business card that serves as your personal ad is one big step better than the minimalist version. In addition to the standard information previously outlined, this business card will have an identifying logo and, perhaps, a branding statement on the face or the flip (usually blank) side. We favor branding on the face because the flip side may then be used for message writing (rather like a Post-it® that does not stick.)

Important points to remember about business card design are:

> A crisp, clean look outshines a cluttered appearance. Less is more in business card design.

> People often "scan" cards into their computers. Italics and some pastel colors do not scan well.

> Use type and fonts people can actually see without a magnifying glass.

> If you must make a choice, print for quality not quantity.

Sort through your own supply of cards from vendors, customers or small businesses for an idea of what you like. Examples of business cards may be found on the Internet. Free cards are available. We like vistaprint.com. Visit your local copy center.

Business plans for small business.

What you need to know.

The Small Business Administration offers a comprehensive, downloadable version in English and Spanish for those who choose, or need, to prepare a formal business plan. Their 36-page document, found at www.sba.gov/starting/indexbusplans.html offers you an excellent stand-alone, highly focused opportunity to describe your business, your marketing plan, your financial management plan and other details as to how you plan to run your business. If you need a government loan, the completion of this particular document will be a requirement before the SBA will consider funding your small business. If you don't need a loan, it is an excellent model to use to keep you focused on the details of starting your own endeavor.

Peter Patsula's top seller at Amazon.Com is *Successful Business Planning in 30 Days* for those who wish a hard copy version of business planning. We like this well-written book because it recommends that you time-frame your business plan writing within 30 days.

The Successful Business Plan: Secrets and Strategies by Rhonda Abrams is a worthwhile reading experience. You may also wish to check out her website at www.rhondaonline.com for tips or to subscribe, for free, to her online newsletter.

Contracts and agreements for independent agents and executives

The more important your contribution is,

the more likely the work will be performed

under explicit terms and conditions as

agreed upon in advance of the assignment.

Most, but by no means all, contracts for independent professionals include the following information:

Term

This is the length of your agreement. It includes both a beginning and an ending date. It may also include automatic renewals in order to avoid the writing and re-writing of agreements when the organization and the individual wish to extend the agreement.

Scope

This describes the purpose of the assignment as well as the breadth and depth of the project.

Definition of Success

A well-written definition of success manages the expectations of both parties and ensures that both know when your work has been completed satisfactorily.

Deliverables

What are you expected to deliver? Written reports, milestone accomplishments and the final products are the deliverables you will wish to define.

Place of Performance

Where is the work to be accomplished? Their place? Your place? Cyberspace?

Internal Liaison

This is the organization's representative with whom you will interact. It may, or may not, be the same individual to whom you will report.

Ownership, Confidentiality and Trade Secrets

This determines just who owns what at the end of your assignment. It details what information must remain confidential to either or both parties. It outlines any restrictions about working with competitors in similar assignments. It clarifies what trade secrets you must keep.

Fees

How much and when is payment due?

Typical fee payments include:

Pay by the hour: In this case, the client pays only for actual time spent. Unless there are a maximum number of hours negotiated, the client pays for all time associated with the project.

Pay by the project: In this case, the client pays a flat fee for the project itself. Often favored by the client because it allows them to manage total project costs, fees may be underestimated by the contracting professional.

Pay by retainer: In this case a monthly, or quarterly, retainer is agreed upon in advance by the client and the contracting professional. The client usually links retainers to milestone accomplishments.

Expenses

What will you cover? What will the client be responsible for in terms of travel, lodging, or other related business expenses?

Materials and Tools

What will you supply and what will the organization provide?

Third Party Assignability

Can you bring in help if you determine you need it? What happens if illness or injury prevents you from completing an assignment? Can you replace yourself with the third party of your choice?

Incentives and Penalties

Is there a financial benefit to you if you meet or beat certain deadlines? Conversely, is there a penalty if you miss a deadline?

Change of Control

In this era of fast and often furious change, what happens if management or organizational changes get in the way of your completing your agreed-upon assignment successfully?

Cancellation

Likewise, what happens if the organization cancels your project, either "for cause" (failure to perform) or, "not for cause" (organizational change in direction). Can you cancel? Will you receive compensation if either party cancels under any number of conditions?

Governing Law

In the case of a disagreement, which State's laws govern the outcome of any dispute? Be careful, State laws vary widely and where you agree to accept governance is where you must fight to a win, lose, or draw conclusion. If you are doing work in another country, and the contract confirms that their laws will prevail, you may find traveling to Hong Kong or Australia, in order to win a dispute, beyond your ability to finance.

Arbitration

Should you reach an impasse, will both parties agree to binding arbitration to settle any such dispute, or must you go through a painful and expensive legal process to determine the prevailing party?

Reporting Relationship

Who represents the organization in determining whether your work is satisfactory?

Signatures

Is the signing party for the organization legally able to commit the organization to the terms and conditions of the agreement? Did you think to ensure that your copy of the agreement has an original signature affixed? Will an electronic signature suffice?

Now that you have read about the several terms and conditions found in many professional contracts, you may find the idea of executing the contract itself somewhat daunting. Contracts may be short or long, but they are important to success. Take the time to have all contracts reviewed by your legal counsel. It is not an expensive proposition to take the small amount of time for a simple contract review by a subject-matter expert, i.e., an employment or contracts lawyer.

Whether you are offered a contract or not, a written understanding of the project is important to you. If the organization does not offer such a written communication, you can write to them outlining your understanding of the project tasks and other aspects of the job that are important to achieving a successful outcome.

Regardless of the formality of any contractual agreement, signed confidentiality and trade secret agreements are almost universally required.

And, then, you must remember the I.R.S.

The I.R.S. has many factors it considers when determining if you are an independent professional or an employee. There is no way that we can answer your concerns about I.R.S regulations. We can say with confidence that there are significant penalties for organizations and individuals who fail to meet their standards. The I.R.S. itself will provide you with a complete list of the factors it uses. Take care to learn the rules of the independent professional's road. I.R.S. lessons can be quite harsh.

What do you need to know about executive agreements?

Unlike the recent past, executive agreements are no longer the domain of just the "C" level officers of an organization. Today, agreements are often the preferred method of engagement for senior level professionals whose talents are so critical to organizational success that the organization might be in danger of failing without their unique talent.

Who should ask for an Executive Agreement?

1. "C" level officers and Senior Vice Presidents.

2. Uniquely talented senior professionals whose critical talents are in short supply.

When should you ask for an Executive Agreement?

1. Executives: Always

2. Executives and others: During startup

    During turnaround

    At times of critical change — such as during merger or acquisition

What are the most recent terms and conditions that executives (and others) seek to see in an agreement?

1. Scope of responsibilities
2. Scope of authority
3. Change in command (what happens when changes occur in the reporting relationship)
4. Change in location (how far and, under what circumstances, must the executive move?)
5. Change in control (what happens when changes occur such as during M&A)
6. Governing law (which state controls)
7. Arbitration (what happens when things reach an impasse)
8. Clear definition between no-fault and at-fault terminations
9. Transitional assistance, including severance and a position-appropriate level of outplacement.

Push-back.

Don't these agreements negate the "at-will" employment clause in most states?

This is a common misconception. "At will" simply states that either party may terminate a relationship for cause, or not for cause, at any time. Contracts and agreements describe the agreed upon terms and conditions of the job itself and the benefits of separation to both parties should either, or both, decide to execute an "at-will" termination.

Similar to a pre-nuptial — where after all, 60% of us still get divorced, the work agreement reflects what the parties agreed upon while they were still "in love." In other words, it is mutually beneficial to spell-out the terms of separation while you still anticipate a long work life together.

And, commit yourself to taking a courageous stand because, after all is said and done, a long work life with one employer may last only as long as 2-3 years! Shorter than many marriage contracts last, wouldn't you agree?

Why shouldn't I craft my own contract?

Of course, you can. But, have your contract reviewed and finalized by your attorney – the attorney who must defend the contract when, or if, it should become necessary.

What if the prospective employer or client insists on using their own contract or executive agreement?

Treat it like a proposal. Once you sign their contract, it is binding. Make it a practice to thoroughly review and offer amendments to any proffered contract before you commit yourself to terms and conditions that make no sense to you. Again, have it reviewed by an attorney.

Is the information in this section all I need to know about contracts and executive agreements?

The information provided is intended as a guide to some, or all, of the content you will wish to consider when entering into a working arrangement. It is not intended as a model for a contractual arrangement.

Proposal development.

Sales proposals.

A sales proposal is a document that supports your marketing efforts by using the written word to achieve favorable business outcomes.

Words and phrases are the tools you use to communicate volumes about who you are and about what is important to you.

Start by stating their business case. Add an executive summary that demonstrates that you understand the business case. Cite your objectives in order to meet their needs. Describe your services or products that will meet their needs. Confirm your competencies to handle their requirements. Add fees.

The following 10 rules apply to sales proposal writing:

1. Write to the reader not to yourself.
2. Use everyday words over fancy words and use short words over long words.
3. Use visual words; words people can "see" while reading.
4. Connect with the reader in the opening line or sentence.
5. Lead each paragraph with your most important information.
6. Make a point, stick to the point, and reinforce the point.
7. Vary the length of paragraphs and sentences to maintain interest.
8. Control any next steps in the last sentence of any communication.
9. Ask yourself whether your communication is as short as you can make it while still making your point?
10. Have your work edited by a third party.

Sound simple?

The choices you make when writing reflect your:

Ability to present yourself in writing	Interests
Attitude, either positive or negative	Philosophy
Clarity of purpose	Self-confidence
Creativity and innovation	Talent
Feelings	Values

It is not simple to write good proposals.

Writing is an art and a skill. It is visual and visceral.

It is too many things to simply "wing-it."

Take a class on proposal writing and proposal selling. It is the only way to ensure that your proposal writing will produce results.

Grants.

A grant is a proposal that is submitted principally to either a government agency or a philanthropic organization in order to obtain funds, conduct a project, or start a non-profit organization.

The time and money connected with preparing grants is daunting! Anyone who can prepare, differentiate, edit, and submit effective grants may lay claim to a real skill as well as an artist's touch. Research the subject of grant writing before you take another step and attempt the task yourself.

For Internet access, type: http://www. followed by the web address.

> *Grantanalyst.com*
> Grant Analyst is an online grant proposal system that helps you to submit paperless grant proposals, save time and money, edit proposals with ease and reach a broad market of investors and donors. They also function as a one-stop shop that will connect you with experienced grant writers.
>
> *cfda.gov*
> A government site that offers a process for grant proposal writing to Federal Agencies.
>
> *Grantproposal.com*
> Grant Proposal.com offers advice and resources for grant writing consultants.

A good book for the neophyte grant proposal writer is *The Foundation Center's Guide to Proposal Writing* by Jane Geever and Patricia McNeill.

RFIs, RFPs and RFQs.

Responding to Requests For Information, Proposals and Quotes is an involved process that can lead to great rewards in securing new business.

RFIs.

An RFI (Request for Information) is a formal way of responding to large-scale sales opportunities. It is used when the buyer wishes to "see what you've got."

Responding to a Request for Information

When a government entity or a company is considering a procurement of products or services, but is not sure about specifications or methodologies, it often issues a Request for Information (RFI). An RFI provides you with the opportunity to make recommendations with regard to what the organization should include in a future RFP. It also gives you an opportunity to show the customer that you are qualified and responsive to its needs. Responding to an RFI is often required if you want to qualify to respond to the future RFP.

When responding to an RFI, there are a number of items that you can attempt to influence in order to gain a competitive advantage in a future RFP. These include:

Specifications. Make recommendations on items with which you can comply, but might be difficult for others.

Technical scope. Try to include requirements that will limit the field of competitors.

Past Performance. If a government entity is initiating the RFI and you don't have any government project experience, make sure you recommend that it considers relevant commercial experience.

Methodologies. If there is a particular approach you would take, describe it so that they can make it a requirement.

Certifications. If you have any relevant certifications or licenses, recommend them as requirements to limit the competitive field. Conversely, if you don't have specific certifications, suggest that they not be required because they are not relevant, would limit the amount of competition and could increase the price.

Pricing. With many projects, decisions made early in the process can have a major impact on pricing. Here is your opportunity to influence those choices.

By describing your recommendations in language that can be included in the RFP, you will be ahead of your competitors in being ready to respond quickly and effectively. Be aware that if you make recommendations and they are included in the RFP, your competitors will see them and bid accordingly. Some recommendations should be saved for when you are responding to the RFP, so that you can retain the advantage and hopefully stand out from your competitors.

Develop a list of questions and call the contracting representative. Not only will you show them that you are very interested in supplying information, you also increase their familiarity with you and your company. Because it is not an official procurement yet, you may find that they are willing to discuss intentions, alternatives, and other important issues that they would not be willing to talk about after the release of an RFP.

RFPs

An RFP (Request for Proposal) is a standardized way of responding to large-scale sales opportunities and it is used when the buyer wishes to entertain several proposals by standardizing and comparing responses.

How to Respond to a Request For Proposal (RFP)

The goal of a proposal is to persuade the reader that their organization's needs are met by your company's products or services. The proposal may first be read by a proposal evaluator from the purchasing department who is not the ultimate decision-maker. Make their job, and the job of the decision-maker(s), as easy as possible by responding to their request as clearly and briefly as possible. Always be thinking about communicating the benefits of your products and services, not just their features.

Before starting to write the proposal, read through the entire RFP and make notes about items that you do not understand along with any issues relating to how the organization wants information communicated back to them. Contact the appropriate individual to get answers to these questions.

The RFP is usually in the form of a series of questions or requests for statements and facts. In preparing your response, incorporate these questions/requests into your format down to the exact number and letter of each heading and subheading. That way, you are making it as easy as possible for the reader of your proposal to match-up your firm's capabilities with their needs. This is especially helpful when a purchasing department's evaluator is using a checklist. The goal is to give them what they want in the order of how they want it.

Tell them what they want to hear in each section. Communicate upfront what you feel is the most important aspect of the information requested, then include the additional data that they are specifying. Explain what your particular approach will do for them and what the benefit will be before actually telling what the approach is.

By stating conclusions that reflect the evaluation criteria, you are showing the reader that you understand their needs and have the solutions to their problems. This is the key to effectively developing winning proposals.

RFQs

An RFQ (Request for Quote) is simply a way for organizations to determine whether your fees meet their budgets. The RFQ is usually incorporated in the RFP.

The Purchasing Manager's Association is a good starting point to learn more about writing and submitting these documents.

CapturePlanning.com is an excellent Website that provides a wealth of information on proposal writing, including responding to RFIs and RFPs.

Resumes.

Great resumes are designed TOP DOWN not Bottom up!

Objective
What you want to do!

What are you selling? May be left on resume or inserted in cover letter.

Support your objective with words that describe how you "fit" your objective.

Qualifications
Support Your Objective

You may add a skills section to promote technical savvy. Add "branding statement."

Use chronological for search firms or when your latest experience supports your objective.

Select Format
Chronological or Combined!

Use combined when you want to feature experience from several past positions.

Embed Your Key Words

Select Accomplishments
Support Your Qualifications

Use only those accomplishments that support what you are selling.

Insert education and credentials with highest listed first.

Education & Credentials

Do not date education and/or credentials

Resume recommendations for mature workers.

1. Do not inadvertently date yourself. For example, many people add statements that say something like this: "Over 30 years of experience..." or, they use obsolete terminology, or they date their graduation from high school or college.

2. Limit your chronological history to avoid the possibility of the prospective employer focusing on how old you might be. 10-15 years of recent experience is more than enough to feature as it is highly unlikely that older experience is what they are buying in any event.

3. Stay focused on the expertise you are selling and do not add superfluous information. Don't digress or you will weaken your case.

We recommend either of two resume formats, the chronological resume or the combined format resume.

The chronological resume

This format provides the reader with a reverse chronology of your work experience. In other words, your last position and company or other business affiliation appears first on your resume. This is the format many search firms prefer as it aligns the dates of your employment history with your responsibilities and accomplishments at a specific company, in a specific position and during a specific time frame.

When selecting this format, please remember that it is not necessary to list every job in every company where you've ever been employed. For example, it is likely that your first few years of employment bear little resemblance to your later work experience. This early experience is unlikely to add much value to your candidacy for your next position. It is a better idea to concentrate on amplifying your relevant experience – experience that your prospective employer needs to know. Very few people care to note that you rose from the mailroom to the head of a department. For those few who might see this as important, add this old data selectively on their behalf.

The combined resume

This format combines the chronological and functional formats by re-positioning critical information from the previously described format where it was embedded in chronology. The combined resume features your best selling points (your relevant experience) at the forefront of your resume. It incorporates a "Significant Accomplishments" section after the qualification statement so you can list specific achievements in order of their relevance to your objective versus including them in the job where they occurred. Sub-headings may be used to list supportive accomplishments by function such as "Financial", "Sales", and "Operations".

Regardless of the type of resume you prepare, you must remember to make each and every resume key word searchable. This means that you will try to "embed" all the possible words in the body of the resume that the employer could possible use to retrieve the resume from electronic storage. Again, be specific. If you are responding to an Internet ad, use their key words to ensure you make the electronic cut.

There is a 3rd resume format with which you may be familiar.

The functional resume, the format many Chief Executives (or other top level officers) use is substituted (by us) with the professional biography as described earlier in the book.

What you need to know about objective statements.

Your objective is your statement of what you want to do next. You will use your objective in conversation, in cover letters and/or on your resume. Whether you choose to leave this objective on your resume, or use it in a cover letter, this is the statement you will use to ensure that your entire resume supports this objective. It should be modified to fit the prospective employer's stated needs.

Objective statements include the position you aspire to as well as the type of company or industry most likely to benefit from your contribution. Your objective may also qualify the size of company (small, mid-size, or large) and highlight the geographic preference you seek. It may describe your interest in a global assignment or feature your international business acumen.

What you need to know about qualification/summary statements.

Your summary statement supports your objective by capturing the highlights of information the balance of your resume features. It is your "Ad." Vocabulary you choose for your summary statement should be carefully chosen to include both aspects of your personality or style as well as your functional contribution to a prospective employer, search firm, or client. When well crafted, it is the summary statement that entices the reader to want to read the balance of your resume.

What you need to know about the body of your resume.

Next, your resume should expand upon your claims in your summary statement with bona-fide accomplishments. For example, if you lay claim to be a hands-on leader, please provide an accomplishment to support such a claim. Briefly describe each accomplishment by describing your actions and quantifiable results in support of the accomplishment.

Let's assume your summary statement claims the following: Hands-on leadership and cost-effective contributor during significant organizational restructuring.

Make a heading out of each claim and support it with a quantifiable accomplishment.

Hands-on leadership:

"Managed the efforts of 4 direct reports in supporting the Call Center activities of 100 employees. Instructed direct reports in telephone techniques in the gentle art of working with difficult people and in maintaining an aggressive number of daily phone calls to customers. Physically worked side-by-side with each and every report, coaching and mentoring their efforts. One result of this hands-on leadership was that turnover was reduced to less than 2% per month in a high turnover field where 15% turnover per month is considered an acceptable industry norm."

Break it down. The first two sentences describe the situation. The third sentence describes the actions taken by the claimant and the last sentence quantifies the results.

Each claim needs to be supported by one such quantifiable accomplishment. Read the following excerpt for another example of what we mean.

Cost effective contributor during restructuring:

"Tasked with developing a comprehensive strategy to move the firm out of its long-term period of loss. Created a strong, team-based organization armed with a shared vision, and restructured the sales approach by developing a distributorship sales model. Within 12 months, grew revenue by 25% and was a key contributor in returning the firm to a consistently profitable position by the end of the second year; a position it continues to maintain 4 years after the turnaround efforts."

The following design checklist is intended to help you to test your resume against the assigned tasks.

Ask yourself:

> Is your objective clearly and concisely stated?
>
> Does your objective balance your goals from both a fit and a functional perspective?
>
> Does your objective indicate the level of responsibility you can handle?
>
> Does your summary statement support your objective?
>
> Is your summary statement written in up-to-date terminology?
>
> Does your summary statement reinforce the level of responsibility you can handle?
>
> Do your responsibilities and accomplishments support both your objective and summary statement?
>
> Are your accomplishments "action-specific?"
>
> Are your accomplishments quantifiable? (Do they support how you can improve business outcomes, make money, or outdistance the competition?)
>
> Have you eliminated unnecessary detail and cookie-cutter terminology, using adjectives that specifically apply to your talent, skills and accomplishments?
>
> Have you included responsibilities and accomplishments that will be clear to almost any adult reading about these achievements?
>
> Have you listed education, training, and other credentials that are relevant?
>
> Did you begin the educational section with your highest level of academic certification?
>
> Did you leave graduation and other dates off of the education section?
>
> Is the reader's eye drawn to the most important information on the resume?
>
> If you were reading – not writing – this resume, would you like the way it looks and reads?

If you have responded with a "yes" to all of the items on the checklist, it is time to have your resume edited for both content and typos.

Ideas to remember when working on your resume include:

> Stay focused on what you are selling. Too many messages are confusing.
>
> Use an 11 or 12-point easy to read type and font.
>
> Limit the use of italics.
>
> Use simple, direct language and powerful short sentence structure.
>
> Remain aware that people usually "scan" before they read. Lead each paragraph with your most important point.

Use words that the targeted audience typically uses.

Be very careful with selecting words. The right words send the right messages. Poor choices mislead and confuse.

Design for "eye" appeal. Use white or off-white paper. Always use the best quality of paper you can find.

Limit the length of any paragraph to a maximum of 6 lines, even if you must "break" the usual rules of grammar.

Use words and sentences the target audience can "see" as well as read or hear. (For examples, turn to the section on suggested words and phrases in the biographical section to help your reader to "see" the real you.)

What you need to know about electronic resumes.

The most frequently used electronic version of a resume is a Word processed version. This version can be sent as an attachment to an email message or posted into the body of the email message depending on how the prospective employer or recruiter wants it sent.

When responding to openings at corporate websites or job boards, you may be requested to submit a plain text version of your resume in place of a Word version. This version is typically copied and pasted into the body of your email or onto the website directly. Check the website for directions.

When asked to forward a "text" (ASCII) version of your resume, Microsoft Word users can quickly convert the word resume to text. Refer to your MS-Word user's guide. This is not a difficult task but it requires a series of steps that you will have to follow if you are to successfully convert the Word document to text. If you want to see how your text version resume will look, send a file to yourself and, perhaps, to another individual with a different email program. This allows you to test for readability and to make necessary changes.

There are other important aspects to creating a text version of your resume, but generally your computer will help you to submit your text version. Typically, you will click on "file" and, subsequently, click on "save as" giving the file your name. Then click on "save as type" selecting "text only with line breaks" and, finally, click on "save" and submit. Sound a bit confusing? This is a time and a place to ask your teenager to help. It is only confusing until you've actually tackled this task once.

Any electronic version used will require that you understand that most employers use a system to search resumes electronically. Most employers today are looking for a focused number of keywords using this systems approach. Be careful to use as many of the employer's own words in the body of your resume to help your document get through the system. Check targeted employers' websites. Review the descriptions of all their open positions and search and replace words that mean something similar with words that target their needs.

You can't fake job titles, but you can use comparable job titles in your resume under a keywords section to ensure that the prospective employer's system screens in your resume. For example, if you are a senior marketing professional, you might include a keyword section that includes the following comparable titles:

KEYWORDS: Marketing Executive, VP Marketing, Senior Marketing Manager and so forth.

Websites.

Websites lend credibility to independent workers. It is increasingly common to find that prospective buyers of services expect websites as one way to validate that you are seriously in business.

We have been working with candidates in transition who are now including website addresses on the first page of their resumes in order to demonstrate their expanded portfolios. If you are in Marketing, or an artistic field, this is an especially good way to show-off an expanded sampling of your work.

While the costs of elaborate websites are daunting, there are excellent low cost resources available. Through the local colleges and universities, accomplished students may work for you at as low a rate as $15-20 an hour and you will be surprised and delighted by their design talent. This is one area where "young" and inexpensive talent may prove to be advantageous to the buyer.

The online companies where you register your URL (Website name) such as Register.com, NetworkSolutions.com and GoDaddy.com, provide services to assist you in quickly establishing a basic website. There are also resources available where a designer will customize a Website for you from an array of standard designs. A resource you may wish to investigate is: BigBlackBag.com where, for less than $300, they will help you develop your own site.

Next Steps – Where in the World do We Go from Here?

All aboard the spinning world of work!

Within us all rests the spirit of hope for the future.

The spirit of "hope" opens you up to the possibilities that lie ahead.

General Index

401k, 4, 139
AARP, 2, 5, 38, 47, 185
Accomplishments, Career, 22, 23, 24
Acting, Extra, 95
Advisory Boards, 68, 72
Agreements, Executive, 260-261
Agreement, Letters of, 113
American Council on Life Insurance, 203
Angel Investors, 66-67, 87
Arts and Crafts, 56, 143
Baby Boomers
    Buying Habits, 43
    Retail Market, 55
Biographies, 243-253
Biotechnology, 55
Boards of Directors, 68-70
Brands, Personal, 231, 237-238, 253
Brochures, 255
Bureau of Labor Statistics, 2, 10, 47, 50, 53, 54, 58, 122
Business Cards, 255
Business Plans, 256
California State University, 203
Census Bureau, 34, 38, 47
Child Care, 56
Civic Ventures, 192
Coaching
    Business, 73
    Career, 73
    Financial, 74
    Life, 74
Consignment Stores, 56
Consulting, 79-82
Contractors, Independent, 112
Contracts, 113, 257-259
Corporate Executive Board, 186
eBay Sales, 194
Employment Policy Foundation, 186
Employment
    At Will, 201
    Contingent, 201
    Interim, 58
    Just-In-Time, 39, 50, 175, 200
    Permanent, Full Time, 201
    Regular, Full Time, 201
    Temporary, 50, 178-180, 201
Entrepreneurship, 85
    Small Business Ownership, 160-162
Ethics Officers, 57
Executives, Interim, 112
Fancy - Free Work, 93-96
Foundations, 131
Franchises, 39, 57, 97-99
Free Agents, 112
Gallup Poll, 37, 38
Goal Setting, 231-235
Government
    City Jobs, 102
    County Jobs, 102
    Federal Jobs, 102
    Homeland Security Agency, 56, 102
    State Jobs, 102
Grants, 263
Harvard University, 204
Healthcare
    Nursing, 57
    Occupational Therapists, 57
    Physical Therapists, 57
Home-Based Businesses, 107-109
Hospitality/Leisure, 60
Humor in the Workplace, 205-206
Insourcing, 50, 54
Institute for the Future, 53
Institute for the Study of Aging, 4
International Longevity Center, 4
Internet
    Growth of Users, 33
    Sales, 39, 61, 194-196
    Teenage Users, 37
Interviewing, 222-226
Investigators, Private, 59
Just-In-Time Employment, 39, 50, 175, 200
Labor, U. S. Department of, 10, 34, 42, 43, 54, 113, 194, 203
Learners, 120-123

Learning, Online, 121
Life Expectancy, 33, 34, 35
Lifelong Learning, 4
Lifespan, Average, 5
Lifework, 3
Medical Devices, 57, 58
Medicare, 35, 39
Mission Statement, 6
Money Magazine, 160
Motivations, 29, 30, 31
Nanotechnology, 39, 57
National Association of Working Women, 203
National Institute on Aging, 60
National Science Foundation, 40
Negotiating, 227-228
Networking
    Business, 55
    For Jobs, 185, 219-221
Non-Profit Organizations, 131-134
Objectives, 231, 236, 239
Outsourcing, 36, 50, 52, 54, 112
Pay
    For Contributions, 201
    For Longevity, 200
    For Performance, 200
    For Results, 200
Pension Plans, 4, 139
Pet Services, 58
Phasers, 139-141
Philanthropies, 131-134
Pieceworkers, 143-146
Portfolio Careers, 148-152
Professionals
    Contingent, 112
    Independent, 112-117, 175
Proposals, Sales, 262
Real Estate, Investment, 59
Recycling, 59
Reinventors, 157-159
Resumes, 266-270
    Chronological, 267
    Combined, 267
    Electronic, 270
    Functional, 267

Retirement
    Early, 2, 4, 50
    Phased, 51, 139
RFIs (Request For Information), 263-264
RFPs (Request For Proposal), 263, 264-265
RFQs (Request For Quote), 263, 265
Sales, 229-230
    eBay, 194
    Internet, 39, 61, 194-196
    Pharmaceutical, 58
Security, 31, 32
    Services and Products, 59
Self-assessment, 6
Senior Services, 60
Shared –sourcing, 50, 54
SHRM, 2
Six Sigma, 49
Skills, 24, 25, 26, 27
Small Business Administration, 34, 160
Social Security, 5, 33, 34
Stipend Workers, 163-164
Strategic Planning, S.M.A.R.T. Methodology, 231
Stress - Free Workers, 167-169
Teaching, 171-172
Team Ensemble Players, 175-177
Tourism, 60
University of Phoenix, 217
University of Southern California, 185
Venture Capital, 55, 66, 86, 87, 89, 189, 190
Venture Capitalists, 189-190
Volunteering, 132, 191-193
Web Merchants, 61, 194-196
Websites
    Business, 271
    Personal, 271
Wi-Fi, 39, 61
Workforce
    Flexible, 57, 200
    Global, 51, 200
    Growth, 10
    Reductions, 1
Writing, 60
    Freelance, 143
    Marketing Materials, 241-242
    Travel, 60

Name Index

Abrams, Rhonda, 89
Armfield, Julia, 108
Arslain, John, 206
Bellman, Geoffrey, 81
Bezos, Jeff, 85
Biech, Elaine, 81
Birkeland, Peter, 99
Blanchard, Marjorie, 112
Block, Peter, 82
Braebec, Barbara, 145
Brounstein, Marty, 75
Buford, Bob, 151
Carter, Barbara, 134
Caskey, Bob, 170
Charan, Ram, 70
Cohen, M.D., Gene, 193
Collier, Marsha, 195
Cook, Marshall, 76
Cookson, John, 100
Cooper, Sue Ellen, 94
Coyne, John, 83
de Cervantes, Miguel, 64
De Pree, Max, 193
Doucet, Gayla, 147
Dowling, Linda, 76
Drucker, Peter, 53, 63
Dychtwald, PhD., Ken, 193
Edwards, Paul and Sarah, 107, 109, 117, 177
Eldred, Gary, 59
Elliott, George, 6
Freedman, Marc, 65, 192
Frum, David, 35
Gates, Bill, 85
Goodman, Gregg, 135
Goodwin, Ben, 71
Graham, John, 105
Gray, Kelly, 108
Green, Brent, 44
Griffith, Rick, 165
Gurvis, Sandra, 94
Haid, Richard, 127, 129
Hanan, Mack, 82, 177, 230

Handy, Charles, 3, 53, 148, 151
Hatten, Elizabeth Kirkcaldy, 60, 167
Hendricks, William, 127
Hepburn, Katharine, 157
Herman, Jeff, 60
Homer, 126
Hudson, Frederic, 197
Hutton, Stan, 134
Johnson, Harold, 127
Joseph, Jenny, 94
Kadubec, Phil, 145
Kennedy, John F., 131
Klein, Andrea, 124
L'Amour, Louis, 64
Leider, Richard, 15, 159
Lombardi, Vince, 73
Lubechenco, Jane, 40
Mancuso, Anthony, 134
Marsh, Catherine, 118
McIntire, Ron, 153
McLean, Andrew, 59
McLean, Pamela, 197
Means, Howard, 40
Michener, James, 238
Mielenz, Cecile Culp, 76
Miller, Arthur, 215
Moran, Patti, 58
Murray, Alan, 185
Niederer, Jed, 75
Noe, Randy, 77
Norman, Jan, 89
Oakeson, Lars, 157, 158
O'Neill, Mary Beth, 76
Pankau, Ed, 59, 108
Patsula, Peter, 89, 109
Paulson, Ed, 89
Peck, M. S., 159
Peters, Tom, 15, 117
Peterson, Peter, 41
Phillips, Francis, 134
Pink, Daniel, 112, 117
Porche, Germaine, 75

Powell, Colin, 56
Prince, Dennis, 61, 196
Reagan, Ronald, 64, 183
Reinhold, Barbara, 117
Robbins, Anthony, 74
Roosevelt, Eleanor, 64
Roosevelt, Franklin, 34
Roszak, Theodore, 193
Rowe, Mark, 134
Rozak, Theodore, 40
Rubik, Fred, 36
Schacter-Shalomi, Rabbi Zalman, 40
Schell, Jim, 161
Schick, David, 91
Shim, Jae K., 161
Siegel, Joel G., 161
Steves, Rick, 60
Suchorski, Joan, 134
Taylor, Jim, 40
Thoreau, Henry David, 17
Tipler, Brad, 52, 209
Tomzack, Mary, 99
Tyson, Eric, 161
Wacker, Watts, 40, 53, 40, 40
Welch, Tom, 110
West, Janet, 145
Williamson, Craig, 173
Winfrey, Oprah, 49
Wolf, Thomas, 134
Wolfe, Josh, 58

Information and Order Form

For more information on mature workforce issues, and to order more copies of **Boom or Bust!** online, go to www.agelessinamerica.com.

For orders by Fax or Mail, please fill out this form.

Please send me _____ Copy(ies) of **Boom or Bust!** @ $29.95: $ _____

Arizona Residents: Add 7.95 % Sales Tax ($2.38 per book): $ _____

Shipping & Handling ($4.95 per book): $ _____

Total: $ _____

Payment Method: ____Check (payable to "Cambridge Media, LLC")

Credit Card: _____ VISA _____ M/C _____AMEX

Card No. _____ Expires (MM/YY) _____

Name on Card _____

Signature_____

Name_____

Address_____

City/State/Zip_____

Telephone_____

Email_____

Fax this form to: 480-315-0373 or mail to: Cambridge Media, LLC
6520 E. Cholla St.
Scottsdale, AZ 85254